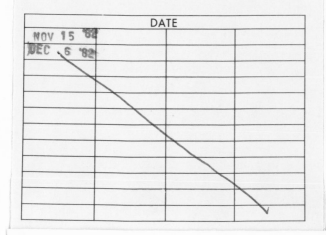

DATE			
NOV 15 '82			
DEC 6 '82			

MACHIAVELLI
AND HIS TIMES

MACHIAVELLI
(From a bust formerly in the possession of the Ricci,
the heirs of Machiavelli).

MACHIAVELLI
AND HIS TIMES

BY

D. ERSKINE MUIR

GREENWOOD PRESS, PUBLISHERS
WESTPORT, CONNECTICUT

Library of Congress Cataloging in Publication Data

Muir, Dorothy Erskine Sheepshanks, 1889-
    Machiavelli and his times.

    Reprint of the 1st ed., published by Dutton,
New York.
    Bibliography: p.
    1. Machiavelli, Niccolò, 1469-1527. 2. Italy
--History--1492-1559. I. Title.
DG738.14.M2M75 1976   945'.06'0924 [B]   74-30928
ISBN 0-8371-7889-4

Reprinted in 1976 by Greenwood Press,
a division of Williamhouse-Regency Inc.

Library of Congress Catalog Card Number 74-30928

ISBN 0-8371-7889-4

Printed in the United States of America

TO MY MOTHER

MARGARET SHEEPSHANKS

CONTENTS

page

CHRONOLOGICAL TABLE OF EVENTS   xi

BIBLIOGRAPHY   xiii

Chapter

I. INTRODUCTORY   1

II. THE STATES OF ITALY IN THE DAYS OF MACHIAVELLI   7

III. MACHIAVELLI'S YOUTH: INFLUENCE OF SAVONAROLA
IN FLORENCE   15

IV. SAVONAROLA   32

V. MACHIAVELLI'S ENTRY INTO POLITICS: CESARE
BORGIA   51

VI. MACHIAVELLI: THE CIVIL SERVANT   77

VII. THE DISMISSAL OF MACHIAVELLI: HIS RETIRE-
MENT AND HIS PRIVATE LIFE   97

VIII. MACHIAVELLI: PLAYWRIGHT AND POET   114

IX. "THE PRINCE": HIS POLITICAL THEORIES   133

X. MACHIAVELLI AND RELIGION   159

XI. MACHIAVELLI AND THE ART OF WAR   170

XII. FLORENTINE FINANCE IN MACHIAVELLI'S DAYS   183

XIII. THE CONSTITUTION OF FLORENCE AND MACHIA-
VELLI'S PLANS FOR ITS REFORM   208

XIV. MACHIAVELLI'S LETTERS: OFFICIAL AND PERSONAL   233

XV. SUMMARY: IMPORTANCE OF MACHIAVELLI'S
POLITICAL THEORIES   250

APPENDICES: GENEALOGICAL TABLES   260

[vii]

ILLUSTRATIONS

MACHIAVELLI   *frontispiece*

SAVONAROLA   *facing page* 28

ALEXANDER VI (BY PINTURICCHIO)   52

CESARE BORGIA (BY PINTURICCHIO)   72

LUCREZIA BORGIA (BY PINTURICCHIO)   92

MACHIAVELLI   108

"FORTUNA" (BY BELLINI)   130

PORTRAIT MEDAL OF CESARE BORGIA AND MACHIAVELLI'S
    SIGNATURE   150

CONDOTTIERE (BY A. DA MESSINA)   172

THE HOUSE OF VANOZZA   190

PORTRAIT OF MACHIAVELLI   242

PREFATORY NOTE

MACHIAVELLI's life falls into two parts. He was first a civil servant, high up in the employment of the Republic. In this capacity he went on various missions as foreign envoy to the King of France, the Emperor, and the Pope. He also took a prominent part in the efforts of Florence to capture Pisa, and he attempted to alter her military system by his foundation of a national militia. He was interested in the reform of the constitution and put forward a scheme for its alteration.

On the fall of the Republic and the return of the Medici he lost his post and was obliged to go into retirement. He then began to write, and until his death lived in obscurity with his books.

This sketch of his life and works deals first with the actual events of his career. It then deals with his ideas on the reform of taxation, of the army and of the constitution, and it takes separately the other side of his writings, his plays and poems, and his political philosophy. His letters are selected to show his private life and his official, and to give an idea of the extraordinarily varied work done by a man of his position in fifteenth-century Italy.

CHRONOLOGICAL TABLE

Italian Affairs		*European Affairs*	
1469	Machiavelli born	1461	Edward IV, King of England Louis XI, King of France
		1467	Erasmus born
		1474*	Isabella, Queen of Castile
		1479	Ferdinand, King of Aragon
		1483	Luther born
		1485	Henry VII, King of England
		1492	Alexander Borgia, Pope
		1492	Columbus reaches the Bahamas
		1493	Columbus reaches Jamaica
1494	Medici expelled from Florence	1497	Cabot, sent by Henry VII of England, reaches North America
1494–8	Savonarola		
1498	Machiavelli made secretary to 2nd Chancery.	1498	Vasco da Gama reaches India by the Cape
1500	Sent as envoy to France	1500	Louis XII becomes King of France and invades Italy
1501	Sent as envoy to Forlì		
1502	Sent as envoy to Cesare Borgia	1500	Pinzon reaches Brazil
1503	Sent as envoy to Cesare and Alexander	1501	Marriage of Henry Prince of Wales to Catherine of Aragon
1499–1509	Operations against Pisa	1503	Julius II, Pope
1504	Attempts to divert the Arno	1509	Henry VIII, King of England
1506	Founds the Militia		
	Envoy to Pope Julius II		
1507	Envoy to Emperor Maximilian	1513	Leo X (de' Medici), Pope
1509	Pisa surrenders Embassy to Louis XII	1513	Balboa crosses isthmus of Panama and sights Pacific
1511	Holy League Pope and Spaniards attack Florence	1515	Francis I becomes King of France and invades Italy
1512	Restoration of Medici Disgrace of Machiavelli	1516	Charles of Austria becomes King of Spain
1513	Writes *The Prince*		Magellan rounds Cape Horn
1517	Writes his play, *Mandragola*		Erasmus translates the New Testament

CHRONOLOGICAL TABLE

Italian Affairs		*European Affairs*	
1520	Writes *Art of War*	1517	Luther publishes his 95 Theses.
1522	Writes *Scheme for Reform of Constitution*		Rivalry of Francis I and Charles of Spain
1524	Writes *Clizia*	1519	Charles elected Emperor as Charles V
1525	Journey to Clement VII to present *History of Florence*	1520	Henry VIII and Francis meet at Field of Cloth of Gold
		1520	Luther excommunicated
		1524	Clement VII (de' Medici), Pope
		1526	Turks invade Hungary and win Mohacs
1527	Death.	1527	Sack of Rome by Imperial troops
			Henry VIII presses for divorce from Catherine of Aragon

BIBLIOGRAPHY

I. BOOKS FOR THE GENERAL READER

MACHIAVELLI, N.	The Prince—trans., Oxford University Press.
Armstrong, E.	Lorenzo de' Medici.
	Italian Studies.
Burd, L.	Il Principe.
Cambridge Modern History	Vol. I, The Renaissance.
Chabod, Fr.	Dal Principe.
Creighton, M.	History of the Papacy.
De Sanctis, Francesco	History of Italian Literature.
Ercole	Da Carlo VIII a Carlo V.
Janni Ettore	Machiavelli.
	Also trans. Enthoven.
Villari, P.	Life of Machiavelli, 3 vols.
	Life of Savonarola, 2 vols.
Yriarte	Cesare Borgia: *sa vie.*

II. AUXILIARY INFORMATION

Barbadora, B.	Le Finanze della Republica Fiorentina.

Berti, P.	Documenti riguardanti il commercio dei.
	Fiorentini in Francia nei sec. XIII—XIV.
Bland, Brown & Tawnay	Economic History.
Burchardi, Johannis	Diarium 1483–1506—ed., Thuasne, 3 vols.
Ceccherelli, A.	I libri di mercatura della Banca Medici.
Deltuf, P.	Essai sur les œuvres de Machiavel.
Dubreton, J.	La disgrâce de Machiavel.
Ehrenburg, R.	Capital and Finance in the Age of the Renaissance.
Goldschmidt	La libertà delle banche a Venezia dal secolo XIII al XVII.
Gossrau, W.	Florentiner Bankiere.
Janet	Histoire de la Politique et de la Morale
Machiavelli, N.	Belphegor, etc.
	Capitoli.
	Discorsi.
	Il Principe.
	Lettere.
	Mandragola.
	Scritti inediti.
Marzi, D.	La cancellaria della Republica Fiorentina.
Mordenti, F.	Diario di Machiavelli.

Norsa, A.	La filosofia della storia nel Machiavelli.
Peruzzi, S. L.	Firenze dal 1200 al 1343.
	Storia del commercio e dei banchieri di Firenze.
Pegalotti	Manuel du Marchand en 1400.
Richardson, G.	Florentine Merchants in the Days of the Medici.
Rodocanachi, E.	Histoire de Rome—une cour princière au Vatican pendant la Renaissance.
Sargous, André	La transformation des méthodes commerciales dans l'Italie Médiévale.
Thevenet, J.	Les idées économiques d'un homme d'état dans la Florence des Medicis.
	La Lutte pour le change au temps de Machiavel.
Turri, V.	Machiavelli.
Von Schubert-Soldern	Die Borgia ihre Zeit—Dresden, 1902.

CHAPTER I

INTRODUCTORY

THE political theories of Machiavelli have interested the world from the time, nearly five hundred years ago, when he first put them into writing, until the present day. Yet the life of the man himself, and the experiences which caused him to arrive at his conclusions, have not been as widely known, and hence to many his works remain only partially understood. To this, in a certain measure, may be attributed the false conceptions which have been attached to him. It surprises some to hear that the man whose name has become attached to a word with a wholly evil connotation, for 'Machiavellism' is generally understood to imply deceit and self-interested wrong-doing, was in real life a steady honourable civil servant of Florence, a man with years of public service to his credit, a citizen whose whole life was inspired by patriotism, and who sacrificed his worldly prospects for his beliefs. In the apparent discord between his life and his writings lies some of the interest of the man. Yet the study of his life shows that the discord is only apparent; a knowledge of his period, and of the events through which he lived, accounts in large measure for his theories.

Further, the record of his life is itself of great interest, especially to the modern mind. Though history does not in any sense repeat itself, yet there do arise, from time to time, curious parallels between one period and another. One of these stretches of time over which certain similarities can be

[1]

traced occurs in a comparison of some of the characteristics of the Italy of the late fifteenth century with our own twentieth century.

The lifetime of Machiavelli coincided with a period of immense vitality, coupled with complete unrestraint in the social life of the times. Thus the Italy of the Renaissance saw great freedom in all sexual matters, a removal of most restraints on behaviour, which coincided with the appearance of books treating in the broadest manner with what modern idiom would define as 'sex-interest.' The tales of Boccaccio, the songs of Lorenzo de' Medici, the plays of Machiavelli himself, are but instances of the treatment given to this theme which runs even through the letters of a scholar such as Bembo. This may be paralleled by the frankness which, in contradistinction to Victorian standards, marks our own time.

Again, it has often been pointed out that there is a certain resemblance to be traced between the violence and carelessness in taking human life, which was found in fifteenth-century Italy and is to be found, for example, in the modern United States of America. Just as the American gangster makes us familiar with the process and idea of 'bumping off,' so the Italian of five centuries ago, organized likewise into a gang, the 'sbirri,' of an underworld of organized crime, took the same simple method of terrorizing the community, and of hiring himself out to remove other individuals. He used the stiletto instead of the gun, and he generally did his work quietly at night, without the aid of noise and speed, but we know from the famous remark of the wood-merchant in Rome, interrogated as to the death of the Duke of Gandia, what the level of safety then was: "He had seen in his day a hundred corpses thrown into the Tiber at that spot, and no questions asked about them."

Nor was the public conscience at all aroused by this lawlessness and savagery. Drama and thrills were the breath of life to the men and women of that day, they enjoyed the sense of 'living dangerously.' They were not in the least brutal savages, they were amongst the most civilized and cultured peoples the world has ever seen, but to them violence, strife and sudden death were all part of the excitement they called life. Again this whole attitude of mind finds greater comprehension when we realize how widespread it was, being more familiar to us when we think of the Elizabethan sea-men, and when we look at the new countries to-day we see this same phenomenon of a civilization possessing great material wealth and luxury going hand in hand with a general lawlessness and lack of restraint.

Another point of similarity, in a different sphere, is to be found in the attacks made, then as now, on the power of the great banking corporations. Money was used as a weapon by the great Italian houses with much astuteness. The Pope himself had to rely on the bankers to negotiate his loans, and one of the most famous conspiracies in history is that of the financial house of the Pazzi against its rivals, the great banking house of the Medici, in which the Pope was involved. The quarrel was brought to a head by the fact that Lorenzo requested his branch in Rome not to advance money to the Pope for the purchase of Imola. The Pazzi at once arranged to supply his Holiness with the funds required, and Sixtus in consequence transferred his banking account from the Medici to the Pazzi, and that fatal intimacy grew up between his influential nephews the Riarii, and the discontented Florentine family, which was one of the features of the famous assassination.

As to the well-marked collapse of established morality and

[3]

religion, it was a commonplace of the fifteenth century. We need no other evidence than the accepted dictum of Luther, that any devout believer, pilgrimaging to Rome, must find his faith stagger beneath the blows dealt by what he saw there. To-day we hear the same complaints that mankind, still wishing to believe, and to find satisfaction for his spiritual aspirations, turns away from organized religion. To-day, as then, a leaven remains striving to restore mankind's reverence in established religion, and to revivify and reform the Churches to which men still would like to cling. We have not, it is true, produced a Savonarola, nor would authority proceed to burn him, if we did, but the intense desire to create a 'chosen' state on earth still manifests itself to-day. It is, under a different guise, the same spirit which causes the Fascist or Nazi to emphasize the desire which they feel to proselytize. In another direction it is to be traced in the corporations founded by Joseph Smith or by General Booth or by Mary Baker Eddy. Men have a natural desire, once they believe intensely, to convert others, and a body of people filled with this intense zeal do take as their ultimate aim the conversion of society and its organization along their lines.

Even the one feature which we sometimes pride ourselves is unique in our era, calling ourselves the 'scientific age,' might be challenged by the Italian of Machiavelli's Italy. For he too lived at a point of time when scientific knowledge was making a great stride forward. Men, then as now, found themselves thrilled with new discoveries, opening to them new possibilities, and Copernicus was then as great a portent as we have found Einstein.

Educational ideas which we conceive of as 'modern' can find their counterpart in those vivid days. Vittorino da Feltre could attend a modern educational conference and find himself completely at home in the debates. He not only preached, he put into practice in his famous school for the 'children of the nobility' such ideas as co-education, no corporal punishment, physical development through gymnastics and games. He used 'letter-games' to teach children of four to read, and he "followed the practice of the ancient Egyptians" in teaching elementary arithmetic by "means of games." He built his school in a beautiful situation, and decorated its walls with frescoes showing children at play, saying that it should be 'a house of delight.' If he found a child unwilling to learn, after fair trial, he would advise a change of education, saying "that nature had not endowed all with the taste or capacity for study." He varied, and alternated as far as possible, the subjects chosen, knowing that the mind wearied if kept too long in one groove, and he included music, singing and dancing amongst his subjects. His aim, shared by all the Humanist Educationalists of the time, was to develop individuality and to create not only 'men of learning' but good citizens.' Girls were educated alongside of, and on the same lines as, the boys, and neither Vittorino nor his contemporaries expected any lower standard of attainment nor apparently believed in any lesser.

Finally, and here we come to the most obvious, as it is at this moment possibly the most widely recognized of all the parallels. Italy in the fifteenth century saw the breakdown in many States of the long-established forms of democracy and the substitution of dictatorship. The Republican form of government, familiar from the most ancient days, had not worked out well against the strain imposed by constant and intensified warfare. Military failure and social misery drove the people in some cases to accept a despotism which gave them safety, and material prosperity, and which to a certain extent earned the description of 'benevolent.' Various types of dictators arose then as now, but love of liberty and the spirit of independence were still forces, and still struggled to survive. It is because Machiavelli, looking on those changes, pondered them in his heart and produced a striking account of their causes and results, that the modern interest in him once more induces us to turn with renewed activity to the reading of his books and to the study of his life and character.

CHAPTER II

NICCOLO MACHIAVELLI is one of the world's famous men. He himself never knew of the immense renown his writings were to bring him. Yet he might have counted himself fortunate in that he lived his life out in one of the most wonderful cities of the world during one of the most fascinating periods of history.

He was a Florentine, born towards the close of the fifteenth century, in 1469. His life therefore began when Florence was in the full enjoyment of her golden age, and the Renaissance was filling Italy with glory. It was a time when art and learning flourished as never before, when men seemed to touch a higher level of civilization than had been known since the great days of Rome. The voyages of the explorers were soon to lay open the New World, but to the Italian of that day no fables of the Indies could surpass the beauties and adventures of life in his own country.

Yet in spite of apparent wealth and security, Italy and Florence herself, though to the outward glance standing on the threshold of further expansion and glory, were both threatened and in danger. The lifetime of Machiavelli coincides with the period in which the Republic went down into ruin. As a patriot and a servant of the State, Machiavelli took part in all the great events in which Florence was involved. He saw the ruin of his country, and he foresaw the greater ruin which was to overtake all Italy. From the events of his life he drew the conclusions which he embodied in his work. To understand his books it is necessary to have some knowledge of his life, and of the world which surrounded him.

Florence, when Machiavelli grew to manhood, was still in form a Republic. The great house of Medici had made themselves the supreme influence in the city, but they observed all the outward forms of the constitution * The citizens were still the rulers of their own city, and the Medici had no title or official dignity to differentiate them from others of their rank. Florence was immensely rich, a great centre of industry and of trade, and above all of finance. Her strength and her influence lay in her wealth, her weakness in her lack of ability to defend herself if attacked. The territory belonging to her which lay beyond the city walls was not very extensive, nor thickly populated. It served her as the source of the food which supplied her swarming inhabitants. She had no easily defended frontiers and she had as her army only such hired troops as she chose to employ. Neither her citizens nor the inhabitants of the countryside were trained to arms. Yet she was surrounded by neighbours who were clearly not her friends, and one of the chief problems of the Medici was to maintain the security of Florence in an Italy composed of potential enemies.

Here the situation of the Republic may be clearly grasped if her actual geographical position is considered, and that of the four other great States which composed the Italy of the Renaissance. For geography played a very important part in deciding the fate of Florence. She lay, a rich but in some ways a weak State surrounded by a ring of other powers, Milan, Venice, the Papal States and beyond them, to the

* See Chapter XIII for details of the constitution of Florence and the position of the Medici.

south, Naples. These five together really made up Italy, while beyond the great barrier of the Alps lay the rest of Europe, hitherto concerned with its own affairs.

Of her immediate neighbours, Florence had most to dread from the power which lay to her south. Here her frontiers met those of the Papal States. Rome, the seat of the Papacy, was also the central city of the territory ruled by the Pope. This consisted of a number of small principalities, ruled over by lords who nominally held their lands as 'vicars of the church,' and whose tyranny and misrule rendered their subjects miserable. With Sixtus IV the Papacy had begun an attempt to consolidate its possessions, and to bring the turbulent lords of the Romagna under its control. Clearly, if the Papacy grew in strength, and developed along these lines, a powerful State might come into existence, and any expansion must bring conflict with Florence, lying as she did across the northern frontier. Weak Popes or holy ones might not aim at the extension of their temporal possessions, but actually the Popes with whom Machiavelli was to be concerned were to prove strong and aggressive, and as such, formidable foes.

To the north-east Florence had to face the great rival Republic of Venice. Venice was even richer and more powerful than Florence. The trade of east and west flowed through her ports, and as she grew in wealth so she had expanded on the mainland, until her territories stretched half-way across Northern Italy. She was strong, and the form of her constitution had given her much-envied stability. She was greedy and she was bold. Once already she had struggled to overthrow Milan, and, though beaten back in the previous century, she now seemed once more likely to seize the opportunity for further aggression.

For Milan, the State which closed Florence to the north-west, was clearly in a troubled condition. She had long since ceased to be a republic and had fallen under the rule of the Sforzas, who had made themselves her Dukes. But family feuds and dissensions had weakened the dynasty, and to the acute politicians of that day Milan was clearly weakening and likely to fall before any determined attack.

Lorenzo de' Medici had been a profound statesman. Ruler of Florence in reality, though not in name, he saw clearly that peace in Italy must be maintained by a balance of allied powers. Thus, seeing in the Papacy a possible danger, he sought to meet that by allying Florence with Naples, the power which lay on the other side of the Papal States. In this way the Papacy was caught between the two, and were she to attack either Florence or Naples the other would take her in the rear.

Again, seeing the strength and the ambition of Venice and realizing how overwhelming would be her position were she to succeed in spreading her territory across the whole of North Italy, Lorenzo allied with Milan, and this conjunction of Milan and Florence served the purpose of keeping Venice in check. Singly she might have been tempted to attack either, but acting together they formed a combination which she dared not face.

Such was the consistent and comprehensible policy of Lorenzo the Magnificent, and while he lived Italy was at peace and Florence was safe. With his death, in 1492, the whole structure fell, ruined by the incredible folly of his son. Piero not only broke the alliance with Milan, he began to intrigue with Naples and plan to attack Milan. The results of that step were far beyond anything he had expected, and yet might have been foretold. To estimate the criminal folly of his action it is necessary to look at Europe and the countries beyond the Alps.

The close of the fifteenth century witnessed the consolidation of the great Kingdoms of Western Europe. France, Spain and England now began to show the lines along which they were to develop. France led the way. The Hundred Years War once ended, and the country at last freed from the English invaders, the French crown began to consolidate its power. Charles VIII, who became King in 1483, brought in the last outstanding piece of territory when his marriage to the heiress of Brittany secured that country to the French crown. His army, trained and toughened by the long series of English wars, was a formidable weapon, and conscious of power, Charles longed to use it.

Spain too was at length becoming united and powerful. The marriage of Ferdinand of Aragon with Isabella of Castile had created a strong monarchy. The country thus at last brought under one rule had, as it believed, increased its strength by attacking and defeating the Moors of the South. The conquest of Granada gave Spain the unity she desired. Her King, Ferdinand, was one of the craftiest of the age, he knew how to utilize every opportunity to her advantage. The voyages of discovery, and the chance which gave to Spain the control of Columbus, were to give her wealth and dominion beyond the imagination. Spain was to be the great rival of France in the coming century.

Central Europe was under the jurisdiction of the Emperor Maximilian. Himself a Habsburg, and founder through his policy of dynastic marriages of the fortunes of his house, he was by election head of the Holy Roman Empire. In this capacity he was overlord of the German princes, and in theory of parts of Italy. He spent his life in struggling to assert himself in Italy, and to subdue the insubordination of the German princes. He could not succeed in either, for there was no Imperial army, and he had no means of enforcing his rule. His weakness, and the failure of the Empire to achieve any real unity, showed the other rulers of Europe how little they had to fear, large though his dominions seemed. Nor could Italy in her turn expect any help from her overlord should she desire it. Maximilian was neither a foe to be feared nor an ally of any value.

In short, the significant fact which we can see dawning upon Europe was the rise to power through union of the various nations. Even England, removed as she seemed from the rest of Europe and isolated by her long period of the civil wars of the Roses, had now begun to follow along the same path. Henry VII had ended the disastrous wars, the Tudor dynasty had taken its place on the throne, and before England lay the prospect of peace, of unity, and of increasing strength.

Now the misfortune of Italy lay in the fact that national unity was denied her. She was split up into these various States, each independent, and fairly equal in strength to the others. Naples, the Papacy, Venice, Florence and Milan could not unite under one rule. No one of them was strong enough to carry through the absorption of the others. Moreover, the fact that the Papal States lay right across the centre of Italy made it impossible for any of the powers to consolidate the peninsula by conquest. To war against the Papal States meant not only war against a temporal power, but war with the Church herself.

Thus denied the possibility of such natural unity as Spain, France, and England achieved, Italy might yet keep herself safe, so long as her various States allied together against the foreigner. This had been one of Lorenzo's objects, and again

with his death this policy was abandoned Milan, deprived
of her alliance with Florence, and threatened with war by
Naples, sought for help across the Alps, and by allying herself
with France, called in the foreigner. Naples, attacked by
France and Milan, in her turn was to seek help from Spain.
Thus France and Spain, called in by these two Italian States,
entered Italy. They came as allies, and naturally, once the
weakness of the country was made clear to them, remained as
conquerors. Italy, which at Machiavelli's birth was a collection of Italian powers, bound together by alliances, was at his
death a country torn in pieces by France and Spain, doomed
to lose her existence as a nation, and to be nothing but the
battlefield on which these two invaders fought out the question
as to which of them should be her master.

Yet none of this was apparent when Machiavelli grew to
man's estate. Florence under Lorenzo de' Medici was more
prosperous and more famous than ever before. Her citizens
were sharing in that immense zest and joy in living which
characterized all Renaissance Europe, but which Italy felt
in an especial degree.

The whole world seemed stirring into new life, and the
boundaries of men's horizons seemed immeasurably wider.
The new learning, the new inventions, the discoveries of new
worlds helped to give that impression of an immense step
forward in the progress of mankind. Vasco da Gama had
rounded the Cape, Columbus was soon to discover America.
The study of Greek had given a fresh impetus to learning in
every city and in every country. England in those days seemed
to the continental a backward and barbarous country, and yet
even in England we can see beginning the pale dawn which
in a few more years was to brighten into the day of Erasmus
and More and Colet. In our feeble reflection we can glimpse

the reality and from our poverty estimate the riches of Italy of the Renaissance.

Machiavelli's Italy was the land whence the learned drew their inspiration, where art flourished, where Botticelli, Michael Angelo and Leonardo found patrons eager and jealous to employ them. There poets and sculptors were honoured by all men, beauty and leisure and happiness seemed the characteristics of Italian life, and at no period has a country seemed to stand so clearly at the beginning of an era of prosperity and advance in all the arts of civilization.

Yet, within the space of his not very long life Machiavelli saw all that promise brought to naught. The Florentine Republic fell in ruin, Italy herself became the prey of invaders. Her art and her manners did nothing to save her. Because Machiavelli "saw with his eyes, and heard with his ears, and pondered these things in his heart," he came to write his books and formulate that philosophy which has so profoundly impressed the world.

CHAPTER III

MACHIAVELLI'S YOUTH: INFLUENCE OF SAVONAROLA IN FLORENCE

"I HOPE, and hoping increases my torment; I weep, and weeping feeds my tired heart; I burn, and my burning is hidden beneath the surface."* Thus Machiavelli wrote when he looked back and summed up the experience of his life.

Despite the misery which he breathes through this cry, we may envy Machiavelli when we realize the men and the events he had seen pass before his eyes. Lorenzo de' Medici, Savonarola, Cesare Borgia, Julius II, Leo X, Gonsalvo de Cordova, what a roll of names! He could recall the passing away of the greatest patron of art the world has ever seen, the burning of the 'prophet,' the poisoning, imprisonment and violent death of the 'prince.' He could reflect that he had seen the rise of a new race of rulers, of a type of government new to Italy, founded on the success of parvenu adventurers or foreign militarism. Despite the ruin and disgrace which his personal loyalty to Republican forms paradoxically enough brought Machiavelli, we must feel how immense was his gain in living in such a period. Nor can any sort of estimate be formed of the sincerity and value of his famous book, *The Prince*, unless we realize from the study of his life that his conclusions were drawn from his practical experiences, his acute intelligence thereby sharpened and induced to lay stress

* "*Io spero, e lo sperar cresce il tormento:*
Io piango, e'l pianger ciba il lasso core.
Io ardo, e l'arsion non par di fuore." (*Capitoli.*)

[15]

on what he realized was actually possible, so that while he saw clearly that independence and freedom were the ideal, he felt that in order to attain them man must sometimes accept the pressure of circumstances. He never, in reality, preached that the 'end justifies the means,' rather he bade men consider what end' and, as a man accustomed to government routine, he appreciated the difficulty of adjusting the means. His life, passed entirely in the service of the State, began on May 3rd, 1469. It was to be that of a highly intelligent, conscientious civil servant, with the background of a happy home life, and in no way foreshadowing the posthumous fame which was to be attached to his name.

He came, as do many of our higher government officials, from a family with a long tradition of moderate prosperity. The Machiavelli might be described as analogous with the English family connected with the countryside, owning a small property and with a respectable record in public life. His father, Bernardo, could trace back his family tree to the year 1120, and derived from the lords of the little castle of Montespertoli. That the Machiavelli were reckoned to be of good birth is shown by the fact that they were entitled to the use of a coat of arms, a cross azure, field argent, with four nails, likewise azure, at the four corners of the cross. Their name is to be found in the list of 'notable persons of the popolani' sent into exile in the year 1260. As his share of the Machiavelli inheritance Bernardo owned lands in the commune of San Casciano, and houses in various parts of Florence, near the Ponte Vecchio. He was in a comfortable station of life, not wealthy, but certainly not poor. It is difficult to estimate the modern equivalent of his income of 110 florins, but probably it represents what to us is £500 a year. This income was later to descend to Niccolò—and the knowledge that he had these 'private means' behind him perhaps helped the civil servant when the revolution in politics deprived him of his appointments.

Bernardo had married a widow, Bartolommea, born of the ancient Florentine family the Nelli, and there were four children of the marriage. Niccolò was the second, there being an elder son Totto, of whom very little is known. As Niccolò became his father's heir, presumably Totto died young and unmarried. The two younger children were girls.

In appearance Niccolò Machiavelli was, in Villari's words, "of middle height, slender figure, with sparkling eyes, dark hair, rather a small head, a slightly aquiline nose, a tightly closed mouth."

No contemporary bust or portrait has survived, the plaster cast in the Uffizzi having no claim to authenticity beyond the fact that during the nineteenth century it was found in the house in Florence in which Machiavelli lived and died— No. 16, Via Guicciardini. The early editions of his works have various engravings, the best of which, dated 1550, is called the 'Testina,' and from these and the stucco bust belonging to his heirs our knowledge of his looks is derived.

Nothing is known of his childhood or education. In 1495, when he was twenty-six years old, he suddenly appears, acting as representative of the whole Machiavelli clan, writing a long Latin letter to one of the Cardinals with regard to the presentation to the benefice of Santa Maria della Fagna, which the Pazzi family were trying to wrest from the Machiavelli.

We know therefore that he had the elements of scholarship, and that his relations recognized that his abilities gave him the lead in the family circle. We do not know how he lived, nor whether he had trained for any career, but almost immediately after this his entry into public life was brought about when he sought and obtained an appointment under the new Government called to power after the fall of Savonarola. The rise and fall of that 'unarmed prophet' is of great importance in Machiavelli's life. He naturally was a witness of, though not a participator in, that extraordinary experiment in creating a Holy City. His later writings show that he drew certain conclusions from that disastrous attempt.

While living in Florence throughout the period of Savonarola's ascendancy, Machiavelli was not one of his followers, and having gone to listen to the sermon of the preacher, he came away convinced that the Friar was an opportunist and a humbug.

His writings show that later, as he looked back and reflected on the real outcome of Savonarola's efforts, he continued to think the Friar did harm to Florence. "Under the influence of his prophetical doctrines no unity could be hoped for,"* and unity was the one absolutely essential aim, so Machiavelli came to believe.

The rough notes which he left behind him contain some brief but from their tone, contemptuous, reference to all the visionary side of Savonarola's life.

"Fra Girolamo at this time played the devil in Florence." "Fra Girolamo went on procession from his convent, getting himself publicity"; and in the *Discorsi* he says: "Although the people of Florence are neither ignorant nor uncultivated, nevertheless they let themselves be convinced by Fra Girolamo Savonarola that he spoke with God. I do not wish to form any judgment as to whether that were true or not, though I do not wish to speak of such a man without due respect."

We can draw our own conclusions from these brief notices, to all of which Machiavelli committed himself on this subject.

---

* *Decennale primo*, op. 5, 362.

Clearly he was quite out of sympathy with the type of man who was now to dominate Florence. Equally clearly the events of the next two or three years cannot but have exercised great influence on Machiavelli's theories, in that they gave him unique insight into the processes of revolution. Perhaps they helped to strengthen his disbelief in the goodness of mankind in the mass. Certainly they impressed upon him the need for unity in the State. Certainly, in the expulsion of the Medici and later in the change of government which coincided with Savonarola's fall, Machiavelli found the opportunity to enter public service on which his subsequent career was based.

A modern writer has said: "Florence of the Renaissance is one of the places and epochs which have been richest in revealed personalities." Few other periods provide us with individualities who still seem to make themselves felt across the centuries, with whose appearance and characters we acquire a familiarity that seems to make them alive and known to us to-day. Something dynamic seems to radiate from them; their intelligence, their wisdom, their strength, still have power to impress themselves on our minds. We can feel, as has been said of Shakespeare's characters, how much we should enjoy meeting them in the flesh and beginning—if we dared—an argument with them.

Amongst all these vital personalities Savonarola is one of those of whom we have the clearest impression. He is one of the most arresting, as he is one of the most original, of the men of the Renaissance. His power, whether exercised through his preaching, or through the intensely dominating effect of his personality on individuals, arose from his complete and burning sincerity, a sincerity in which we may believe, though Machiavelli did not. It derived from his belief in sin,

and his overwhelming fear of the power and of the consequences of sin, from which mankind must be forced to turn
and to seek salvation. Perhaps this strength of conviction and
its effect may be comprehended through the words of John
Donne, in whose mentality and Savonarola's there is a certain
resemblance, and in whose sermons and poems Savonarola
would have found much that he could understand and which
would express his own feelings. When Donne writes, "I have
a sinne of fear that when I have spunne my last thread, I shall
perish on the shore," he expresses the same spirit which
haunted Savonarola from his childhood. The emphasis on
sin which was the theme and constant preoccupation of the
friar is exactly expressed by the poet:

> "Despair behind, and death before doth cast
> Such terror, and my feeble flesh doth waste
> By sinne in it, which it t'wards hell doth weigh."

or:

> "Oh! my blacke soule!
> Thou art like a pilgrim, which abroad hath done
> Treason, and durst not turne to whence he is fled."

When Donne writes:

> "I am the man which hath affliction seene
> Under the rod of God's wrath having beene,
> He hath led me to darknesse, not to light,"

he gives the desolation of spirit which we know descended
upon Savonarola when he realized the failure of his work.

No words can better point to that supreme touch of
misery suffered by those who have striven, as they believe,

to do the task laid upon them by God, and have failed, than
Donne's:

"My strength, my hope, unto myselfe I said,
Which from the Lord should come is perished."

Savonarola's whole nature, passionate and highly-strung,
led him to believe that he had in a very special sense direct
communion with God, who had laid upon him a sacred
mission, and to him the crowning horror of his end was the
perception that somehow he had failed to carry out this task.
That sense of spiritual failure, transcending all worldly disaster
and the perception that it was due to his concerning himself
in worldly politics, even though he did so in no worldly
spirit, finds its truest expression in Donne's terrible cry:

"To see God only, I goe out of sight:
And to scape stormy days, I chuse
An Everlasting night."

*   *   *   *   *

With this intense background of fear and burning desire
to save, Savonarola entered upon the career which was to have
a vitally important effect upon the history of Florence.

He was not himself a Florentine. He came from Ferrara,
and had entered the Dominican order, where his life would be
devoted to teaching and to preaching. He gained his early
experience in Lombardy, chiefly at Brescia, and on his
earliest coming to Florence, in the lifetime of Lorenzo de'
Medici, he at first met with no success. His style did not
appeal to the taste of the Florentines. He did not model
himself on classical lines, he did not quote from the humanists.
He based his 'message' on the Gospels, and it was invariably
one of the need for repentance and salvation. The Florentines

at first found both his person and his preaching uncouth, and greatly preferred the polish of his rival, the Augustinian Fra Mariano da Gennazzano, the protégé of Lorenzo.

Yet in spite of his early failure to please and his consequent recall from Florence, he was in 1490 once more asked to return, and was now made Prior of San Marco. This was brought about through Pico della Mirandola, friend alike of Savonarola and of Lorenzo de' Medici.

Pico is of interest in that he is the exact antithesis of the ruffianly, bloodthirsty fierce Italian which the phase 'age of the despots' conjures up to our imagination. He is instead the prototype of the youths who look out from Botticelli's pictures, and whom too often we forget when we envisage the Italy of the Borgias. Sir Thomas More so loved and admired Pico's religious meditations that he translated both them and a life of Pico. Here is the description given in More's words of this beautiful young man: "Of feature and shape seemly and beauteous, of stature goodly, his visage lovely and fair, his colour white, intermingled with comely reds, his eyes grey and quick of look, his teeth even and white, his hair yellow and abundant."

Not our conception of a typical Italian, and yet Pico was of a type perfectly familiar in Italy of that day. He had lived as most young men of his station then lived, a gay and pleasure-seeking life "wandering over the crooked hills of delicious pleasure" and he had combined this with a love of learning that led him to a study of Greek, of philosophy, of the languages of the East, of law and natural sciences.

Platonism was his special interest, and he had first gone to Florence, in 1463, at the age of twenty to visit Marsilio Ficino. Gradually to Pico came the realization that pagan myth and philosophy did not satisfy him. He set to work in an attempt to reconcile them with Christianity, trying to harmonize Plato with Moses and comparing the Timæus with the Book of Genesis. He knew all the best scholars of his day, he was himself soaked in the 'new learning,' and yet he could find no spiritual peace in his life. Pleasure had long ceased to satisfy, now the intellectual knowledge he had acquired seemed insufficient for happiness, and he turned to religion. His writings sought to "define the stages by which the soul passes from the earthly to the unseen beauty," and he ended with the conclusion of the mystic: "We may rather love God than either know Him, or by speech utter Him. Yet men had liefer by knowledge never find that which they seek, than by love possess that thing which without love were found in vain."

In the course of his wanderings throughout Italy, and in his restless anxiety to find a solution of the spiritual problems which so troubled him, he of necessity had forced upon him the difficulties put in the way of one anxious to believe, by the moral failures of the Catholic Church of the period. He had written in criticism of the Papacy, and his works had been condemned for lack of orthodoxy. One of the agreeable pastimes of the day was the arranging of public debates between all sorts of opposing parties. Attending such a debate between lay speakers and members of the Dominican order, Pico had heard Savonarola denounce the corruption into which the Church had fallen. He came at once under the sway of that powerful personality, and it was he who now begged Lorenzo de' Medici to recall the preacher to Florence.

Here Pico became the intimate friend of some of the most learned and cultured men, both young and old, who all believed in his sincerity and were attracted to him, thus once more illustrating the fact, true in Renaissance Italy as in our modern world, that intense religious feeling, combined with education and knowledge, has an appeal which men of all types find irresistible. Marsilio Ficino, the great scholar and Platonist, Poliziano the humanist, Lorenzo Credi, Botticelli, and Michael Angelo, were all his intimates. To-day San Marco remains perhaps the most completely satisfying part of Florence. Here no noise, no touch of modern invention, has come to intrude upon the quiet picture of bygone days. Fra Angelico's clear bright frescoes light up the plain walls, the tiny cells. The little garden is as remote, as simple as it has always been. Here, could they return, these great men of the past would feel themselves once more at home. It is as they saw it. Here Lorenzo himself, in the first early days, must have come to visit the new Prior of the foundation he loved, and here Savonarola was to realize the nature of the task he had set himself. Here he once prayed, here he preached, and here he suffered his last overwhelming disaster.

To Pico della Mirandola Savonarola's return to Florence brought spiritual peace. Yielding more and more to the Friar's influence, he abandoned the world, entered the Dominican order, and fulfilling the prophecy of Cammilla Rucellai, died 'in the time of lilies'—as the French *fleur-de-lys* were borne through the city gates. Lorenzo himself died before he could realize that in the short ugly heavy-featured friar he had brought to Florence the man who was to destroy the power of his House.

For Savonarola, intent on his work of salvation, could hardly become an inhabitant of Florence without coming at once into conflict with the Medicean standard of morals and behaviour. Lorenzo had encouraged in every way the sensual side of Florentine life, but it must be admitted that everywhere in Italy at that period the standard of morals and behaviour was low. The luxury which material prosperity due to expanding trade had brought was very great. The nobles and bourgeois enjoyed every comfort of a splendid and comfortable existence. Their houses, furniture, clothes, and way of living, all attested their wealth and their taste. Their manners reflected the apparently universal rule that rich people with little to occupy their time do not fall back on 'high thinking.' The amusements of the Borgian Pope were a cause of scandal, public opinion felt that the Holy Father had gone too far in taking his guests after dinner to watch the behaviour of the stallions in the stables, and that it was clearly vulgar to fill the bosoms of the ladies' very low-necked gowns by cramming sweetmeats down them. Yet if this was done in the highest circles, it is clear that the code which made such jokes possible was a low one. In Florence the Medici themselves never sank to such a level, Lorenzo's taste was too good. The ordinary wealthy citizen, however, was extraordinarily free in his behaviour, and in the lower ranks of society coarseness had very disagreeable manifestations. The very fact that so many readily brought bawdy books and pictures to be burnt in Savonarola's 'bonfire of vanity' shows both that the more decent feelings of the people were roused to get rid of what they were really ashamed to own, and that they did in point of fact buy and possess many things which had nothing to recommend them but their obscenity. Savonarola was no hater of learning or art—he proved this later when he used the funds of San Marco to save the Medicean collection of Greek codici and miniatures—but he did hate their degeneration.

In addition Florence was, even in the eyes of the Italians, notorious for and disgraced by her carnivals. Here Lorenzo's actions came directly into conflict with Savonarola's ideas and ideals. Lorenzo had quite deliberately helped on, both by lavish gifts of money and by himself writing songs and encouraging others to do so, the development of these municipal festivals into pagan orgies which no reformer could pass by. These festivals cannot be defended even by those who appreciate the survival of folk-songs and dances. The fifteenth century was not one of restraint, there was no need to encourage the populace to "get rid of repressions," and Lorenzo did no service to his fellow-citizens by encouraging bawdy songs and more than bawdy plays.

In addition Savonarola, while hating with all his soul this degradation of a people by coarse pleasure, had intelligence enough to see what lay behind it. Lorenzo did not seek to divert the people through pure love of seeing the poorer classes enjoy themselves. His subsidizing of the carnivals had its political aim, and Savonarola fully appreciated that point. If the democracy was pleased, it was likely to be contented under the ascendancy of the man from whom its pleasures flowed. With popular support behind him, Lorenzo could carry out his schemes for political rule. Therefore Savonarola, in whom, as in many great Italians, there still lingered an innate love of the old ideal of liberty, felt his moral prejudices reinforced by his political ideals. The people of Florence were being corrupted in manners and in morals, and by a man who in reality was destroying their liberty.

Here Savonarola found himself in a position of extraordinary strength. Many in Florence shared his distrust and dislike of the Medici, but most people dared take no action. They could not run the risks which open opposition to Lorenzo entailed. But Savonarola was free. He summed up the situation in one sentence in answer to emissaries sent by Lorenzo to point out the inadvisability of criticizing Medicean rule. "You," he said, "having wives and children, have good cause to dread exile; but I have none, for it matters nothing to me whether I dwell at Florence or elsewhere."

With this feeling of independence, driven on by his fervour, strengthened by all the burning convictions of his passionate nature, Savonarola set himself the task of opposing the Medicean influence and of drawing together all the forces which opposed it. During Lorenzo's lifetime he preached, he taught, he made personal converts. His power grew until it became immense. It was based partly on his complete contrast to the other well-known clerics and preachers of his day. As a Dominican he had been of course carefully taught and thoroughly trained in the art of dialectic and preaching. He was a firm believer in the power of reasoning and the need for education. He knew all the intricacies of the faith, he was no simple good man, making an impression and obtaining his effects by 'sweetness and light.' He was a born arguer, ready to dispute and maintain his views, and his earliest teachers had warned him against his tendency to subtlety. Now he had become the exponent of missionary views. People were to be reconverted and brought back to the faith. He had as his rivals preachers of the other orders, Fra Mariano the Augustinian, and Fra Domenico da Ponza the Franciscan. Of these the one preached in the accepted 'classical style' with artificial divisions of his sermon, following upon the old Roman rules of rhetoric. Fra Domenico was of the opposite way, he tried to startle and amuse, and in so doing, in the opinion of many, degenerated into the grotesque, reminiscent to us of the strange evangelists of some modern sects.

Savonarola preached the doctrine in which he believed, the need for redemption and for change of life. He preached it with simplicity, with eloquence, and above all with complete conviction. Here was the secret of his power. This was a man who was never thinking of his reputation, his success as an orator; he was a 'prophet crying in the wilderness,' a man whose whole energy and strength and all his gifts were poured out in his burning determination to 'save his people'— 'Repent, for the Kingdom of Heaven is at hand' had brought crowds to listen to St. John the Baptist in the wilderness, it brought crowds to listen to Savonarola's sermons in San Marco. To these sermons Machiavelli came, but he came as a scoffer, and as a scoffer he went away. To his cold clear mind, the preacher's eloquence did not appeal, and the involved, long-drawn-out arguments failed to convince. Later in his political writings Machiavelli was to urge the same message in the sphere of politics that Savonarola now urged in the spiritual—harmony and consistency of life, subordination to an ideal, and hope. Now he saw in "the prophet's" utterances "nothing but lies," as he wrote in a letter to a friend. Yet both Machiavelli and Savonarola were to give their lives to the study of the same subject, the happiness and welfare of their fellow-men. Savonarola's solution of the problem failed, and has perished, Machiavelli's has prevailed.

It may be noted here how Machiavelli accounted for Savonarola's ascendancy. In the *Discorsi* (i. xi) he says: "People believed in him, *because of his way of life*," meaning that they were swayed by his personality; "*because of his doctrines*," that is to say, the immense appeal made by a call to live a better life on a people who though corrupt were both appreciative of the fact and respondent to a desire for something better; and "*because of the subjects with which he dealt*," and here is meant the reform of the constitution after the flight of the Medici, a matter in which every

[28]

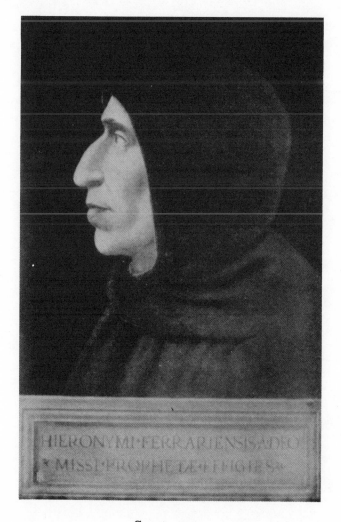

SAVONAROLA

Florentine was passionately interested.

The physical personal characteristics of the man who was now to sway the whole city are of interest, and one of the curious points is the impression made by his portrait, and the conclusion, reached in considering his later career, that this portrait misrepresents his inner self. His face, once seen, can never be forgotten, and at first must repel, by its plainness and heavy ugly features. Yet there is strength, harsh obstinacy, self-control and something which makes one look, and look again. The type can still be seen reflected in modern Italian faces, but the portrait emphasizes every detail. It must in actuality belie the man it portrays. For one of Savonarola's outstanding characteristics was his sympathy. He was never harsh to those with whom he came in contact. He had the gift of winning love. And, unhappily for him, he had not the physical courage and toughness the strong features seem to betoken. When the time came, he could not stand the physical horror of torture, and he could not face the thought of an agonizing death. His nerves, and his body gave way, and his last writings and utterances tell the saddest story in the world, when one who had believed so ardently and intensely in his mission was driven by sheer physical agony to doubt and to deny his own beliefs. "When I crie out, he out shouts my prayer," wrote Donne. Savonarola, in his cell, condemned to death, came to think that his strength had come not from his Lord, but from the devil. His prayer now might well have been:

"That Thou remember them some claim as debt.
I think it mercy if Thou wilt forget."

In 1494 these days were still to come. Savonarola had no doubts, no hesitations. He went on his way like a great storm. Florence crowded to San Marco, entranced with his eloquence, and drawn to sympathy by the real, if unacknowledged, wish of mankind to rise above its worse self.

The doctrines he preached were, in the main, always the same. First, the Church would be punished. Second, she would be renewed. Third, this would come quickly.

By this he did not mean solely the Church as a religious corporation or order, he meant the whole of Christendom. He declared that the Christians of the day, far from being a society of those saved from sin, were a society of persons, who were committing sin. The wrath of God having been incurred would overtake the world, but it would not destroy, it would renew. He was in no sense a precursor of the Protestants, and should not be claimed as such. He was entirely orthodox in dogma. He held that the Church, as a religious body, could not be reformed, for it was the vehicle of revealed truth and the administrator of the Sacraments. Neither dogma nor the Sacraments would be touched, in the coming purification, only laws, customs and the way of life.

Further, he held, and here he began to draw towards danger, that the punishment he foretold would come from the State, from the civil power. Now he began to enter the domain of prophecy, and as his fervour grew, and that of the huge crowds that flocked to hear him, visions began to appear before him. To a vast awestruck congregation he declared how he had seen a great sword, suspended in the sky, which fell crashing upon the earth. This, he said, was the truth revealed to him as a prophet that he might warn the people.

He spoke to troubled ears. Florence was aware of her sins, and she was aware too of the difficulties and dangers which were threatening her. She knew that a sword was in very fact threatening her, and that a fleshly enemy was approaching her walls.

For in 1494 the dreaded tide of French invasion rose, flooded across the Alps, and poured down upon the plains of Italy. The foreign invasions which were to destroy Italy and for four hundred years hand her over to be carved up by alien powers had begun.

CHAPTER IV

SAVONAROLA

THE coming of the French had been foreseen for some years by the politicians of Italy, and it is one of the commonplace historical problems as to why, seeing the obvious results, such wily politicians as they were, not only took no adequate steps to prevent it, but actually encouraged it.

Ludovico, Il Moro, usurper of Milan, is one of the villains of the piece. He was ruler of the Key-state, commanding the routes over which the French must enter Italy. Why, instead of uniting with the other powers, did he commit the incredible folly of calling in the foreigner? The answer is one which lies behind many of the fatal acts of history. He did it because he believed it suited his own personal ends, and he had no breadth of vision to enable him to see the ultimate results likely to follow from his selfishness. Self-interest is not always the best policy, and narrow nationalism, then as now, based solely on what is really animal instinct, by denying all the benefits of co-operation between States, ultimately cramps and ruins the strictest adherents to the doctrine of selfishness.

Ludovico was engaged in making himself lord of Milan, keeping in subjection his nephew, Gian Galeazzo, rightful Duke, whose untimely and suspiciously opportune death was soon to make Ludovico lord in name as well as in fact. The only attempt to check him came from a woman. Here an extremely human element came into play. Gian Galeazzo was acknowledged to be incompetent just as his uncle Ludovico was readily recognized as a capable and intelligent man, well able to guide the State and exercise all real power, while leaving his nephew titular ruler. Ludovico was not aggressive, and it is barely possible he might have contented himself with this. Unluckily for Italy he married, in 1491, that famous young beauty Beatrice d'Este, whose charms and accomplishments have so endeared her to posterity that the mischief she did has been glossed over. For Beatrice, arriving as the bride of the man known to be the real ruler of Milan, was resolved to have the prestige as well as the power. She must be the acknowledged head of Milanese society. But there, occupying the throne which Beatrice was convinced she could most adequately fill, was the figure of another woman—the young Duchess Isabella, wife of the incompetent young Duke, now twenty years old, mother of a baby heir, and daughter of a proud fierce man, Alfonso, King of Naples. That feminine vanity mixed with stronger feelings cannot be denied. Isabella found herself relegated entirely to the background. It was Beatrice who became the central figure in society, Beatrice who held court, for whom marvellous parties and pageants were arranged, with 'stage effects and decorations' by no less a person than Leonardo da Vinci. Possibly Isabella might have accomplished little, but she was driven on not only by wounded pride; she had the better impulse of fighting for the rights of her little son. She had no party to support her in Milan, and she began to implore, more and more fiercely, as the situation grew more threatening, the aid of her father, the King of Naples. Here was the fatal possibility of danger, and from this quite comprehensible pretext for the interference of Naples in the affairs of Milan sprang such overwhelmingly disastrous results. In this threat from

Naples Ludovico saw danger to himself, and probably excused his action to his conscience by the plea that his duty to Milan made the most desperate remedies expedient. He ought, if traditional policy and alliances had still held good, to have been able to rely for help on Florence, his great neighbour, who lay between Alfonso and himself.

For the past half-century Florence, Naples and Milan had formed a league which really guaranteed the stability of Italy and her immunity from foreign invasion. No power across the Alps would care to face such a combination. We can easily see the resemblance to modern conditions in the Balkans. If the small powers of a peninsula, with a difficult mountain frontier to guard it, are leagued together, it is hardly worth while for an invader to force that barrier and descend into a hostile country. But if those small powers fall out, and if one should make advances to the foreigner, the nature of the danger becomes clear.

This is exactly what happened in Italy in 1494. Piero de' Medici, incredibly stupid son of Lorenzo, possessed every fault which could bring disaster on the politics of his country. He was thick-headed, violent, inaccessible to reason, touchy, and with bad friends to whose advice alone he listened. He would not dream in his conceit of following in his father's footsteps, he must strike out on his own line. So he deserted the Milanese alliance, broke it off and leagued himself secretly with Naples.

Ludovico felt himself in peril. He is a good example of the man who can almost excuse his conduct as we mentally arraign him. Unquestionably he was the ablest man in Milan, and the one best fitted to rule. He had lost his ally, Florence, he was threatened by the violent and unscrupulous King of Naples. France had often in the past been held over Italy as the formidable figure in the background whose aid might be invoked to quell tiresomely quarrelsome neighbours. Ludovico must have convinced himself that his policy was necessary for his own interest, justifiable in those of Milan, and not necessarily dangerous to those of Italy. He was wrong in his judgment, and naturally his ill success had put him at a disadvantage. Like many others who have acted in a way we call 'wrong,' it was his failure which really covered him with disgrace.

In 1493, however, he made his fatal decision. He entered upon negotiations with France and urged Charles to revive the claims of the House of Anjou to Naples.* That the King of France had a claim was familiar to every politician in France and Italy. Hitherto the Kings of the House of Anjou had not thought it worth their while to assert their claims. But with Milan, Florence and Naples no longer united, but all quarrelling venomously, and with Milan, the border State, welcoming him to Italy, Charles VIII overcame the reluctance of his more sensible advisers in France, and crossed the Alps to make himself King of Naples.

He passed through Milan, and advanced on Florence. The news of his approach brought about an immediate upheaval, and now Savonarola steps from his pulpit and from his cloister on to the stage of the political scene. For with the advance of the French it became clear that the Medici would fall. The family which had dominated Florence was held responsible for the danger which threatened. Piero was directly responsible, for it was he who had deliberately broken with Milan and joined with Naples. He now piled Pelion upon Ossa. He slipped out of the city, went to meet Charles, and in the vain hope of placating him handed over the keys

* See Appendices.

of the great fortresses Sarzana, Pietra Santa, Pisa and Leghorn to the French, who hereafter occupied them.

Florence broke into an uproar of anger, mixed with fear. On his return, the doors of the Palazzo Pubblico were shut in his face, the street urchins pelted him with stones. He saw worse violence must follow from the grown men and he fled. Next day his brother, the future Pope Leo, who had shown more courage and more sense, saw that the city was too hot even for him. He too escaped, and Florence found herself free of the Medici and left to follow the advice of the leader who now took their place as uncrowned wielder of authority.

Savonarola had that singular experience which sometimes attends the vague prophet of misfortune, his prophecies had come true. He had foretold disaster, war, even the drawing of the sword. He had prophesied the coming of an avenger, and the avenger was here, his sword in his hand, war following behind. "You are sent by God," so he informed the King of France, "and you have caused all the servants of Christ to rejoice—for we hope that God, through you, will lower the pride of the proud, and exalt the humility of the humble—will throw down vice and set up virtue—and put right all that is wrong."

The people of course saw in this the proof of his divine mission. The city fathers, now responsible for the safety of the Republic, saw more. They were many of them personally acquainted with Savonarola, and they appreciated his brains, his strength of character, and his sincerity. They chose him as one of the delegation now sent to treat with Charles. Perhaps they felt too that the French King would look with a specially friendly eye on the man who had so earnestly foretold his coming—who had therefore exalted him as the chosen "instrument of God."

Florence, as things were, could not resist. Charles entered the city, but as a guest, not as a conqueror. George Eliot's *Romola* is dull as a romance, yet contains vivid and excellent descriptions of the entry of the slobbering misshapen figure riding beneath his magnificent banner marked with the lilies which ironically derived from the same flower as Florence's own *Lys rouge*, and of the ill-concealed furious discontent of the Florentines. Appearances were kept up, however, and Charles, bribed with an immense subsidy, and still retaining the sea-fortresses, agreed to leave. His attempted delay led to another interview with Savonarola, who, confirmed in all his own beliefs, assured Charles that it was now the will of God he should 'move on.' Accordingly, influenced perhaps rather more strongly by his general's advice that enough time had now been wasted, Charles left the city on November 30th and Florence set herself to create the new form of government which has become famous as being attributed to Savonarola.

The constitution now to be drawn up under Savonarola's guidance and inspiration was the one under which Machiavelli's life as a public servant was henceforth to be lived. It created the machine of which Machiavelli became a part. It stood the test of time and experience sufficiently well to last until the return of the Medici caused a reversal of its democratic principles. Into the full complexities of the Florentine system of government it is not necessary to enter here.* In outline the Republic was governed through an elaborate system of Councils, based on the organization of the training and manufacturing guilds. It was not a pure democracy. Men who were not members of a guild had no share in the

---

* Full details are given in Chapter XIII. It may be remarked that a celebrated Oxford tutor, Edward Armstrong, consoled an anxious pupil who was puzzled by the intricacies of the Florentine constitution thus: "Well, my friend, if you don't understand it, neither do I, but take comfort, neither do the examiners." (*Italian Studies*, E. Armstrong.)

government, and at the other end of the scale the nobility were largely debarred from office and power. Indirect election was employed, and laws, before they came into force, had to pass through many stages, coming before one Council after another. The executive power rested with the Signoria and the Collegi, most important bodies. The Signoria carried on all the important work of government, and in its hands rested largely the control of the city. It was a body consisting of the Gonfalonier of Justice, who acted as the ceremonial head of the State, with eight Priors, two from each quarter of the city. It held office for two months, and its members, though unpaid, lived during their period of office in the Palazzo Pubblico at the public expense.

The Colleges (colleagues) consisted of twelve Buonuomini, acting as a sort of Privy Council, and check on the Signoria, and of the sixteen gonfalonieris of the militia companies, with nine assessors.

The appointment to these highly important offices was in theory by lot, the names being drawn out of *borse*, or purses, containing the names of those who were eligible. In actuality these *borse* could be manipulated, by the omission of the names of persons from the lists of eligibles. The Medici were accustomed to exercise their influence and obtain their power by such manipulation. Eligibility was decided by a Scrutiny, conducted by a board, and people could be held ineligible for various reasons, including having been 'warned' (*ammonito*) for any political offences. This system finds its modern parallel under the Soviets, where only persons of proved loyalty to the State can be on the electoral register.

Florence was now eager for a more democratic form of government, and after the first patchwork attempt had proved a failure, Savonarola, though reluctantly, was called in to

take a share in the constitution-making. He gave utterance
to his views through his famous series of sermons preached
in the Duomo. It seems perhaps a little odd to us that he was
able to explain the system of rule which he considered
suitable for the city in a series of addresses given on the
prophets of the Old Testament, but it was so. "Aggeo"
(Haggai), "Salmi" (Psalms) and "Giobbe" (Job) all helped
to make clear to the Florentines what reforms were desirable
and why.

Savonarola hoped, of course, to set up a true City of God,
and he intended to do so not by establishing a theocracy, but
by giving power to a reformed and truly Christian democracy.
Thus his constitution, while largely adopted from that of
Venice, which was held to be the model for all Italy, since
under it Venetians were the most peaceful, contented and
wealthy of all Italians, was given a less oligarchic and more
democratic twist. His most beloved and most famous institution was that of the Great Council open to all 'eligible'
citizens (i.e., those whose relations for three generations had
held or been eligible for office), and with the equally famous
Council of Eighty, which was elected by the Great Council,
and from now on chose the members of the Signoria. These
steps, extremely simple in themselves, did give the body of
the citizens more share in the control of government. The
plan which seems to us so absurd of appointing these great
magistrates for such a short term of office as two months
was in reality meant to help on the same object, for rapid
rotation in office both prevented any man getting too firm a
grip on the machine, and it also increased the power and
pressure which could be exercised by the voter who elected
to the office. He never aimed at giving power to the mob.
The franchise was restricted, as before, and he succeeded in

abolishing the appeal to mob rule hitherto made possible in that final resort of the constitution, the Parlamento. No longer could any party in the State summon the crowd to the Piazza and severe penalties threatened anyone who attempted it.

Savonarola tried to make his followers realize the responsibility of political power. The vote was to be regarded as bringing with it a serious, almost a sacred responsibility. The elector—and this was indeed a counsel of perfection—was never to vote for party reasons, but always for the best candidate, irrespective of party. Nor was the 'best' to imply religious goodness, without intelligence; indeed if the choice was unfortunately between the wise man and one who is good but foolish, the elector, in the interest of the State, must choose the wise.

These changes in the constitution were of great interest to Machiavelli, whose mind was incessantly dwelling on the problem of 'the best form of government.' He definitely disapproved of some of the more democratic alterations, such as of law of 1494, allowing an appeal to the Grand Council on behalf of anyone condemned to death. Savonarola himself, while desiring to establish a court of appeal, did not really favour it being such a large body, but accepted the idea as better than nothing.

In general, the chief lesson Machiavelli drew from these reforms was that anyone desiring to make reforms permanent must have the power to enforce them. He believed that Savonarola failed because he was 'unarmed'—"his new institutions came to nothing, since he had not the means to keep his followers steadfast." Il Principe, 6.)

Dear as his creations in the sphere of government were to Savonarola, only a part of his energies went to them. His real passion was for reforming the citizens to whom he gave these powers. He was foredoomed to fail, for he could not battle against the fact that religion had lost its ancient hold upon the people. Yet he made the attempt, and acting in the belief that laws can make mankind good, he invoked State aid. Drunkards were driven off the streets; gambling, 'the favourite Florentine amusement,' if carried on in public was punishable by torture; swearing in public was to bring the penalty of piercing the tongue. "The foreigners," said Machiavelli (*Opere P.M.*, Vol. II, p. 245), "say that we have escaped from the hands of the Medici and have fallen into those of the Friar."

Besides the actual laws, enforced by the State, Savonarola relied on an intensive campaign to revive religion and morality. In the place of the Carnival, the year 1496 saw the famous Bonfire of Vanities, when cards, dice, false hair, cosmetics, obscene books and pictures, all went up in flames on the Piazza.

The bands of small boys and youths who went from house to house collecting these vanities show how every reformer soon learns the importance of enlisting the enthusiasm of the young. Indeed, his organization of children met with the warm approval of most decent people. The street-arabs of Florence were a disgrace and a nuisance. They went about in bands, put poles across the streets and demanded blackmail from the passers-by. They spent the money in feasts which often ended in pitched battles between the rival gangs and occasionally, as a result of these contests, the defeated party would withdraw, leaving some of their band actually dead upon the stones.

The people of the Renaissance loved children and devoted much time and thought to their education. The curious distortion of ultra-Protestant views was yet to come, which by stressing 'original sin' and treating children as 'vessels of wrath' brought with it a tradition of severity and harshness which in Protestant countries is only now passing away.

In England we are so accustomed to the after-glow still cast by the Victorian age that we hardly stop to reflect that the severity towards children of the last century was not shared by continental nations nor that it was one of the worst legacies of Puritanism. But it is to be noted that as that harsh conception has passed away, so there have grown up all the various movements and organizations designed to enrol the children by enlisting their sympathies and encouraging their enthusiasm. We may rather tepidly approve of Scouts as useful in absorbing energies which may otherwise become tiresome; we may allow ourselves to become irritated by accounts of slightly smug gatherings of Young Communists or Young Conservatives; we may, turning our eyes elsewhere, regard the German or Italian youths with disfavour, but all preachers of creeds, political or religious, now accept the conversion of youth as one of the cardinal points. The Dominican of the fifteenth century realized that, and his enrolment of his bands merely shows his progressive and essentially practical mind.

For a time the fervour of religious ecstasy, reinforced on the one hand by joy at having got rid of the Medici, on the other by relief that the foreign invader had gone on his way doing so little harm, carried all before it. The churches were crowded, money was poured out on charity. Enemies were publicly reconciled, merchants and bankers 'gave up what they had unjustly acquired.' Florence became "a city of penitents and ascetics," and on Palm Sunday, 1496, Christ was proclaimed "King of Florence."

No longer did the carnival songs echo between the houses
in the narrow streets. One of the few beautiful little songs
which have come down to us had been written by Lorenzo
himself. Instead of the refrain, as haunting now as then:

> "*Quant è bella giovinezza*
> *Che si fugge tuttavia!*
> *Di doman non c'è certezza:*
> *Chi vuol esse lieto, sia!*"

the population went along singing the hymn:

> "*Viva, Viva in nostro core*
> *Cristo re, duce e signore*
> *Ciascun purghi L'intelletto*
> *La memoria e voluntate*
> *Dal terrestre e vano affetto*
> *Arda Tutto incaritate*
> *Contemplando la bontate*
> *Di Gesù Re di Fiorenza.*"

Florence had indeed become regenerate.

Once more time has made it easier for us to drop the attitude
of impatience at the rather childish futile efforts to change
the nature of a people through intensive propaganda. We
have "seen with our eyes, and heard with our ears," modern
nations following on the same lines. One might say that since
Revolutionary France filled Europe with the sounds of the
Marseillaise, the importance of song has come into its own.
Certainly modern Germany and Italy have impressed upon
us the power of anthems which imprint themselves in the
minds of the masses, and which fulfil, as they are intended
to fulfil, the object of rousing mass enthusiasm.

Moreover, here Savonarola's theories, underlying all the

outward business of organized religious feeling, were approximate to the theories which Machiavelli was later to embody in his famous works and which must be considered in detail later. Niccolò himself was completely aloof from the revival of religion. He regarded Savonarola, at this time, as an impostor, deceiving others and himself. Looking back long years after he might have done him more justice, and realized that, though so dissimilar in character and life, their aims had something in common. For both sought to identify man, the individual, with the community, the State. Both, being chiefly concerned with Florence, had in mind the city-State, but their theories apply equally to Italy the nation-State. Both believed that the individual only enjoyed happiness and only obtained his fullest and highest development when he subordinated his interests and his welfare to that of the community. Both, above all, held that the community was entitled to demand and to receive recognition of the supremacy of its claims. The State was to be all, man to exist only as a member of that State.

Savonarola's ascendancy, his forcing of a 'holy' city upon Florence, clearly could never be maintained. He owed his rise to power to the reaction felt against the influence which the Medici had exercised on the government of the city. His 'constitution' was popular and successful and to this his early predominance must be attributed.* Now his influence began to wane and his hold over the people to weaken. His failure to maintain his position must be attributed mainly to two factors. He had engaged in politics, and had identified himself definitely with the alliance with France and with antagonism to the Papacy. As the futility of the French alliance became

---

* Savonarola's reform of the constitution is important. It is studied in detail in Chapter XIII.

clear, so his policy was discredited. Further, the French had obtained Pisa and had not returned it to Florence, and the whole city resented bitterly, and rightly, this loss of a vitally important possession.

To these purely political considerations was added the weakening of his hold over the religious feelings of the people. Primarily his position had been won by the appeal he made to the instincts of morality and religion. If he ceased to maintain his domination in those spheres he had no claim on the allegiance of the Florentines. Hence the fact that he united various sections of religious opinion against him was highly dangerous, and when the mass of indifferents saw that his political schemes had gone awry, they illogically ceased to believe in his claims to act as a religious reformer.

His loss of influence in this sphere may be largely attributed to the enemies who from the outset he had raised up amongst those of his own calling.

Friars of other orders resented the power of this Dominican, and they had naturally many loyal and devoted disciples on their side. The Franciscans were to be the actual instruments of his downfall, but they were only representative of the vast body of orderly religious folk who loathed the extremes and religious excesses into which the city had plunged. The secular clergy, too, were quite genuine in their opposition to his methods, and many of them believed firmly that religion was best served not by attacking all worldly ways, but by trying to find some means of reconciliation between the two spheres.

Naturally Savonarola was not slow to make political reference to the close resemblance between these 'Tepidi,' as he called them, and the Pharisees of old. "False brethren," he said they were, more concerned to get money for masses than to save souls. It was the eternal cry of the enthusiast

[45]

against that organization of religion which has created a connection between performing the services of God and gaining money.

Joined to these were all those whose politics ranged them against him. There were the friends of the Medici, anxious to work for their restoration. There were the great merchants, who distrusted the affairs of a vast commercial city being so deeply influenced by a visionary and impractical Friar. There were the aristocrats, who disliked mob rule. And, ready to be used by any or all were the disreputable young ruffians who would stick at nothing to shake off this highly disagreeable rule of piety, and be able to return to their old rostering ways.

The wisest of his opponents knew that time was on their side, and some foresaw the direction from which trouble would come.

Savonarola had prophesied "the Church shall be reformed," and he had believed that Charles VIII would overthrow the Pope, Alexander Borgia. But no reform of the Church had followed, Alexander came to terms with Charles and continued placidly his life of pleasant and domestic enjoyment of the temporal good things of the Papacy. Savonarola had not wished to touch doctrine. "We do not wish to change our faith; nor do we wish to change the law of the Gospels; nor the power of the Church; but we wish that men should become better." But men did not become better, and outside Florence no one showed any signs of taking the faintest interest in either the revival of religion or the purification of life.

So frenzied became his sermons and his denunciations of the Papacy that at last, though reluctantly, the Pope took action. He was the head of a 'corporate State,' of which

Savonarola was a member. Such unruly behaviour must be checked. Yet Alexander recognized both the sincerity and the merits of the Friar; he appreciated his teaching while unprepared to follow it. Hence at first he gave Savonarola ample warnings. He once more joined San Marco to the Lombard congregation, thus depriving Savonarola of independence in his office. He then summoned him to Rome, that he might 'give an account' of his prophesying. This summons Savonarola disregarded. He went further, and when ordered to desist from preaching, after some inward doubt, disobeyed and appeared in the pulpit. This was defiance, and inevitably led to a bull of excommunication, which Alexander, again with reluctance, issued in May 1497.

A brief respite occurred, and to Savonarola's distracted mind a gleam of hope must have shone, when a sudden tragedy at Rome gave strange hope of Papal change of mind. In June the Pope's dearly loved eldest son, Duke of Gandia, was murdered in circumstances which, for mystery and drama, cannot be surpassed. Alexander was completely heart-broken and almost frantic with grief. Remorse for his sins rushed upon him, he vowed to change his whole life. Savonarola was, as we have seen, no harsh bigot. He had a marked strain of affection and humanity in his composition. He could, and did, sympathize with the misery and anguish suffered by a man whose natural affections were the overwhelming passion of his nature. One of the strangest letters ever written must be that which now passed from the Friar, already harassed and saddened by approaching failure, to the Pope, grief-stricken by the death of his son.

The hope faded, Alexander's immense vitality reasserted itself. He remembered that he had other children. Life at the Papal court began again on the old lines, and all chance of reformation passed.

Now came the moment for which Savonarola's political enemies had waited. The Signoria was controlled by the Arrabiati, the anti-Medicean party who had seen Savonarola snatch from them all the benefits they hoped to gain when Piero fled. They had lost their awe of the Friar, whose prestige had been immensely shaken by the failure of Charles's expedition, and who had now no influential party or foreign friend to save him.

Savonarola played into their hands. Driven on by his belief in his own innocence and uprightness, he committed the grave error of celebrating mass, and himself communicating while under sentence of excommunication.

Rome, forced to action by this serious step, threatened to place Florence under interdict. The Signoria, as magistrates of the city, would have been bound to take some action, but all was precipitated by the challenge issued by the Franciscans. Fra Francesco di Puglia challenged Savonarola to walk with him through a blazing fire. The ordeal would show which of them would be protected by God as His servant; the righteous would pass through unharmed, and the wicked would perish. Unwillingly, for either his common sense, or a lingering doubt whether he had indeed departed from the right path, caused him to hesitate, Savonarola at length agreed. He himself would not go, but his follower Fra Domenico would. The piles of wood were arranged in the Piazza. The Franciscans with their champion marched into the great square. The Dominicans came in procession, singing the Psalm, "Let God arise and let his enemies be scattered." No doubt they chanted with the same fervour as that with which Cromwell's Ironsides sang the same words before they charged at Dunbar, but here it was no prelude to victory.

The Franciscans refused to allow Fra Domenico to walk between the fiery piles in his robes 'lest they be enchanted,' nor would they agree that he should carry the Host with him. While theological argument raged, a terrestrial storm broke. Heavy thunder-rain soaked the bonfires and put an end to all chance of the spectacle. An angry, disappointed, disillusioned crowd yelled derision and threats as the Dominicans returned to San Marco.

Alexander would have rested satisfied. He only wanted the recalcitrant preacher silenced, and after the failure of April 7th Savonarola could preach no more in Florence. The politicians, however, were determined that he should be destroyed. At this very moment Charles VIII died, and the accession of his cousin Louis XII, who had strong claims on Milan itself, and who was known to have every intention of attacking Italy, meant fresh danger for Florence. Charles VIII had at least frightened the statesmen of Italy. They knew now how fatal was weakness, and the Signoria of Florence were determined that their city should cease to be torn by dissension. They may have believed that the 'freedom of Italy' was at stake; they certainly believed Florence must be rid of Savonarola, and that only by his death could she be made secure from him. He was arrested, not by the Pope and the Church, but by the State, and was charged with uttering false prophecy and having treasonable political relations. He was put to the torture, and broke down under it. He had always hated physical violence, and he had been haunted by a fear of violent death. Like Joan of Arc, he was brought to admit, and possibly to his own anguish to believe, that his 'visions' had not come from God. He agreed that his gift of prophecy had not been genuine, that he had issued false prophecies in order to be thought holy, that ambition, not the

Holy Spirit, had been the source of his inspiration. He was also accused of threatening to appeal to a general council.

As to his political crimes, they were said to be that he had sought to overthrow the constitution.' This he denied, but admitted he had thought it would strengthen the constitution were there to be a Gonfalonier for life.

Nothing was really proved against him to render him worthy of death, but his death was voted because his enemies were resolved upon it, and his friends dared not face popular indignation and vote for him. He retracted the depositions made under torture. Alexander sent him absolution, but his civil enemies showed no forgiveness. He was hanged on May 23rd, 1498, on a gibbet set up in the Piazza, and the boys of Florence were allowed to stone his body as it hung. After death the body was burnt, and the ashes thrown into the river. The government treated the execution as a public holiday, providing wine and food for the onlookers. His followers, scattered and miserable as they were, had hoped that even at the last a miracle might come to pass, or at the least he would speak to them from the scaffold and leave them some words of explanation and hope. They were disappointed and Savonarola died in silence.

CHAPTER V

MACHIAVELLI'S ENTRY INTO POLITICS: CESARE BORGIA

(1)

AT this very moment Machiavelli entered upon his public career, almost as though the death of Savonarola unlocked a door hitherto closed. Certainly the influence of the Friar ran directly counter to Machiavelli's own tendencies, and the triumph of the opposing party evidently meant the rise to power of persons who knew and approved of Niccolò.

In May, 1498, Savonarola was tried and condemned. In June proposals came before the Florentine government to nominate a new secretary to the second Chancery. The post was vacant, owing to the removal of Braccesi, a strong supporter of Savonarola. Four names were now laid before the Council of Eighty, and of those four the one to receive the majority of votes was that of Niccolò Machiavelli. The Great Council next voted, and again he was elected, and in July the Signoria ratified his appointment. The post was important, for the Chancery, known as "the ten of liberty and peace," managed foreign affairs, and sent envoys and ambassadors to carry out Florentine policy. His salary was 200 florins a year, but this was not as large as appears, for official salaries were paid in a specially depreciated florin, worth only 4 livres, and not 7 as were the ordinary florins. The rate of pay in our modern English coinage would work out at about £500 a year.

Machiavelli was now to be sent on repeated missions, to the most important people, at a most critical juncture in Florentine history. He had found the career for which he was best suited, and in reality the posthumous fame which his later writings were to bring him is due to the experience he was now to gain. He tells us himself in one of his letters that he knew nothing of trade or business, he did not care for art or poetry, but he did care intensely for the study of politics, and especially for its underlying study of human behaviour. He was at once to be brought into contact with a man who presents for all time the picture of ruthless efficiency, undeterred by moral considerations.

Nor can we doubt that the experience had a very marked and important effect upon Machiavelli. Throughout *The Prince* he refers again and again to Cesare Borgia, and devotes the major part of one chapter to his career. He was, as will be seen, to go on many missions to the Duke and was with him at some of the most decisive moments of his career, and after his fall actually discussed with him, in his Roman prison, the cause of his downfall.

Moreover, it is necessary, in order to understand the background of Machiavelli's political life, to have some knowledge of the Borgias. Not only was Machiavelli brought into close and frequent contact with them, but they do sum up the political and moral ideas prevalent in Italy of those days. Alexander's personality and conduct inevitably influenced Machiavelli's ideas on the Papacy, while from Cesare he learnt some of the lessons which affected the whole of his political philosophy.

Cesare Borgia was a brilliant epitome of one of the most striking sides of the Renaissance, and the impact of his personality was the more terrific because his character seemed

ALEXANDER VI
By Pinturicchio (from the Vatican).

to be one where every high-light was emphasized and every outline stood out clear, hard, and brilliant. The name of the Borgias must always act as a slight irritant on the mind of any student of the Renaissance. The family has earned an infamous reputation, which all the mild attempts of historians have failed to eradicate from the popular imagination. To 'dine with the Borgias' carries but one instantaneous flash of meaning. Yet how great would be the surprise of the average man did he know exactly why the Ferrarese ambassador wrote in his dispatch, "To sup with the Pope is reckoned a severe penalty," for the truth was, as the ambassador goes on to say, that Alexander Borgia was an extremely abstemious man, he ate but little, and his meals were very simple—"the Pope has but one dish at his supper," so the letter continues, "although there is plenty of that one." Thus greed, and not the fear of poison, induced the reluctance shown to dine with the Pope. Facts, being more reliable than gossip, also do their share in clearing Alexander's reputation. The Cardinals have been supposed to be the chief sufferers from his alleged poisoning propensities, as being the persons from whose death he would profit, the Pope being able to seize what revenues they had in hand, and being also able to nominate their successors, again to his financial advantage. Many of them were not regretted in the circles they left, as the epitaphs circulated in Rome show. One, on Cardinal Ferrari, runs, "Say not 'Light lie the earth,' neither scatter flowers, but if you wish to give me rest, clink money on my tomb." But, whatever their characters, and however welcome their demise, Alexander ought not to be accused of hastening the event. The register of the deaths of the Cardinals, together with the number of new creations, shows quite conclusively that the mortality amongst them was no higher under the Borgias than under that of any other Pope. Under his predecessors the rate works out at roughly two deaths for every year, and it remained the same under Alexander, and was higher under his successor.*

Moreover, though poisoning was much talked of in Renaissance Italy, it was not at all an effective weapon to use. We have only to look at the recipes kept in the famous secret "Cabinet of poisons" by the great Ten at Venice to realize how greatly gossip exaggerated the possibility of 'death in the bowl.' Venice was popularly supposed to be the most successful employer of secret poisoning, and 'tenders' sent in by would-be employees asked for very high salaries, 1,500 ducats a year, and "all expenses." Yet here is one of her best 'recipes':

"Take 2 lb. of sublimate of silver.
6 grossi of arsenic (1 grosso $= \frac{1}{10}$ of 1 square inch).
6 grossi of salts of ammonia.
6 grossi of salts of hartshorn.
4 grossi of verdigris.

Mix well, and then add 4 grossi of aconite root, and add 1 scruple of this mixture to one glass of wine."

The directions wisely went on to say that it was necessary to see the 'patient' did not drink more than two glasses of the 'doctored' wine, or he would be sick. In fact, if the stuff ever passed his lips, which seems unlikely in view of the extra-ordinary flavour it would acquire, no stomach could retain such a mixture. It was indeed simply made by piling together

* Pontificate.	Duration.	Deaths.	New Creation.
Sixtus IV	13 years	27	35
Innocent VIII	8 ,,	11	13
Alexander VI	11 ,,	27	34
Julius II	9½ ,,	36	27

(Given in Creighton's *History of the Papacy*.)

every known poison and had no scientific basis or any skill whatever in its composition.

If we can get rid of any preconceived notions, and look the reputation of the Borgias squarely in the face, what do we find? First, far too much weight has been given to the idle gossip of diarists, such as Sanudo, whose information was all second-hand, and who being a Venetian was naturally one of the most bitter opponents of the Papacy. Few of us would care to have our characters established by the diaries kept by our enemies. Then, we must reckon with the low standard of the period. The author of a pamphlet called "The right that princes have to compass the lives of their enemies" in dealing with political assassination says, and his words seem to carry with them a touch of shocked astonishment, "the complaints of the Duke of Ferrara almost amount to a declaration that actions of this sort are entirely illicit and unjust." Again, Alexander's character was baffling and alarming to his contemporaries, not by reason of any subtlety or sinister cruelty at all, but because they simply could not comprehend the intense vitality and zest which would cause him to rebound after any act of violence or tragedy, even if it affected himself. The Venetian ambassador put his finger on this trait when he wrote, "The Pope loves life, he has a joyous nature, and though he is 70 years old, he grows younger every day." Wild grief on the death of his eldest son, furious resentment and horror at the murder of his son-in-law, would all burst in a storm upon the onlooker, to be replaced in what seemed an extraordinarily short time by cheerfulness and fresh power of enjoyment. It was this which horrified the observer. Yet looking at Alexander's character as a whole, we see it is perfectly consistent and perfectly comprehensible. He was a Spaniard, of the rare fair type, a most magnificent physical specimen. He was over six feet tall, strongly built, bursting with life and health and strength. He was extremely handsome, very dignified, and possessed a most beautiful speaking voice. His manners were very attractive, and he clearly had a gaiety and charm which made him love society and triumph in it. He had no trace of cruelty in him; on the contrary, he was very easy-going, and did not readily take offence or even seek to avenge injuries. "Rome," he said once, "is a free country, where any man may write or say what he will. Much is said against me, but I do not interfere." He was a very competent financier and man of business. During his pontificate all salaries of officials were paid punctually. He left the finances of the Papacy in excellent order, and he carried on the routine of business with the most exemplary diligence. His presence and dignified mien on ceremonial occasions were always remarked upon favourably.

Why then has his name become a byword? Partly because he was unlucky in the weight posterity has wrongly given to the gossip of certain of his contemporaries; partly because his faults and sins, though not unduly horrifying to his age, have come to be more severely regarded by posterity. His predecessors had not been of holy or austere habits. They, like him, had mistresses, and illegitimate children, whom they did their best to advance. Alexander gained notoriety because he was more spectacular than they. His nature was so over-flowing, the force of his affections was so immense, that his love for his children overshadowed everything else in his life. Had he been a secular prince, we should have had no legend of infamy, but his career has shocked mankind just because it was based on feelings from which he should have been debarred by his vocation.

[56]

Moreover, we touch reality when we come to the effect of his political action. Alexander's pontificate was of great importance because he carried on the work begun by Sixtus IV and pushed forward the great consolidation of the temporal power of the Papacy. His capacity and his energy made him embark upon the conquest of Central Italy. He intended of course to create a kingdom for his own son, and in that he failed. But the seed was sown by him, and being cultivated by his successor, grew into a great tree. Julius II was a man who turned to the advantage of the Papacy what Alexander had meant to be for the advancement of his own family. Yet he only continued along the path which the Borgias had marked out. Had it not been for Alexander we should have had an entirely different political history of Italy.

The achievement of the Borgias was made possible by the rare combination of two men in very peculiar circumstances. Alexander would probably never have embarked on his policy of conquest had it not been for his wish to raise up a kingdom for his family. Cesare would probably never have achieved his successes had he not been backed by all the wealth and power of the Papacy. It was because the Pontiff threw all his energies into the task, and because in Cesare he had the exact type of man to use the means placed at his disposal, that the situation arose which for the next ten years was to terrify all Italy. The effects produced on Machiavelli, who was to be drawn into frequent and close personal contact with Cesare, were profound, and through the results embodied in his political writings they have in turn influenced the thoughts and actions of all mankind.

Cesare's career stands out in all the welter of political confusion in Italy as a clear, sharply defined whole. His achievements are like great rocks, rising threateningly above the treacherous sea of political intrigues. So obvious were his aims, so definite his advance, that no one, then or nov·, can doubt that in him we have a perfect example of the prince whom Machiavelli desired.

"I can find no fault with him," he writes; "nay, it seems to be reasonable to put him forward as I have done as a pattern for all such as rise to power by good fortune and the help of others" (*The Prince*, ch. 7), and again: "There is no brighter example than in the actions of this Prince for whosoever judges it necessary to rid himself of enemies and to prevail, by force or fraud, to make himself feared yet not hated by his subjects, respected and obeyed by his soldiers, to be severe and affable, magnanimous and liberal."

A touch of irony reinforces this dictum. Cesare's device, or motto, which he even had inlaid upon his sword, runs, "Fays ce que dois, advien que pourra." He translated this into deeds, but in the sense that he always acted as seemed to him best in his own interests, and certainly entirely disregarded the moral judgment of mankind upon his actions.

Cesare's character, which seemed to Machiavelli so admirably suited for the rôle of ruler, was in great contrast with that of his father. Where Alexander was open, Cesare was reserved. "The Pope cannot keep a secret," wrote the Ferrarese ambassador, "he cannot resist pouring out his thoughts." Cesare, on the other hand, confided in no one and was both silent and unapproachable. He would frequently go about Rome in a mask which could not conceal his identity, made conspicuous and recognizable by his long golden hair and golden beard. Where Alexander let people give free expression to their thoughts Cesare said fiercely, "I will teach the people of Rome to hold their tongues." In their personal lives the difference is striking. Alexander was warm-blooded and sensual, extremely affectionate, and full of gaiety. Cesare, on the contrary, seems to have had no feelings of affection to anyone. He was not on good terms with his brothers, and posterity was to accuse him of the murder of Gandia. His father, Alexander, gave to onlookers the impression of being afraid of him. The stories of his love for his sister Lucrezia have no foundation in fact. He was not given to mistresses, and though sometimes present at Alexander's notorious parties we are never told that Cesare was licentious with women. He was accused by Guicciardini of homosexuality, but even in this case the account does not make it clear whether his action was not one of revenge and cruelty directed against the defeated Manfredi. He married, for political reasons, Charlotte d'Albret of Navarre in order to cement the alliance with the French King. From this marriage came his only child, a daughter, but we find no trace in his life of any affection or interest in either wife or child. Nor do we find that he took any interest in art or literature. He was no patron of learning. His métier lay in military achievements, and in administration. When he had conquered his territory he threw his whole energies into practical measures for restoring its prosperity. Hard, cold, efficient, without friends, without love, caring only for his advancement as a ruler, such was the man in himself.

Physically, Cesare was as fine a specimen as his father. He was tall and well-built, and very active. In colouring, like all his family he was fair, with golden hair and beard and light complexion. Castiglione wrote, "The Pope's son is most gallant to behold and amazingly beautiful to see." Although Alexander was a pure Spaniard and Cesare was half-Italian, his mother being Vannozza dei Catanei, of an old Roman family, yet Cesare conforms far more closely than did his father to our conception of the sixteenth-century Spaniard, made known to us through Philip II and Alva, a fierce, ruthless, hard type, verging on cruelty. His character presents some typically Spanish traits, such as his intense pride, and terrible resentment when, as he thought, any personal insult was offered him. This is well illustrated by the story of the murder of his brother-in-law, Alfonso, second husband of Lucrezia. Alfonso was living in the Vatican with his wife, now aged twenty, to whom he was attached, and whose later conduct shows she returned his affection. He was wounded by some bravos, on the steps of the Vatican, and taken to his rooms, where his wife nursed him and where he began to recover. He and Cesare were on bad terms, and one day seeing Cesare walking in the gardens below he seized a bow and "shot at the Duke intending to kill him. But the Duke, seeing who had done this, sent his men-at-arms up to his brother-in-law's chamber, where they put an end to him." So run the Venetian dispatches. Creighton, dealing with the matter in detail, concludes that Cesare "would not commit a deliberate crime except for some good reason." No such reason existed here. Cesare did not benefit in any material sense from Alfonso's death, for his lands passed, and were allowed to pass, to the little son born to him by Lucrezia. Nor was any political purpose served, and Creighton concludes that it was "simply the result of sudden passion."

This story of course brings us to the accusations brought against the personal relations of Cesare, and even of Alexander, with Lucrezia. All modern historians agree that the rumours and hints of incest rest on no basis of reality. Lucrezia was in no sense a woman of loose character, and the charges against her and her brother are too flimsy to bear any examination. Her first husband, Giovanni of Pesaro, was an unmitigated brute. She then married Alfonso of Bisceglie, and at his death she showed the greatest distress. When twenty-three years old, she was married, for political reasons, to Alfonso d'Este, heir to Ferrara. He was very unwilling to marry her, but necessity forced him to agree. Yet the match proved success-ful in every way. Lucrezia gained his affection and his respect. Given a home and a sphere of her own, she showed herself a completely domestic character. She was absorbed in her children, and in her good works, and after twenty years of a blameless and inconspicuous existence, she died really lamented by her husband and his people. "The Ethiopian does not change his skin, nor the leopard his spots." What Lucrezia was for the whole of the twenty-odd years of her married life, she had been in her girlhood. If we may judge her character and inclinations from the life she led after she had left Rome, we can only conclude that she never desired notoriety, all she wished for was a home and children. Her portraits show her as she really was, not the beautiful fiend of distorted romance, but a gentle, rather doll-faced girl, pink and white and golden-haired, placid, amiable and pleasing, but insipid. She was never interested in politics, showed no ability in them, and was nothing but a pawn in the game. The only time she was ever known to assert herself was on the journey to her wedding at Ferrara, when she insisted on holding up the progress for an entire day while the long golden hair which was her chief beauty and her great source of pride, was specially washed and dried in order that she might enter the city with it flying loose.

No affection ever manifested itself between her and Cesare, who indeed is never recorded to have shown any affection either for father, sister, wife or child. Alexander loved her and was proud of her, and to this day his delighted affection rings in his exclamation to the Ferrarese ambassador at the ball held to celebrate her betrothal, "Come! Look at the new duchess dancing! One can see that at all events she is not lame!" Such affection was however only natural, and had Alexander been a secular prince he would only have been praised for the love he felt for his children, and for his efforts to advance their worldly prosperity. Cesare indeed rather repelled this affection, though he took advantage of it to swing all the influence and wealth of the Papacy in the direction of his own aggrandizement. Ambition was the mainspring of his life, and ruthlessness the key-note of his character. He never sought to please, nor to win applause. His only concession to any policy of gaining popularity in Rome seems to have been by his introduction of the spectacle of the bull-fight. Here again his conduct illustrates the Spanish strain, for he not only took pleasure in the sight, he also went into the ring himself, and on one occasion is said to have dispatched six bulls, five with the sword and one with the lance. The sport, cruel as it was, called for courage, strength and agility, and of all of these Cesare possessed an ample share.

The effect of this strong fierce character upon the Renaissance Italian was profound. Though violent and bloodthirsty enough in some ways, the Italian preferred, if he could, to use intrigue rather than force. The great republics of Venice and Florence considered themselves adepts at the work of deceiving their opponents, and at temporizing when expedient. Such policy however came to grief when met by Cesare's resolute ambition and capacity for swift violent action.

(2)

Cesare's political aim was clear. He meant to subdue the lords of the Romagna, and set up a Central State. How far its boundaries would stretch depended on whether he would be able to attack Florence, lying to the north. Florence, fully aware of this, sought to check Cesare's hopes by allying herself with France. Louis XII, who inherited the throne in 1498, had naturally inherited the claims of Charles VIII to Naples, and in addition he had himself a claim to Milan.* To prosecute these claims successfully he needed the friendship or at least the neutrality of Florence and the Papacy, for without this in any advance on Naples his rear would always be threatened.

Thus we have the position with which Machiavelli as envoy had to deal. The Pope and Florence were outbidding each other for French support, while Louis hesitated to alienate either the one or the other. Perhaps we may reckon it a triumph for Florentine diplomacy that Louis stood by Florence, and it was his intervention which saved her in various crises. Indeed it was only when Louis' power was clearly waning that Cesare felt emboldened to launch his last and most threatening attack on the Republic.

The conflict between Cesare and Florence began in the preliminary stages of the conquest of Romagna. A key-town to the roads leading north was Forlì, ruled by Caterina Sforza, a lady who was "bloody, bold and resolute." She had been faced with rebellions against her and had shown her fierce disposition in her famous retort when the rebels threatened to force her to surrender by killing her hostage children. "If you

* For the French claims to Milan and Naples see Appendix V.

slay these I can give birth to more." To this lady Florence now, in 1499, dispatched Machiavelli on an embassy. He was to negotiate for the engagement of young Ottaviano as condottiere, and for the purchase of gunpowder and salt-petre. The real object of the Republic was to establish friendly relations and thus check any advance on the part of others into Northern Italy. Caterina, aware of this, asked that Florence should "guarantee her security." This Machiavelli was not empowered to do, and he was obliged to return, unsuccessful and slightly discomforted, to Florence. The wily representative of a city so often spoken of as a "fickle woman" could not outwit this woman in the flesh.

Cesare meanwhile hired 4,000 men from the French, who were now preparing to invade Milan. The Pope declared that the 'Signori or Vicars' of the Romagna holding their lands from the Papacy had failed to pay their dues, and their dominions were in consequence forfeited.*

Cesare's advance at the head of his foreign army produced an immediate effect. Forlì was surrounded and Caterina was forced to surrender. "Beneath the banner of the lilies," wrote Machiavelli, "he made himself lord of Imola and Forlì" Caterina's strength and courage gave her a hold on Cesare's respect. He treated her with all courtesy, and she was sent to Rome, whence after eighteen months she was allowed to retire peacefully to Florence. The French troops being now withdrawn, the campaign ended with the first step taken towards conquest.

The next phase showed the real reason for the success with which Cesare was to meet. In 1500 he advanced on the other cities he coveted, and now the lords of these States fled before him, yielding their cities without any attempt at defence.

* His list included Forlì, Imola, Rimini, Pesaro, Camerino and Urbino.

They were rulers whose cruelty and violence gave them no hold over their people. Machiavelli emphasizes this when he writes (*Discorsi*, III): "The lords who ruled in Romagna were examples of all evil living; on the slightest pretext they gave themselves to rapine and slaughter, due not to the depravity of their subjects but to the wickedness of these princes. Being poor, and wishing to live as rich, they resorted to plunder. They made unjust laws and reduced the population to misery."

By the inhabitants of these lordships Cesare was welcomed and having once got rid of the smaller lords, Cesare established some measure of law and order in the district. "He was reputed cruel, yet his cruelty restored the Romagna, united it, and brought it order and obedience, so that it will be seen he was in reality merciful" (*The Prince*).

Now the victorious soldier was made 'Duke of Romagna' by his father and with this the whole scale of operations seems to become larger. Events seem to take place from now on, upon a more important stage, the lesser lords have retired to the background, and the greater powers take their place.

For first Cesare tried a bold experiment. He "resolved to depend no longer on the arms and fortunes of others," says Machiavelli, and by this he means that Cesare prepared to emancipate himself from dependence on France by engaging his own troop under tried condottieri. So good was his reputation as soldier and as paymaster that he was easily able to get together a first-rate army. He advanced on Bologna, showing that he was not content to be lord of Central Italy. Machiavelli believed that he aspired to the lordship of Tuscany, and that this was but the preliminary swoop upon Florence. "He was desirous to follow up and extend his conquests, and was about to attack Tuscany, from which design King Louis compelled him to desist." For Louis, now established at Milan, had no wish to see Cesare advance too rapidly, and at once intervened and stopped him. Cesare, therefore, turned against Florence, not of course with threat of conquest, he was not strong enough for that as yet, but with the intention of extorting blackmail. He wanted money, for he meant to take into his service the greatest condottiere he could obtain. Florence was rich, and she was weakened by her struggle with Pisa. He calmly asked that he should be taken into Florentine pay and given a *condotta* of 36,000 ducats. Florence hesitated, and Cesare advanced to Campi, within seven miles of the city. The Republic then gave in, and agreed to his terms. Cesare moved off to Siena, and there Machiavelli went as the Florentine envoy and the agreement was carried through. Triumphant, Borgia returned to Rome, where a new policy was to be inaugurated.

The importance of the change now introduced by Louis XII cannot be over-estimated. Louis had conquered Milan with ease, but his attack on Naples brought him face to face with far more difficult problems. He was not really strong enough to maintain his hold in a part of Italy so far removed from his base. Moreover, as Machiavelli does not fail to point out in his mordant criticism of Louis,* he had made several irreparable blunders. By his treaties with Alexander he had alienated all the Romagna. Then he had failed to make Alexander a true ally, by his support of Florence against the aggressions of Cesare. Now he committed his worst mistake. Not happy in his allies, he tried to save himself by calling in a more powerful supporter. He actually suggested to Ferdinand of Aragon that Spain should assert her own claims to Naples, should send an army to Italy, and that after jointly conquering

* *The Prince.*

that Kingdom of Naples, France and Spain should divide it between them. On this Machiavelli comments: "The wish to acquire is no doubt a natural and common sentiment, and when men attempt things within their power they will always be praised rather than blamed. But when they persist in attempts that are beyond their power, mishaps and blame ensue. If France could have attacked Naples with her own forces, she should have done so. If she could not, she ought not to have divided it."

Upon that fatal mistake, however, Louis now rushed, and concluded the treaty of Granada (1501), whereby France was to have northern Naples, and Spain the southern part. Alexander, unable to help himself, ratified the treaty, and the Spanish troops, under the 'Great Captain' Gonsalvo de Cordova, appeared in Italy. They were destined to conquer the whole of the south, to expel the French, and to set up the rule of Spain, and ultimately of the Empire, which was to keep Italy divided and subject for the next four hundred years.

It is impossible to doubt that Cesare, whose ability Machiavelli ranked so high, should not have perceived the folly of France. He could not, however, devote much of his energies to the affairs of Louis, for at this very moment he was approaching the climax of his own career. He had decided that the moment had come when he must make a supreme effort to establish his lordship in Central Italy, and he did not hesitate now to use the weapon of treachery.

(3)

Machiavelli was an eye-witness of much that followed; he approved Cesare's actions, and it is this very approval, openly expressed, after mature consideration, in *The Prince*, which has brought so much blame upon him.

It is quite impossible to understand the bearing of Machiavelli's comments, unless we know the specific facts which he was criticizing. The whole of Machiavelli's theories are based on the contingency *"in certain circumstances, certain acts are permissible."* Hence, the importance of understanding this phase of Machiavelli's life, and the effect of Cesare's actions upon the later writings.

Cesare believed that his own interests were paramount to all considerations of former friendship and loyalty. He was now about to commit the deeds which called forth one of the most famous of the sayings in *The Prince*. "If all rulers were good, you ought to keep your word, but since they are dishonest, and do not keep faith with you, you in return need not keep faith with them."

Thus he began by attacking Urbino—ruled over by a prince whom all loved and whom Cesare had treated as a friend. Yet, when he appeared before her walls, Urbino yielded and the Duke fled without a blow being struck in his defence.

The sensation in Italy was overwhelming. Everyone thought Cesare was irresistible. Florence was aghast, she feared her ruin must come next. Most important of all, Cesare's own captains grew alarmed. They began to plot against him. Florence knew of their treachery, and sent Machiavelli as envoy to Cesare to see how matters would turn. He was, therefore, actually at hand when the great plot came to a head.

Machiavelli went to the court Cesare was keeping at Urbino, and there Cesare in conversation with him uttered the saying which was his sole justification: "I am not here to play the tyrant but to extinguish tyrants." In truth the evils created by the multitude of small States were so great that the establishment of strong rule was the lesser of evils.

Yet Cesare's triumph over Urbino was short-lived. Even while he talked with Machiavelli, his captains had all leagued against him. They met and formed a conspiracy, at Magione, on Lake Trasimeno. They joined their forces into one large army, and appealed for help to other States. The news spread and Urbino revolted against Borgia and recalled its own Duke. It seemed as if the complete ruin of Cesare's plans was at hand, when the army which he sent against the conspirators was totally defeated at Fossombrone.

This was the moment when both Cesare and Alexander showed their courage and strength. Quite undismayed and unflurried, they made their plans. Machiavelli was now in Rome, trying to take advantage of the Borgias' disasters to win concessions for Florence. By agreeing to the Republic's demands for trade concessions, Alexander kept her from siding with the rebels, who were desperately trying to win her support. He sent to Louis for a supply of troops, and so important had his diplomacy made him to the French King, that the troops were forthcoming. When the news of the arrival of the French at Cesare's camp before Imola reached the conspirators, they lost their heads and decided to open negotiations. Now Cesare made his master-stroke. In one sense we are amazed at the obviousness of the trap into which these thoroughly experienced men walked so readily. The Duke agreed to treat with them. He offered to receive them back into his service, though the captains had apparently sense enough to stipulate "they should not be compelled to appear in person before him unless they so desired." Machiavelli tells us that he personally was aware that the

Duke's proposals were not genuine, and he had good grounds for his statement, since at this juncture he was with Cesare, and accompanied him to Cesena. There the Duke sent word to the conspirators, and arranged a rendezvous at Sinigaglia.

The condottieri, led by Vitellozzo and the Orsini, captured the little town on December 26, and prepared to welcome Cesare there, no doubt believing their success in taking the place would advance their credit with him. He set out from his camp, and met them outside the walls. Pretending to leave his own troops without, he bade them do likewise, and they agreed. All rode together to the Palace, and entered, but Cesare's own guard of gentlemen had already arrived there. No sooner were all in than the guards arrested the four captains. Vitellozzo and da Fermo were put to the torture. They were unable to stand it and confessed their treachery and were strangled that very night, the two Orsini were put to death a few days later. "It is well," said Cesare in discussing this very matter with Machiavelli, "to beguile those who have shown themselves masters of treachery." "The Duke," so runs Machiavelli's report, "with the brightest face in the world, expressed his satisfaction in his triumph . . . and he explained his reasons for now desiring friendship with our Florence in words which excited my imagination." Machiavelli was indeed full of praise for this bold stroke, and his dispatches home to the Florentine government reflect his feelings quite plainly. "Consider the Duke," he wrote, "as a new potentate, with whom it is better to make a league than with a condottiere," and later: "I do not say that the Duke is not a man of honour, he is a man rather with whom you ought to be circumspect, and look out lest you be deceived." As to the severity shown, first in the execution of Ramiro, and then in those of Oliverotto, Vitellozzo, and the Orsini, he says: "It was of the Duke's nature not to pardon, nor did he leave his vengeance to others." He clearly felt that here was an excellent instance of a man acting upon the principle later to be expounded in *The Prince* that "he who quells disorder by a very few signal examples will in the end be more merciful than he who from leniency permits things to take their course."

Nor need we really feel anything beyond surprise at the stupidity of the captains, and scorn for their cowardice. They had been led to plan their conspiracy from fear of Cesare; they had deliberately plotted against him while in his pay, and they were led to abandon their enterprise again by their fears. If, with their experience of the man, and their realization of what they had done, they could go unguarded into the Palace they deserved their fate, for here we must agree with both Cesare and Machiavelli that faith need not be kept with such men.

The "affair of Sinigaglia" resounded throughout Italy, indeed throughout Europe; even in France "men held it a liberating of the country from tyranny." Now Cesare seemed to go from strength to strength. He was lord of Romagna and Urbino. His treacherous captains were dead. Perugia and Siena were both captured by his troops. Florence felt the danger coming nearer.

First she tried to strengthen herself by improving her system of government. The measure which Savonarola had been accused of favouring, namely the appointment of a Gonfalonier for life, was carried. This gave stability, though the man chosen, Soderini, did not prove strong enough.

The Borgias meanwhile decided that they could do without French help. Louis had already fallen out with Ferdinand and his troops were being defeated by the Spaniards. Machiavelli's last negotiations with the Borgias were undertaken at the end of April, 1503, when he was entrusted with the task of trying to come to terms with the Pope and Cesare.

(4)

Yet now, the element of "fortune" to which Machiavelli attached such importance, played Cesare false. In August, after dining in the open air one evening with Cardinal Adrian of Corneto, Bishop too of Bath and Wells, the Pope, his son, and their guest were taken dangerously ill. Modern opinion sees in their symptoms some fever, either malaria or typhoid, due to the poisonous state of Rome, where people were dying daily from the unhealthy conditions of the city. Cesare of course had foreseen the contingencies likely to arise at his father's death and had provided against them. A large block of Spanish cardinals had been created, to sway the election of a new Pope; troops were to have been at hand; Cesare himself had the keys of all the Papal fortresses. In reporting the last interview Machiavelli ever had with Cesare he says: "He told me himself that he had foreseen and provided for everything else that could happen on his father's death, but he had never anticipated that when his father died, he too should be at death's door."

That severe and completely incapacitating bout of fever ruined Cesare for ever. The Orsini flocked back to Rome, and Cesare as soon as he could be moved was obliged to fly from the city. All his conquests fell away from him—the lords of the States he had conquered returned in triumph to their possessions. Only the Romagna, which under him had attained more peace and order than ever before, "waited for

CESARE BORGIA
By Pinturicchio (from the fresco in the Vatican).

him one month." Then it too fell away. He could not control the election of the new Pope, and after the brief reign of Pius III, lasting only three weeks, he was compelled to fall in with the successful candidature of his enemy Giuliano della Rovere. He suffered the last irony of fate when he put his trust in the word of his enemies.

Giuliano signed a convention with him, on October 29th, promising to make him Gonfalonier of the Church and to allow him to govern the Romagna. Cesare in return secured Giuliano's election through the vote of the Spanish cardinals whom he controlled.

Machiavelli's admiration for Cesare, which had been based on his success, now abated most rapidly. Hitherto, he had never failed to praise Cesare's boldness and activity. With the total collapse of the Borgia's power, Machiavelli's belief in him likewise vanished. His friends in Florence had always considered his praise excessive. One of his closest intimates had gone so far as to say plainly, "in general you are laughed at for writing too eulogistically of the Duke, and some even believe you hope to secure some benefit for yourself from him."

In one sense this is hard to credit, for Machiavelli was a devoted Florentine, and would never have left the employment of his city, as his subsequent career fully proves. Yet the fact remains that no sooner had Cesare fallen from his high estate than Machiavelli completely changes his tone. He speaks of Cesare with bitterness and contempt, writing home: "Your Excellencies can neglect him as you will . . . indeed we need trouble ourselves no more about him. His sins have found him out . . . I took leave of him as quickly as possible, for it seemed to me a century before I could leave his presence." He spoke thus, knowing he was dealing with a ruined man. Della Rovere, now elected Pope as Julius II, found he dared not use Cesare as an ally, for fear of the bitter enmities it would arouse all over Italy. He therefore made the Duke a prisoner, and only allowed him eventually to leave Rome in return for the Romagna fortresses which his captains had still held for him. Cesare, trusting to a safe conduct, granted him by Gonsalvo the Great Captain, withdrew to Naples. There Ferdinand of Aragon, Gonsalvo's master, the most unscrupulous prince in Europe, bade Gonsalvo break his word. Cesare was arrested, and sent as a prisoner to Spain.

His spirit still undaunted, he made a dramatic escape, climbing from a high tower down a rope-ladder by night, falling and breaking his leg, was saved by the help of a faithful servant, and despite the pain of his injury endured a wild ride to safety in Navarre. He died four years later, fighting for his brother-in-law, King of Navarre, and was killed in a single-handed battle against a troop of Aragonese. His body when found was so covered with wounds as to show the determination and courage with which he had fought to the end.*

Thus the Borgias vanished from Italy. They had been a sign and a portent.' The scandals which their enemies attached to their name have been allowed to obscure their real political importance. For they had pointed the way to a measure of unity, and they laid the foundations of a central Italian State upon which Julius II was to rear the building of the temporal power of the Papal States.

To give credit where it is due, and where so much discredit

*Historians had for long said that he was buried in the cathedral at Pampeluna, but the researches of Yriarte have proved that he was first given a splendid tomb in the church of Santa Maria at Viana, but that the tomb was later, in the seventeenth century, desecrated and destroyed. No trace of it now remains. A persistent local tradition affirmed that his bones, turned out of the tomb when the church was restored, had been buried at the foot of the three steps leading up into the church. Digging at this spot Yriarte found the skeleton of a man, laid in a very rough grave made of brick. No proof of course can be given that these were the bones of Cesare, but apart from them, all trace has vanished.

has been attached, both father and son showed themselves excellent administrators. Alexander had performed all the business transactions of the Holy See competently and well. He had stopped the recurrence of famines in Rome by his measures of prevention and relief. He had worked hard and had not devoted his energies solely to his own advantage. Machiavelli's dictum on him runs: "He was the first who showed how greatly a Pope, by the use of money and of arms, could make his power prevail." He had, in fact, made possible a new development of the Papal power.

Cesare, on his side, had governed the territories he had conquered with real ability and success. The Romagna, freed from the miseries caused by its host of petty tyrants, prospered under him. He drew up a code of laws, reformed the administration of the towns, developed its industries. He did what none of the earlier lords had done, when he tried to give relief after famine. At Forlì he not only ordered free grain to be distributed to the poor, he also started works in the city to give employment to men who had lost their work. He bought food for the people in want, and throughout the Romagna encouraged the establishment of State-aided pawnshops, to tide the poor over bad times. At Fermo he allocated the municipal revenue for a period of ten years to be paid not to him but to repair the damages done to the city in the wars, and to rebuild the ancient aqueduct. He forbade the judges to take 'presents,' or oppress litigants. He encouraged the manufacture of wool at Faenza, of terra-cotta at Rimini, of pottery at Pesaro, of printing at Fano. He carried through commercial treaties, lowering the duties on trade with Venice and Florence. Machiavelli says that "he gave good government to the Romagna, seeing that the country was overrun with robbery, tumult, and every kind of outrage," and that thereby he "endeared himself to the people." Summing up his reflections on the lessons he thought he perceived in Cesare's career, this is what Niccolò says: "He acquired his state through his father's position, and when the one was lost, he lost the other, although he had done everything which a prudent and virtuous man ought to do to establish himself firmly in that position which armies and money had won for him."

This significant summary is an indication of the flaws in Machiavelli's arguments, and of the blind spots in his outlook on life. "Armies and money" are "not enough," and to found a stable government more is required. Machiavelli based his theories on the essential baseness of mankind, and on his belief that, left to themselves, men always act from selfish and generally evil motives. That theory has often been disproved. Mankind's most striking attribute is not the desire to do evil, but its stumbling efforts to do good. Cesare's kingdom was won by force and fraud, and it was lost exactly by the same instruments. What was good in his policy, hidden and distorted as it was, is to be found in that attempt towards unity, that faint foreshadowing of a distant future when Italy should unite, and in uniting free herself from the foreigner.

That germ of good lived on, but the evil which Machiavelli believed to predominate proved less potent. Italy ceased to admire Cesare when it need no longer fear him. The evil side of his life and character brought him into disrepute. Because he failed, men were no longer blinded by his success. Italy, like the Papacy itself in the next generation, showed that men did not gain immortality by self-interest; that they still recognized the difference between good and evil and were still capable and determined to struggle for some higher standard.

CHAPTER VI

MACHIAVELLI: THE CIVIL SERVANT

(1)

Foreign Envoy

IT might be expected that his connection with foreign affairs, and the many embassies which brought him into personal contact with the most outstanding figures of the day, would form the chief interest in Machiavelli's life. This is, however, emphatically not the case. When in retirement he looked back and saw what he had done with his life, the part on which he reflected with most satisfaction was not his journeys or his experiences of courts, but the comparatively humdrum task he had tried to carry through in Florence itself.

He was above all else a patriot, devoted heart and soul to his city-State, and to him the work of his life, the best justification that he had not misspent his time was the creation of a Florentine militia. This may strike us as extraordinary, indicating a parochial outlook on the part of a man who was, in point of fact, widely travelled. It is, however, entirely characteristic of the Renaissance Italian. To such a man his own city made a passionate appeal, his whole energies and intelligence were devoted to furthering her interests. All Machiavelli's extensive experience forced him back on one conclusion: Florence must be given some surer means of defending herself against the dangers which threatened her from every side. His whole life was passed at a time when the Republic was perpetually in a state of alarm, and when every Florentine felt uneasily that the city was not strong enough to hold her own. In his creation of a national militia Machiavelli believed not only that he had carried through a sound and useful piece of work, but he also believed that he had forged the weapon which should save the city.

He arrived at that conclusion because his travels and embassies impressed upon him not only the relative weakness of Florence, but, as he thought, the true source of the strength of her enemies. Over a period of more than ten years he was employed as envoy, not only at the minor courts of Italy, but also at the courts of Rome, of France and of the Emperor Maximilian. The Florentine 'foreign office' conducted its business on a highly developed system. Machiavelli, were he to be reincarnated to-day, would not find much difficulty in adjusting himself to modern conditions and coping successfully with modern methods. The envoys wrote detailed dispatches, which were duly filed and preserved. All the endless stream of letters, instructions, minutes of meetings, reports of decisions, were tabulated and filed. Literally thousands of such documents exist in the Florentine archives, signed by Machiavelli, and in some cases entirely written by him. The industrious, competent, and business-like civil servant can find no better prototype than the Florentine secretary of the second chancery.

Machiavelli left behind him, in addition to his official correspondence, the "Discourses," which have been variously described. Some we should call 'reports'—such as the 'Discourse on the best method of dealing with the rebels of the Val di Chiana.' Others, such as that dealing with the raising of fresh taxes in 1503, read like speeches, to be made not by Machiavelli himself, but by his superior, the Gonfalonier, before the Great Council. Others are summaries, written after his return, of the impressions made upon him by his chief expeditions as envoy to foreign countries. These are of interest as showing how in his travels Machiavelli ceaselessly tried to discover whence the countries derived their strength, in order that he might benefit Florence by his conclusions.

Thus in 1507 he was sent to negotiate with the Emperor Maximilian, and for the first time travelled into the country known to us as Tirol. He went up first through Geneva and Constance and across Switzerland to what is now Bolzano, and to Innsbruck, where he met the Emperor. He later summed up his impressions in his "Sketch of German Affairs" and his "Report to the Signoria" on his mission. Like many other travellers his impressions of Tirol were of delighted enjoyment. He admired the country, the people and even "the stoves which they have to protect themselves from the cold." Then, as now, the charms of a simple country life, lived by mountaineers who were above all things cheerful and independent, appeared most evident. In 1507 he observed what in essence can be noted to-day: "They are frugal in all things, for they affect no luxury in either their buildings or their attire, and have but few chattels in their dwellings . . . they sell things fashioned by their own hands and their gains are the greater because earned by labour with very little capital." For the luxurious Italian, accustomed to the lavish comfort and sophisticated beauty of Florence, was capable of appreciating this totally different existence. Moreover, he saw more than an idyllic country life: he perceived that the basis of these people's content lay in their feeling of liberty and security. "They enjoy their rough life, and their liberty . . . they spend little on administration and nothing on soldiers, for they train their own subjects to arms. On festival days, instead of playing games their youth seeks diversion in learning the use of the pike and of other weapons . . . they would not go to war save for the decrees of their own communities."

Their self-reliance in military matters struck Machiavelli as of overwhelming importance, and he drew the same moral from his repeated visits to France. He actually took part in four major embassies to Louis XII, and though, in contrast to his feelings towards the Tirolese, he disliked and despised the French, yet he once again noted their military strength and independence.

"All the nobility are devoted to the military life, and the French men-at-arms are the best in Europe . . . the Gascons have proved themselves rather thievish than valiant, yet they behave well in the defence and attack of fortresses, though badly in the open field. In this they are the reverse of the German and Swiss, who are unrivalled in the field but worth nothing in the attack or defence of fortified places." He goes on to notice the peculiar economic and social structure of France, fastening on the characteristics which in an intensified degree were to precede the great Revolution. "The country is very rich in agricultural produce, but everything goes into the hands of the nobles and bishops, who absorb two-thirds of the riches of the kingdom and have great power . . . the people live at very slight expense . . . they dress coarsely and in garments of small price." He concludes with a paragraph showing the dislike he always felt for this neighbouring nation: "The French nature is greedy of others' goods, and in addition is also prodigal of its own and others' property. The Frenchman will steal in order to devour and waste, and will enjoy his booty with him from whom he has stolen—a nature contrary to that of the Spaniards, who steal but who never let you see any trace of what they have robbed from you." In other words the Frenchman likes to acquire property and then to demonstrate his glory in his new acquisitions.

All the information which he acquired, and the conclusions at which he arrived, were devoted by Machiavelli to the improvement of his own country's position. He wanted to study other countries in order to benefit his own. He aimed chiefly at giving to Florence the security others palpably enjoyed. He thought, planned, wrote, entirely with an eye to the work he could do for Florence. This patriotism is the glow which lights up and warms his otherwise cold intellectual character. No one can read *The Prince* without being aware of, and slightly repelled by, the feeling of ruthless detachment, the tinge of cold indifference which pervades it. When he set his mind to consider the problems of government in the sixteenth-century Italy, Machiavelli used his brains and showed no feelings When, however, he came to treat of Florence, his attitude changes. Here is the inspiration of his life, and here he shows himself a patriot in the best sense, willing to toil and drudge in attempting to carry through the one definite piece of work he believed he could do for Florence.

(2) *Warfare by Condottieri*

He was impelled to take up his project by the perception which every year forced upon him, that weakness was fatal and that dependence on others was disastrous. We know that his opposition to Savonarola was based on the fact that Savonarola brought division to the city and so weakened her. We know that he admired Cesare Borgia because he brought unity and strength to the Romagna. He knew that Florence was struggling against powerful enemies and that she must be prepared to fight for herself. Conditions of warfare made him conclude that she must strike out on a new line; she must try to render herself independent of hired condottieri, and with this object in view he bent all his energies into providing her with a national militia.

This proposal was in a sense as great and remarkable an innovation as the levée en masse called forth by the French Revolution. For in Italy in those days, men did not fight for their country. Each State relied for its defence upon mercenary troops, hired out in bands. Such men were usually Italians, enrolled by Italian captains. This was not however invariable; French, Swiss, Germans, all appeared in the great bands, and one of the most famous leaders of the late fifteenth century was the Englishman, John Hawkwood, whose name appears rather delightfully rendered by lips which could not cope with 'Hawkwood' as "Giovanni Acuto."

In many ways these condottieri showed a thoroughly sensible outlook. War was to them a trade; it was carried on, not for glory but for cash. It was, therefore, not only absurd to risk one's life, it was unnecessary. Blows and wounds of course entered into the contract, but not death, and if possible not privation. These views were shared by trooper and by leader. If the private soldier did not wish to risk too much in return for his pay, the leader was equally unwilling to risk the loss of his valuable men. It was not altogether easy to get together a band of good soldiers, and their loss was not easily made up. Therefore, a code was evolved, and followed by all the condottieri of Italy, which aimed at making warfare as little bloody as could be achieved. Battles were fought on this understanding, and casualties were comparatively few.

Quarter, of course, was always given. There were no night-attacks, and no winter campaigns. Men who were heads of a good reliable band could hire themselves out, receiving a *condotta*, or annual salary, and naturally long-drawn-out operations paid them best. Their employers, however, frequently grew impatient, and sometimes, not without reason, accused their captains of taking bribes from the enemy and of not showing sufficient energy in their campaigns. Thus, in the famous instance of Carmagnola, Venice believed his withdrawal to the baths of Abano was not due to ill health, but to bribery. Florence, too, condemned Paolo Vitelli for supposed treachery and many other instances could be multiplied.

Florence suffered to a greater degree than some of the States. She was rich, and she had no military leader or even class to protect her. Her chief official, the Gonfalonier of Justice, held office by election and only for two months. Her nobles were debarred from office altogether. In the unsettled state of Italy, and with foreign invaders crossing the Alps in the north and swarming across from Spain in the south, her position grew more and more precarious.

Cesare Borgia's career filled her with terror. She bought him off once, but she must have watched his steady persistent advance towards her frontier with great apprehension. She could use her wealth to hire other troops, but it was becoming increasingly difficult to find any leader who could stand against Borgia. Moreover, the career of Francesco Sforza, who, being originally hired as a mercenary of Milan, ended by making himself lord of the city, was a warning. Finally, her bitter experiences in the Pisan war were now to compel her to take action, and it was Machiavelli's truest source of pride that to him were due both the inspiration and the accomplishment of the formation of a national army. In the development

[83]

of his plans we may also see both the weakness of Florence and the flaws in Machiavelli's own judgment.

The story of his official career, involved in all the tangle of Italian politics and inter-State warfare, may be made clearer if these points are kept in mind. First, Florence was, but the exigencies of her situation, forced to rely on France, and constantly invoked her aid. From this arise Machiavelli's frequent embassies to the French. Second, she was most apprehensive of the Papal advance, as personified in the conquests of Cesare Borgia and his steady approach towards Tuscany. After the death of Cesare she still feared the policy of Julius, and how just were her apprehensions is proved by her ultimate collapse before the Medicean Popes. Thirdly, while struggling with these enemies beyond her frontiers, she was being drained of her strength by the war with Pisa, and the discontent and faction which the prolongation of that struggle created within her own walls. Considered on these lines, Machiavelli's career, and the policy of Florence, became clearer and more consistent.

In especial the Pisan war is of interest in Machiavelli's life, because here we have a totally different aspect of his character. He was the busy secretary to the second chancery, and posterity knows him as a political writer, but in addition he became through these campaigns against Pisa familiar with every detail of soldiering, and he ended as practical if not theoretical commander of the army which finally won success.

(3) *Pisa*

Pisa, by its very position on the Arno, between Florence and the sea, was of the utmost importance. The trade interests of

Florence necessitated the control of this city, and she had never rested until she had subjugated it. The Pisans, however, were equally resolved to struggle for their independence and when Charles VIII came into Italy in 1498, and the Medici fled from Florence, Pisa seized the opportunity and revolted. Her loss, and the bitter fury it aroused, had been one of the contributory causes of the unpopularity of the government influenced by Savonarola. The Florentines considered that the 'prophet' ought to have been able to bring about the re-conquest of Pisa, and from that date onwards the struggle for domination was to continue, for fourteen weary years.

Pisa, like all the other small Italian States, really consisted of a city, and a country district. When attacked by Florence, she withdrew the country population within the city walls, and withstood a siege. The enemy could, and did, ravage the countryside, burn and pillage and destroy. Machiavelli's directions to the troops ran: "Let them carry off all the corn, and what they cannot remove should be burnt." But the strength of the fortifications, the poor siege equipment of the attackers, and it must be added the cowardice displayed by troops called upon to adopt storm tactics, kept the city itself safe. Indeed, it was to be one of the defects which time brought to light, that Machiavelli's militia gained an undeserved reputation for efficiency and bravery just because they were really only called upon to harry a defenceless and largely deserted countryside, and never actually took part in hand-to-hand fighting with trained soldiers.

This was not, however, to be apparent for many years, and when Machiavelli first obtained office, after the fall of Savonarola, none of the difficulties before him were clearly visualized.

In 1499 Machiavelli had received his appointment as

secretary to the second chancery, in whose hands were both the conduct of foreign affairs, and of war. He was sent at once to Forlì, on his mission to Caterina Sforza, and it is significant that almost immediately his subordinate wrote to him urging him to use all possible dispatch and return, "remaining away is not good for you, and here there is such a deluge of work as never was." This pressure was caused by the trouble over the Pisan command.

Florence had engaged as her captain in the enterprise Paolo Vitelli, a celebrated condottiere. She had been lavish in expenditure of funds; more than 64,000 ducats had been voted and spent and, indeed, the 'Ten' had thereby won for themselves the nickname of 'the Spendthrifts.' Money was not to be grudged, however, if it brought success, and when the walls of Pisa were breached, all Florence thought victory was at hand. What, then, was the horror and rage excited when reports came in describing how Vitelli had forbidden his troops to mount the breach, and had actually driven back the few who wished to attempt it! On the top of this came the news that boats sent to the Florentine camp with arms and stores had somehow sunk in the Arno, but that the Pisans had succeeded in fishing them up. Machiavelli was now the man in authority in the appropriate department of Florence. He was convinced that Vitelli was a traitor, acting against the interests of his employers. "All our trouble," he reported indignantly, "has been brought to nought by his shuffling and deceit." Convinced by his arguments, the Signoria ordered the arrest, and subsequently the execution of Vitelli, as a traitor. At the time some doubted the Florentine case and declared Paolo was only following the accepted practice "to spare his men and avoid exposing them to peril," but actually time has proved that Machiavelli was right. The Venetian archives have shown that Vitelli was, as Machiavelli believed, in communication with Venice and was on the point of deserting to her.

This episode had far-reaching results. Vitelli's brother, Vitellozzo, never forgave Florence. He was one of the condottieri engaged by Cesare Borgia, and this personal animus against the Republic was utilized by Cesare both to harass Florence and to mask his own designs behind the actions of his captain. Even more important was the decision made by Florence to engage not Italian but French troops. Furious at her lost opportunity, eager to renew the attack at once, and thoroughly distrustful of all Italian condottieri, Florence sent to the French king and hired an army of French troops, including 500 lances, 2,000 Gascons, and 4,000 of the Swiss who had enrolled themselves under Louis.

This horde poured into Tuscany in the early summer of 1500. They were to be paid for by the handing over to Louis of no less than 24,000 ducats. Florence having sent her money to Louis was not directly responsible for their pay, but Louis probably meant to make her indirectly support his men in addition. In any case they marched towards Pisa, plundering and ravaging Florentine homes as they went along, and when they arrived at the camp before Pisa they broke into riot, demanding both food and pay. Florence sent Commissioners to deal with the situation, and Machiavelli went as secretary to the Commission. The reports which he sent back give a vivid description of the outrageous scenes which took place and, indeed, these events made an indelible impression upon him. He describes Albizzi, the extremely courageous chief·Commissar, "disputing for his very life from hour to hour, in the midst of a great mob of soldiers, brandishing their halberds in his face." Albizzi eventually was forced to give his own personal bond for the payment of 1,200 ducats, and having wrung from him this amount, "all the Swiss and Gascons have deserted and withdrawn."

Machiavelli's bitter hatred and contempt of mercenary troops may be said to have dated from this example of their uselessness and the danger of employing them. He saw now that 'foreigners' were no more to be relied upon than native Italians.

Further lessons, however, remained to be learnt. Florence had no troops of her own; she was obliged to hire and proceeded to engage Italian mercenaries. The failure of this policy was soon as evident as that of her experiment with French troops. Cesare Borgia was pushing his advance across the Romagna; and he now took advantage of the Republic's dilemma. He demanded that he should be granted a *condotta* by Florence, the amount to be no less than 36,000 ducats. At first Florence was inclined to resist this blackmail, and volunteers were called for to defend the city. Possibly we have the first germ of the project which was to develop under Machiavelli. But with Cesare's advance to Campi, only seven miles off, at the head of a large army, Florence was obliged to give way. She paid the sum demanded, and Cesare withdrew for the time.

It was now obvious to all concerned that the position was most threatening. No one in Italy was blind to the implications of Cesare's policy. Clearly he intended to found a State, and equally clearly he would eventually attack Florence. Here is the real explanation of the persistence with which Florence clung to the French alliance. She has been accused of betraying her own interests, of relying upon the foreigner, and of earning that hatred on the part of the rest of Italy which was to bring about her downfall when ultimately

France could no longer protect her. The crisis of 1501 is her justification. Venice and the Papacy were only too eager to attack her; in self-defence she must seek help, and her only effective ally was France, who at this time was planning her invasion of Naples, and who would in consequence need to pass through Tuscany.

Endless letters are preserved in the Florentine archives from Machiavelli, dealing with the whole matter. In September the Pope and his son advanced, and all Florence was panic-stricken, but in this dilemma, being firmly resolved to pay no more to Borgia, and with no prospect of hiring effective Italian troops, the Signoria dispatched another embassy to Louis of France. A sum of 30,000 ducats was paid over, and the promise made of another 120,000. In return Louis, whose advance southwards made his word effective with the Pope, forbade Cesare Borgia to take any action against Florence, which he himself undertook to defend.

For the moment Florence could breathe again, and within a few months the revolt of Vitellozzo and the other captains against Cesare, and his triumph over them set her free from apprehension from that quarter. She resolved to make further efforts to recover Pisa. The death of Alexander and the consequent fall of Cesare, the failure of the French in Naples, all added to her determination. She realized that the great powers were too deeply concerned over the rise of Julius II and his determination to drive out the foreigner to interfere with Florence and her rebellious subject.

She had made one effort to strengthen her own hands in the change she made in the constitution by appointing a Gonfalonier for life. Hitherto her chief magistrate, the head of her executive, had held his office only for two months, the idea being to prevent any individual acquiring sufficient eminence to set up a 'tyranny.' Pressure of danger forced the Republic to take a step she hated and Soderini took office as the first permanent Gonfalonier. He was a personal friend of Machiavelli, and threw himself with ardour into the Secretary's plans for ending the Pisan war. Between them they now evolved a plan which met with bitter opposition at the time and which, it must be admitted, seems to reflect unfavourably on their sense of what was possible. They decided to try to bring Pisa to terms by diverting the course of the Arno. This was to be accomplished by the building of a great dam and the digging of two channels to carry away the water. The engineers consulted declared the work practicable, and that "two thousand men can accomplish it in *fifteen* days." When the proposal came before the Ten, they considered it "mere madness" and refused to sanction it. Soderini, warmly supported by Machiavelli, persisted, and ended by carrying the proposal. Sappers were dispatched to dig the trenches, engineers to construct the dam, soldiers to guard the works. Letters flew backwards and forwards between the Secretary and the men on the spot, all of whom incidentally condemned the project. On the first channel being opened, the water duly rushed into it, but then returned to the Arno. For whereas it had been declared that the building of the dam would raise the level of the river, it turned out that the dam being built slowly, the current of the river was increased as the bed grew narrower, and the faster-flowing water deepened the bed and lowered the river-level. The works had been begun on August 20th, 1504, and they were finally abandoned at the end of October. So great was Machiavelli's disappointment that he took to the writing of verse and declares "Fortune is not yet content, Florence desires Pisa . . . my mind is torn between hope and fear. . . . Florence must reopen the temple of Mars."

Actually an intensive burst of fighting was to come. The Spanish troops, having overcome Naples, were now seeking employment. Alviano, as one of the condottieri who had been serving under Gonsalvo, came north and offered help to Pisa. To meet this, after much delay in negotiations, Florence hired and dispatched a fresh army. The walls were extensively breached and a general attack ordered, but the Florentine troops resolutely refused to advance, and rushing back to their camp in utter confusion showed such hopeless cowardice and insubordination that, in despair, Florence recalled them, broke up the camp, and disbanded the men. (1505.)

(4) *The founding of the militia*

Now Machiavelli was at length able to induce the Signoria to listen to his scheme for a national militia. After the disgrace and ignominy of the failure to capture Pisa, the Republic was, in desperation, willing to try this new expedient. The Secretary was authorized to set on foot the plans he had in readiness. On the various occasions when he had visited the Romagna, Machiavelli had already noted the methods of Cesare Borgia in raising troops. A census was taken of all males, and a proportion called up for service. Uniform was supplied by the Duke, and arms. A novelty was the issuing of long lances instead of swords to the infantry, which enabled the foot soldiers to repel cavalry. Drums and banners were provided, and over each twenty men a corporal was appointed.

Machiavelli, in his institution of the Florentine militia,

clearly followed this model. In 1506 a decree authorized him to set to work. Men were to be enlisted throughout Florentine territory as volunteers. The officers, one to each twenty men, were to be citizens of Florence herself, not men from the country. The cavalry likewise were to be drawn solely from the city. The country territory (*contado*) was to supply infantry. Places which had not been part of the Florentine Republic but which had been added by conquest, known as the districts (*distretto*), were not to be armed. No officers were to be allowed to command a troop drawn from the same district to which they themselves belonged. No officer was to command the same troop for more than one year. The command of the whole force was never to be entrusted to a Florentine, but must be given to some outside soldier. This famous institution shows at once all the weaknesses of the Republic. The regulations make clear the lack of unity, and, indeed, the actual distrust existing between Florence and her subjects. Machiavelli believed that Italians were still capable of bravery. He did not think that the cowardice shown in the Pisan wars was any proof that Italians could no longer fight. He thought that training would put the volunteer certainly on a level with the hired professional, and that patriotism would enable him to rise even higher. "How great," he writes, "is the difference between those who are soldiers for choice and those who fight for money only." He failed to realize that discipline and training were not enough, that confidence must exist between leader and men, and, indeed, more than confidence was necessary. If a true patriot army were to be formed, the men must be united and inspired together with their leaders, must be accustomed to their officers and have more mutual knowledge and trust than he ever envisaged. It was, of course, not easy for Machiavelli to see what appears so obvious

LUCREZIA BORGIA
By Pinturicchio (in the Vatican).

to us. The 'companies' of Italy were not bound together by the ties of kindred and blood, or even locality. They had no feeling of allegiance to, or of affection for their commanders. In no country known to Machiavelli was there a national force animated by patriotism, and he failed to see that the true 'spirit' which alone could inspire his volunteers was not adequately encouraged by his ordinances.

The terrible curse of faction was still powerful enough to spoil even Machiavelli's militia. It was this ancient dread which underlay the regulations aimed at preventing any troop from cohering under its leader. In the past Florence, like all Italian cities, had been obliged to call in foreigners to act as judges in the courts. No Italian State saw anything but common sense in the appointment of aliens as Podestàs. Therefore, to the Florentine it seemed natural and obvious to take the same precautions in the army. It was dangerous and risky enough to create this standing army at all, to give its command into the hands of a Florentine, who might use it for his own ends, and once more revive the horrors of civil warfare was unthinkable. Safeguards must be the supreme object, in order to prevent any attempt at a tyranny. So Machiavelli ordained as a check upon the commander that all pay should pass through the hands of the Ten, that in time of war the Ten should control the militia, and that acting *under their instructions* should be a captain of the guard, and "no native of Florence, or of Florentine territory or district, nor of any place within forty miles of the Florentine border, could be nominated to the post."

All this importance attached to a local force may seem petty and trifling, but to Machiavelli it was the very breath of life. He had seen far too much of political intrigue to doubt the reality of the dangers threatening his city. He was convinced that the employment of mercenaries was worse than useless. Now, like a man desperately throwing up an embankment to keep out a great flood, he toiled and drudged at the enrolment of his militia. For the rest of his official career, comparatively short as that was to be, he threw all his energies into this humdrum task.

He wrote round to all the mayors of the commune, calling upon them to enlist men, he saw to the provision of the requisite funds, he ordered and supervised the distribution of arms. Directly the force began to come into being he was inundated with letters from the newly-appointed officers, asking for instructions, for he was the only person qualified as yet to give them. In everything he had the warm support of the Gonfalonier, without whom, indeed, he could hardly have pushed through his ordinances.

One of the difficulties which had to be faced at an early stage was the appointment of the first "Captain of the Guard." Here we have an excellent instance of the way in which Machiavelli acted on his own theories. To him practical results were all-important, and to them he would sacrifice theoretical morality. Thus he was resolved his force should be no amateur body, to bring ridicule on his creation; it must above all things be trained and disciplined by a man who really knew his work. For this reason he succeeded in forcing the appointment of the Spaniard, Don Michelotto, who had served under Cesare Borgia, who had a reputation for extreme cruelty, and who carried through the strangling of the captains at Sinigaglia, but who was likewise known to be a thoroughly efficient and experienced man. Only a short while before Florence had denounced this individual as "a monster of iniquity, an enemy of God and man," but Machiavelli now pointed out, "he having been accustomed to the command

and management of the same sort of men [infantry] . . . we think he will soon be able to turn them to account on active service."

Certainly this policy met with success. Volunteers flocked to enlist; within six months no less than 12,000 had come up for inspection. Of these 5,000 were accepted and inscribed on the lists. They were organized into thirty companies, each with a flag, and eleven 'constables' were nominated as superior officers. Reviews were held, and the men, dressed in new uniforms, paraded in the Piazza at Florence, to the great satisfaction of all concerned.

Michelotto, having trained his men, began to transfer them to the camp before Pisa. An ironical touch is given to the situation by the report Machiavelli speedily had to make to his committee—the new troops made such a good showing that emissaries of other States promptly appeared in the camp and began to tempt them away to take service elsewhere.

The immediate reward of all the energy and zeal Machiavelli had lavished upon his project was now, however, close at hand.

Pisa was surrounded on all sides. Three camps were formed, which completely cut her off by land. A Genoese corsair was hired to blockade the mouth of the Arno, and even when he withdrew the militia were able to command the banks. Machiavelli in person went to direct operations, and brought some criticism on himself by paying no attention to the Commissary Capponi. He superintended the building of a pier across the Fiume Morto, of the sinking of ships in the river to make it fordable to his troops, of the establishment of blockade parties along every path leading to Pisa. Starved into surrender, on May 24th, 1509, envoys appeared in Florence to negotiate terms, and as only unconditional surrender was acceptable, to this they agreed and "at thirteen o'clock, an

hour that had always been of good omen to the Florentines,"
on May 31st, after nearly fifteen years, Pisa once more passed
over to the control of Florence.

Immense rejoicings broke out in Florence, bonfires were lit
in the streets and "every man is mad with delight." Con-
gratulations were showered upon Machiavelli, who was
recognized as the true organizer of victory.' It was the most
triumphant moment of his career, and with wonderful
dramatic irony it was the immediate precursor of the ruin of
both Machiavelli and the Republic.

CHAPTER VII

THE DISMISSAL OF MACHIAVELLI: HIS RETIREMENT AND
HIS PRIVATE LIFE

IN spite of the triumph which the surrender of Pisa brought
to Florence, the relief and safety which she now hoped to
enjoy were illusory. Storms were gathering over Italy, and
the Florentine Republic, which believed itself to have climbed
to a peak of safety and glory, was to be brought to disaster.
Her fall was to come from the policy of the Papacy. Julius II,
the warlike Pope, whose fierce visage looks out from the famous
portrait by Raphael, full of vitality and strength in spite of his
age, had on his election in 1503 inherited the conquests of
Alexander VI. With the single-minded aim of adding to the
Papal possessions, Julius resolved first to crush the Venetians,
and then to expel the French. With these objects in view he at
once embarked on the League of Cambrai to crush Venice.
"In one day the Church has taken power from the Venetians
with the aid of France; after accomplishing this, she has
chased the French from Italy." Thus Machiavelli summed up
the action of Julius. In 1510, having, with the help of France,
crushed Venice, he was free to carry out the second part of
his plan.

Now the quarrel of the Papacy with France would inevitably
affect the fortunes of Florence. The policy of the Republic
was bound up with her French alliance. Faced with demands
from both sides to declare her intentions, Florence had to
make a great decision. Louis XII called upon her to say with

which side she would range herself. Yet if she adhered to France, Julius II, warlike and resolute, fresh from his successes against Venice, would undoubtedly attack Florence. Moreover, there at Rome, chief amongst the influential Cardinals, was Giovanni de' Medici, son of Lorenzo. Soderini, ardent opponent of the Medici, threw all his weight on the side of the French alliance. Ultimately Florence decided to adhere to her old friends; she threw in her lot with France against the Papacy, and thereby settled her fate. Louis XII, casting about for any weapon to use, began to talk of invoking a General Council of the Church. The points to be laid before this Council were as to "whether it is permissible for the Pope to make war against a Christian king without declaration," and whether in any case he may declare it "against the Most Christian King of France." Florence, dragged into the project, agreed, despite the violent protests of Julius, that the Council should meet at Pisa, and was at once placed under interdict by the Pope.

Machiavelli was deeply concerned in all the negotiations respecting these momentous affairs. He was the envoy sent to Louis in France to convey the adherence of Florence to the alliance. He was dispatched to meet those Cardinals who supported the idea of a Council and who came to Pisa when Florence, disliking the interdict, wished to draw back and pacify the Pope. He was sent once more to Louis in order to persuade the king to postpone the Council. On Louis reluctantly agreeing to this, it was found to be too late. The discontented Cardinals, who felt themselves too deeply committed, had already reached Pisa. Machiavelli was once more set to negotiate with them.

He succeeded, but now all attempts of Florence to temporize were unavailing. Julius was her bitter enemy, and he now identified himself still further with the Medici by appointing the Cardinal de' Medici as legate of Bologna, "which added greatly to the divisions and discontent of the people of Florence."

War broke out between the Papacy and France. Julius, eager for victory at any cost, allied himself with Naples, Venice and England in the Holy League, and appointed the Spanish viceroy of Naples, Raymond de Cardona, captain of his forces. This action had far-reaching and quite unforeseen results. The opportunity was given to Spain to advance into Northern Italy, and she was destined ultimately to become the chief power in the peninsula, and when in the future, under Charles V, Spain formed part of the Empire, she was to hand on her preponderance in Italy to Austria. Julius, though he drove out the French, sealed the fate of Italy in paving the way to the predominance of the Emperor Charles V.

All this lay implicit in the war of the Holy League, and amongst the consequences to follow from that pact was involved the collapse of the Florentine republic before the Medici. This in its turn was to produce the dismissal of Machiavelli from public life and his consequent turn to literature and the writing of his books.

For the war against France ended in the complete discomfiture of Louis XII. At first he promised to hold his own. Bologna, a city of vital importance, fell into the hands of the French, and Julius, roused to fury, himself led the Papal army in an attempt to recover it. Then came the news that a great French army had crossed the Alps under the command of Gaston de Foix, the twenty-three-year-old brother of the French Queen, who was one of the "wonders of the age," and who seemed likely to prove a military leader of real genius.

Gaston carried all before him, and reached Ravenna at the head of a victorious army. There he was met by the League forces, under Raymond de Cardona, and there what is usually called "the first great battle of modern times" was fought April 1512. French, Swiss, Spaniards, all fought with the utmost courage and tenacity. The League casualties were at least 12,000, possibly more. The French losses were about 4,000, and the victory rested with them. Gaston de Foix was killed in pursuing the flying Leaguers with too great audacity, and his death ruined the French. They had no one to take his place. Julius rallied his forces, sent fresh armies, and, like a great tide ebbing, the French retreated towards the Alps. City after city fell into the hands of the Pope, including the key to the north, Bologna, and carried onwards by his triumph he determined to destroy his enemy, the republic of Florence.

The Cardinal de' Medici had been with the Papal forces at Ravenna, and had for a short while been a prisoner in the hands of the French. He was now free, and accompanied Raymond de Cardona in his advance. A meeting of the League was held at Mantua to decide the fate of Florence. The Medici produced 10,000 ducats there and then, and promised more to any who should help them to return to their native city. The poor Florentine ambassador, attending the conference, had nothing with which to outbid these terms. The decision of the League was rapidly made; Soderini, the upholder of the French, must be expelled from Florence, and the Medici should return.

The news was received in Florence, and the Signoria met to decide what should be done. Soderini still had great influence, and he in his turn was swayed by Machiavelli's belief in the militia. Close personal friends and joint creators of the national army, Soderini and Machiavelli both believed the city could hold her own. Machiavelli was at once sent round to all the territory to collect troops and organize the defence. He visited Pisa, Montepulciano, Valiano, San Savino, Firenzuolo and other towns. The army of the League, headed by de Cardona and the Cardinal de' Medici, arrived at the frontier. They formally demanded the expulsion of Soderini and the return of the Medici. Soderini now summoned the Great Council, and laid the case before them, urging the citizens to fight for their independence. The assembly "unanimously declared for the maintenance of the popular government and the defence of their liberties." They would have agreed to the return of the Medici as private citizens, but they refused to depose Soderini, feeling no doubt that the point was vital, since it involved definite interference with their constitution.

Money was voted for the defence of the city, men collected and dispatched to bar the way of the advancing army. Many in Florence doubted the wisdom of resistance. Besides the large body of Mediceans, who naturally opposed such action, there were others who had no belief in the militia. Guicciardini wrote: "The militia lacked experience of war, they had no captains in whose merit or influence they could trust, while as for the leaders they were of such sort that never in the memory of man had there existed any less worthy of their pay."

Yet this force was called upon to meet the experienced troops of de Cardona, fresh from Ravenna and all their subsequent victories. Actually one might say they never did meet the Spaniards, for at the breaching of the walls of Prato, without even waiting for the Spanish storm troops to advance, the militia fled. Machiavelli could only report on "the vileness shown by our troops"; the Spaniards themselves spoke with disgust of their opponents' cowardice, and every contemporary, reporting the events, speaks of "the utter cowardice" of the men and "the complete ignominy of their flight." Feelings were inflamed by the knowledge of what such cowardice involved. The Spanish troops were cruel and were speedily out of hand. Prato, abandoned and without defence, was put to the sack, and the horrors which overtook men, women and children shocked and revolted the whole conscience of Italy. The soldiers who fled away through the gates and saved themselves without striking a blow naturally earned undying contempt.

Prato was entered by the Spaniards on August 29th. In Florence all hope of resistance was abandoned, and three days later, Soderini having been deposed and having fled from the city, the terms of the League were accepted, and the triumphant return of the Medici was secured. The terms accepted laid down that the Medici should return as private citizens; that Florence should give up her French alliance and join the Holy League; that she should pay all the expenses of de Cardona's army and should ally herself with Spain.

Though with the restoration of the Medici to Florence the independence of the city in reality vanished, yet for a time the forms of Republican government were retained. The Medici showed themselves to be moderate and conciliatory. It was the more creditable since Ridolfi, the temporary head of the Republic after the flight of Soderini, remarked: "Our enemies have got us in a barrel and can attack us through the bung-hole." The Constitution was at once altered in certain respects, the Signoria was to continue, though it was now not to be elected but nominated, and the Gonfalonier of Justice was, as before, to hold office for two months. The real control of government passed to a *balia*, or commission of forty, mostly selected by the Medici, who at once abolished the Great Council and the Ten, together with the national troops and the Nine of the Militia. Even where the various committees and councils continued to exist, or were revived in modified form, all were elective, and as the control of the elections now passed entirely into the hands of the Medici, to them fell the control of government, and "the city was reduced to the point of doing nothing save by the will of Cardinal de' Medici" (Nardi).

It was of course inevitable that the chief offices in the State should pass into the hands of Mediceans, and Machiavelli must have anticipated his own fall. He had been one of the most eminent employees of the Republic, he had been the personal friend of Soderini, and he had been one of the principal men to urge armed resistance to the forces of the League.

Yet, surprising as it may seem to us, Machiavelli not only hoped against hope that he might retain his post, he entirely refused to accept the prospect of dismissal, and at once set to work in desperate efforts to conciliate the Medici and secure the retention of his services.

The only reasonable explanation for his behaviour is that, like many others who have become accustomed to playing an important part in carrying on the work of government, he could not conceive that such work could continue without him. He believed that his ability and energy must make him indispensable, and that the Medici, showing themselves moderate, would be glad to employ so useful an individual. No sooner were the Medici back in their palace than he instantly sought to win the private patronage of the Cardinal. Three letters exist which he wrote at this time. Two are to the Cardinal himself, and one to a lady of the Medicean family. In all he not only accepts the restoration, he says: "This city is now very quiet and hopes to lead, with the assistance of the Medici, no less honourable an existence than in past times when their father Lorenzo, of happy memory, was at the head of the government." He warns the Cardinal against letting himself be unduly influenced by the enemies of Soderini, and points out that difficulties will arise in the resumption of the Medicean estates if those who had quite legitimately bought them in from the Republic when she confiscated them, were now dispossessed. It is a situation analogous to that which faced the restored Stuarts in England, and Machiavelli gave the Cardinal sound advice when he suggested that one of the first tasks of the new *Balìa* should be to vote money compensation to those owners of the estates now resumed by the Medici.

Neither conciliatory words nor helpful advice could win Machiavelli any place in the regard of the now all-powerful Cardinal. On November 9th a decree was unanimously passed by the new Signoria dismissing Machiavelli from every post which he held, banishing him for one year from Florence, but ordering him to remain within Florentine territory, and to find sureties in a large sum for his submission to the decree. His post as Secretary to the second chancery was filled by the appointment of Michelotto, a strong adherent of the Medici.

Worse was to come. Within three months of these events Julius II died, and as his successor to the Papacy the conclave elected Cardinal de' Medici, who now became Pope Leo X. Naturally this advancement of the family had its repercussions in Florence. Whether rendered desperate by the stronger hold this elevation would give the family, or whether chance brought to light events previously planned, is uncertain. But at this exact juncture a plot against the Medici came to light, organized by Boscoli, a friend of Soderini. Amongst the papers seized was a list, presumably of the conspirators, and amongst them was the name of Niccolò Machiavelli. He was at once arrested and put to the torture. The Medici were at first uncertain as to the extent of the conspiracy and its aims, and wished to clear up the situation. Eventually it was made clear that the plot was wholly vague, nothing had been planned out, and that probably none of the persons whose names were on the list had even been approached. Only the two ringleaders were put to death. The others, including Machiavelli, were held to have cleared themselves, were declared innocent by the judges and released. Machiavelli had endured "four twists of the rack," and writing to his friend Vettori, the Florentine ambassador at Rome, tells him that his hands are still swollen from the torture, but he adds: "It is a miracle that I am still alive, for I have lost my office and have been on the point of losing my life . . . I am really pleased with myself for the fortitude with which I have borne my afflictions, and I think there is more in me than I ever before believed."

Physical courage and the power to face desperate situations Machiavelli had demonstrated. Yet he had not the moral courage to accept his disgrace and fall from office. He obviously considered that he could still serve his country in a public capacity, and he convinced himself that it was right for him to accept the restoration of the Medici. Perhaps here we have proof that the lack of a moral standard which cannot be explained away from "the Prince" was part of Machiavelli's character. The State was to him supreme, and to achieve good government actions which were bad in themselves could be held justified. What he argued in the wider sphere he applied to his own case, and he was resolved to leave no stone unturned if he could win back to office.

His letters to Vettori are explicit. "Try if possible to keep me in the memory of our master (Leo X), so that if it were possible I might begin to be useful to him or his house in some way"; and again: "Cannot I obtain some employment, if not in Florence, at least in the service of the Papacy?"

If he convinced himself that his services ought to be utilized, he also knew that without any official employment his own personal position was desperate. He was now forty-four years of age. He had wife, four sons and a daughter. Though he had now inherited his father's estate, he had debts, and the loss of his salary was a crushing blow. "If nothing can be done for me," he writes later, "I must live as I came into the world, for I was born poor." He was actually summoned for non-payment of taxes, and when Vettori was asked to certify that he was in no position to pay he wrote: "He is really poor, as I can affirm, penniless and burdened with children." An extraordinary vivid touch is given in one of Machiavelli's most depressed letters to his friend: "I would be better dead, and my family better without me, since I am only a burden, being accustomed to spend and unable to exist without spending."

That last phrase lights up with a flash one side of his character. Accustomed to a good position, and fond of pleasure, Machiavelli had even in the past indulged himself in all the ways readily accepted by the period. Fond of his wife, he had never been faithful to her, and often his letters to his official colleagues had been supplemented by stories of his dubious adventures. Villari holds that he often exaggerated the tale of his doings. Certainly many of his private letters show that if a gay friend wrote bragging of his dissipations, Machiavelli, not to be outdone, would counter with a story of his own. In one breath he admits to being ashamed of himself, and yet cannot resist giving an account of the behaviour which he knows was scandalous. Thus in one notorious letter, written a few years before his fall, he describes a visit he paid to a brothel at Verona, and admits that when he struck a light the prostitute he visited was so revolting that he was overcome with disgust when he recalled her. Indeed, in his boasting about his amorousness he resembles Pepys; both were of a type which could not refrain from such episodes, and while never disguising the knowledge that they were scandalous, got enjoyment from reporting them.

In his private life Machiavelli was not able to find any comfort; indeed, his personal difficulties only added to his public disgrace.

He had married in 1502 a young Florentine lady, Marietta Corsini, and very little is known of her. No letters to her from her husband remain. They had five children, and the only one of her letters which has been preserved is one written shortly after the birth of their second son, which took place while Machiavelli was in Rome in 1506. The letter shows that there was affection between the two, and a strong bond of love for their children. Like so many other women whose letters to their eminent husbands have been preserved, she dilates on the beauty of the baby, confident that her husband will want a description of the child. "The baby is well," she writes, "and resembles you. He has a beautiful white skin, and his hair looks like a piece of black velvet on his head. His likeness to you makes me think him beautiful, and he is as lively as if he were a year old. He opened his eyes directly he was born, and he cried so loudly that he filled the whole house with the noise. Our little girl is not at all well.

Be sure to come back soon." This simple revelation of the happy family tie recalls the letter, very similar in tone, which the more fortunate Clarice wrote to her husband Lorenzo de' Medici when he too was absent, describing their children at play, or another written by Henrietta Maria Queen of England giving an account of the birth of that "black-haired boy" whom others thought so ugly, but who to her was beautiful. Marietta cannot have been much of a companion to him as far as intellectual interests went, for we find he obtained all his mental stimulus from his friends, and his letters to them do not even mention her. In later letters to his family he always speaks of her with affection, but now in his great unhappiness he never once refers to any sort of consolation to be found in his home circle. Indeed, the mere pressure of want, and the anxiety as to how to keep his home together, added to his misery.

With his record of dissipation behind him, therefore, it is not altogether surprising that, in his disgrace and poverty-stricken exile, Machiavelli let the lower part of his nature have full play. He was desperate and he tried to find oblivion through a plunge into debauchery. He gave himself up to bitterness and allowed his rebellious misery to find vent in visits to brothels, or in writing indecent plays—anything to distract or relieve him. He says to Vettori: "I counsel you too to throw off all restraint and give yourself up without caring what anyone may say, and this I myself have done."

No one can understand Machiavelli without a knowledge of this phase of his life, for it both brings the reality of his character before us and it gives a human interest which would otherwise be missed. Other men have fallen from the occupying of good positions, from the possession of wealth, and from the performing of honourable work which they love. Some

MACHIAVELLI
(From an early edition of his works).

have let themselves fall, as Machiavelli did, into an abyss of despair and have sunk down into depths of degradation. A few have rallied, and dragged themselves painfully up again. Machiavelli had at bottom the strength to do this. Slowly he emerged from his 'slough of despond,' he struggled up once more, saved by his intellectual gifts. Possibly it was the feeling of intellectual power being wasted and unused which made him so desperate, and which made him stoop to beg for employment from the Medici. In any case his gifts, denied their outlet in the sphere to which he had become accustomed, sought and found fulfilment in other ways. He began to write, and in his exile at San Casciano he composed *The Prince* and set down the political philosophy which has gained him immortality.

The extraordinary future of that book was of course undreamt of by Machiavelli. He wrote it, and presented it to the Medici, but it was never published in his lifetime, and as far as we know he attached no special importance to it. But once launched on his career as a writer, he had found his salvation. He followed it up with his *Discourses* and his *Capitolo della Ambizione*. Helped once more by Vettori he obtained at length a commission to write his *History of Florence*. For this he received a fixed salary of 100 florins, and in addition he sought for and obtained a subsidy from Leo X, who wished to encourage the recording of his father's rule.

Gradually he obtained other employment. He was sent to negotiate on behalf of commercial matters by the great woollen guild. And he had one small piece of work in connection with the Franciscans. He joined a club of literary men in the Orti Oricellaria, and wrote the *Art of War*. He was called in by Leo X to write a *Discourse on the reform of the Florentine constitution*. The memory of his disasters was gradually obliterated, and he worked his way up once more to a position of usefulness.

How closely his history is bound up with that of Italy, and the upheaval due to the rise of great nations in Europe, is illustrated by the close of his career. For he emerged from his obscurity just in time to participate in the great events which now took place. His life was to close at the exact time when the Papacy suffered its eclipse in the terrible sack of Rome. Just as the beginning of his career coincides with the first invasion of the French under Charles VIII, so its end coincides with the final disappearance of the French from Italy, and the establishment by the Emperor Charles V of that domination by the Habsburgs which was to survive until the age of Garibaldi.

Leo X died in 1520, after a Pontificate which marked the culminating peak of splendour in the history of the Papacy. He was followed by the Emperor's tutor, Adrian of Utrecht, known as Adrian VI and hated by the Romans as a 'foreigner.' He in his turn was succeeded in 1523 by the second Medicean Pope, Giulio, illegitimate son of Lorenzo's brother, known as Clement VII. He was to be as unfortunate as it was possible for any man to be. He had to deal not only with the Reformation, and the troubles over the divorce of Henry VIII and Catherine of Aragon, but with the terrific struggle now to be fought out in Italy between those two great rivals, the Emperor Charles V and Francis I of France. Appalled by the situation he had to face, Clement had no better policy than to try to play off one great power against the other. Absorbed in international politics, he yet remained faithful to his love of Florence. As the fighting between French and Imperialists took place in Northern Italy, he realized the likelihood of Florence being involved, and strove to protect the city.

When Machiavelli journeyed to Rome to present to the new Pope his *History of Florence*, now completed down to the end of the rule of Lorenzo, Clement received him warmly. He discussed with the former Secretary the whole question of Florentine defences, and Machiavelli, true to his old beliefs, revived, for the Pope's benefit, his scheme for the 'national militia.' Clement thought it worth while to go into the matter further. He sent Machiavelli back to Florence with a commission from him to consult with the Signoria and see what could be done. He was bidden to draw up a scheme for the protection of the city, and was made Chancellor of a special new body, "The Five Procurators of the Walls." Letters and reports once more began to flow from Machiavelli's pen, the old days seemed to have come again.

Then, with the suddenness of a cyclone, came the attack on Rome. The Pope, after the battle of Pavia, realizing that the French were beaten once and for all, and seeing no hope of resisting the Emperor, concluded a truce abandoning the war and promising a large indemnity to the Imperial General. Believing that by the truce he had made all safe, he disbanded his own forces. The Imperial army, under Bourbon, was clamouring for pay; it contained a large element of German landsknechts, who, as Lutherans, were utterly hostile to the Pope. Unable to control his men, Bourbon let them force him to march on Rome. The Holy City was caught without defenders, was assaulted, captured and put to the sack. The Pope himself fled, in disguise, leaving the city to her ruin.

When the news reached Florence, revolution broke out at once. All those who were opposed to the Medici, hearing of the downfall of Clement, rushed to arms. The Republic was once more proclaimed. The constitution was restored, the Ten of Peace and War re-established. Machiavelli seemed to be living a re-enactment of the scenes which had marked the first expulsion of the Medici. Once more the city was free, and she now prepared for her last great struggle to maintain her democratic institutions and her liberty.

Machiavelli himself did not live to share in that heroic defence. That he hoped to be given once more his old position, we know. The Ten of Peace and War had been re-created, the post of Second Secretary was vacant. But Machiavelli was probably thought too old; he had lost his influence, and he was never nominated. No one seems to have even remembered the man who had been so prominent fifteen years before. Indeed, the efforts he had made to win employment under the Medici, even the trifling commissions he had done for them, now told against him. True he had for months been occupied with the measures for the defence of the city, but he had done so as the emissary of the Pope. Through all his life he wished to serve Florence, and had suffered his misfortunes because of his connection with her democratic government; yet now, when the democracy regained power, he was considered to have forfeited his claim.

The 'Vicar of Bray' turned his coat to keep his position. Machiavelli, in so far as he ever turned his, never regained the office he had once held, and the attempts he had made under the Medicean supremacy now effectually barred him from resuming it under the restored Republic.

Another person was elected to the office he so longed to re-occupy. He had worked hard, he had just returned from a long and fatiguing journey, and the shock of knowing all his hopes were illusory seems to have been the finishing blow. He had for some time suffered from some internal illness. He was now seized with a violent attack, from which he did not rally. His wife and children knew that he was dying, and sent for a Friar. He died on June 22nd, 1527, and was buried in Santa Croce. Later generations have placed over his tomb the inscription:

"Tanto Nomini Nullum par Elogium."

He was fortunate in his death, for he was spared from witnessing the complete downfall of Florence. Heroically as she struggled, she was to fail, and was now to lose even the semblance of her independence. She was to fall under the tyranny, real in name as well as in fact, of the Medicean Dukes. She went down fighting. In this last spurt of patriotism the mists of the past lifted for a moment, and the remnants of Savonarola's party reappeared to take their share in the defence of the city. The *Piagnoni* of Savonarola and the re-created national army of Machiavelli fought side by side in the last desperate effort to save the city both men had loved.

CHAPTER VIII

PLAYWRIGHT AND POET

IF an Italian of the early fifteenth century had been asked whether he had heard of Machiavelli, he would probably have replied, "Do you mean the author of *Mandragola*?" For to his contemporaries Machiavelli was best known as the writer of this very successful play. He wrote others, but this is his masterpiece. It has been enjoyed and praised by men of letters in all countries, and such very opposite persons as Voltaire and Macaulay agreed in praising it. Voltaire declared it surpassed the comedies of Aristophanes, Macaulay that "it is the work of a man who, if he had devoted himself to the drama, would probably have attained the highest eminence, and produced a permanent and salutary effect on the national taste." When we come to consider the theme of the comedy we may be astounded at this dictum of the Englishman, but perhaps Macaulay's classical tradition enabled him to take a broad view. Certainly where the Victorians could never have dreamt of allowing the play to be performed, a modern generation which has seen representations of *The Country Wife* must feel that Machiavelli's comedy does not fall short of that play. His comedy gives us a group of people in whom we recognize, possibly to our astonishment, types that have become familiar to us in the better-known works of later authors. We cannot fail to see that here, on the one hand, is the forerunner of Molière, and on the other, the originator of that class of comic personages who abound in the plays of

Shakespeare. Writing, of course, long before either, he may yet claim to stand at the head of the line from which they are directly descended, and his work sometimes shows the best qualities of both.

His style and his wit give life to his dialogue, and like all great writers in calling up before us the persons whom his imagination has created, he also calls up for us a complete and vivid picture of the life of his times.

Mandragola is constructed round the story of a prosperous merchant, Nicias, who is most happily married to a beautiful, simple, and stupid young wife. Both long for children, and their happiness is clouded by the fact that they have none. A gay young man, Callimaco, hears of the beauty of the young wife, Lucrezia, and desires to become her lover. He also hears of Nicias' longing for an heir, and decides to make use of it to further his own ends. He disguises himself as a doctor, and visits Nicias to give him advice. He tells him to administer to Lucrezia a potion composed of the root of the mandrake, a plant, it may be noted, of the bryony family, much used both in medicine and in the herbal witchcraft of all countrysides. If Lucrezia drinks the potion, he can assure Nicias that she will infallibly bear him a child. Nicias is delighted at such a simple remedy, but is much dashed when he hears of the drawback attending this use of the mandrake. Whoever shall spend the first night with Lucrezia after she has taken the potion, will die during the next eight days. However, Callimaco tells the dejected husband all may be well, for he knows of a reckless young man who, for love of adventure, will come and incur the risk. Nicias agrees, and it then remains to induce Lucrezia to consent. She is both simple-minded and good, and the persuasions of her mother, who is in favour of the scheme, are not sufficient. She does not like to be the cause of the death of a young man, she says. This leads to the introduction of Fra Timoteo, who as Lucrezia's confessor has sufficient authority to remove her scruples. She agrees under the Friar's directions, and the young man, who is, of course, Callimaco in disguise, spends the night with her. The next day we see the happy reunion of Lucrezia and her husband—all in fact are happy, all have attained their ends and prepare now to enjoy a prosperous future. Such a plot was perfectly in keeping with Renaissance ideas of comedy. To a people with a tradition based on the comedies of the Greek and Latin authors, and accustomed in daily life to the far broader stories enacted at the carnivals, there was nothing at all to shock and everything to amuse. Provided, that is, that the theme was well treated, and it is here that Machiavelli shows an extraordinary gift. One characteristic of his dramatic work is its immense zest and vitality. Just as in Shakespeare directly certain characters such as Bottom and Falstaff appear upon the stage, everything seems to burst into life and reality descends upon the scene, so we find with Machiavelli this marvellous sense of vitality coming into the play with the entrance of such a character as Fra Timoteo. He is of those who take command of the author himself, and thrust their personality upon him willy-nilly. He appears late in the play, for he is only called in when other efforts have failed. Callimaco has had to overcome a regular hierarchy of persons, first Nicias, then in order to persuade Lucrezia, her mother, and the mother refusing to burden her conscience, the confessor must soothe her doubts. The Friar is to be bribed, and must be well bribed, "for these Friars are crafty and keen-witted, because they know their own sins and ours as well." The plotters find him in the church, chatting to a country-woman, who has dropped in for a moment, but who declares she cannot spare the time to make her confession. "If you wish to confess," urges Timoteo, "here I am ready for you." "No—not to-day. I am in a hurry, and it has been quite enough to pass the time of day with you without going down on my knees and all that. But have you said those masses for my husband?" "Yes, indeed I have." "Then, here is a ducat, and I wish a mass to be said for his soul on every Monday for two months. He was a regular good-for-nothing, but after all, the flesh is weak, and I feel rather sorry for him when I think of him. Do you think he is really in Purgatory?" "I'm perfectly certain of it." "Well, I don't know. You know how he used to behave to me and how I used to come to you about it?" . . . "Never mind, the mercy of God is great. If man wishes to repent, he can always do so." And as the woman, having taken up much time without performing her religious duties, prepares to depart she turns back and says: "I suppose you don't think there is any likelihood of the Turks invading Italy this year?" "They will if you come chattering without making your confession."

In this dialogue we can see the whole social scene, and the woman who is there but for a few minutes shows herself as the prototype of a whole race reaching down to the chattering Miss Bates and the inconsequent Mrs. Nickleby, always ready to talk and generally to go off at a tangent. The Friar himself is bent on doing his best for the Church in the way of getting business. Approached by the plotters, he is perfectly ready to do their business for them, provided it is sufficiently well paid. He gives to Lucrezia and her mother, who now appear to ask his advice, a justification for his actions. Lucrezia cannot believe "that it can be right a man should die by disgracing her." Her mother assures her there can be nothing wrong in the affair, for she "would never persuade any child of hers to act wrongly," and in any case, "If Fra Timoteo tells you it is not sinful, you may set your mind at rest." Timoteo does declare there is no sin in the proposal, and in his arguments we have what has been called the essence of Machiavellianism.

"I have consulted all my books for over two hours, and I find many points in our favour, both in general and in particular. First, as to your conscience, you must stick to this generality, that where there is the alternative of *certain* good, or *uncertain* evil, we must not lose the good for fear of the evil. Now take the certain good. You know that you will bear a son and thereby gain a soul for the Lord God. Secondly, it is the intention rather than the act which creates sin, and the will rather than the body. You will sin if you refuse to obey your husband, who orders you to do this, but if you obey you will be pleasing him. You would sin were you to enjoy this deed, but you do yourself penance as you dislike performing it. Besides, we must always consider the end in view. Your end is to create a soul for Paradise, and to make your husband happy."

"Oh! father, what do you urge upon me?" says Lucrezia, bewildered by these arguments, and still secretly convinced such actions cannot be right.

Left to himself, Timoteo meditates on what he is doing. "The saying runs, and true it is, that bad company leads to the gallows. It is as easy to go wrong through being too obliging, and indeed too good, as through being too wicked. Lord knows I never mean harm to anyone! There I was in my cell, saying my prayers, hearing my penitents. Then comes in this wicked fellow and persuades me to touch this wicked deed, at first with the tips of my fingers and now my arm has been dipped in crime, and indeed my whole body! And I don't see yet how much further I shall have to go!"

Next day, knowing that the intervening night has been decisive, one way or the other, the Friar is in a fever. He talks to himself as he waits in the church for news. "I have said matins, I have read the lives of the Holy Fathers, I have been into the church and relit a lamp that had gone out. I have changed the veil of the miracle-working Madonna. How many times am I to tell the brethren to keep her clean? How can they expect people to pray to her if she is dirty? I remember when she would have five hundred offerings and now she hasn't twenty! All our fault for not seeing how to keep up her reputation! We used to recite prayers and organize processions and get plenty of fresh pictures and offerings. Now we have let all that slide and yet wonder that people aren't as devout as they used to be. Oh! What imbeciles these brethren of mine are! Ha! I hear an uproar in Nicias' house!" and in burst all the family, bringing Lucrezia to be purified with holy water from the 'venial sin' she has committed. All are joyful, all are satisfied, and the Friar, equally delighted and reassured, recites the prayers and gives his blessing. "Oh!" exclaims Lucrezia's mother, "who would not rejoice at all this?"

The other outstanding personality is Nicias. Macaulay says of him: "Old Nicias is the glory of the piece. . . . Shakespeare has a vast assortment of fools but Nicias is a *positive* fool." In him at once we see the prototype of M. Jourdain. The likeness is unmistakable, and Machiavelli, like Moliere, can give us both the ludicrous and the human side of such a man. Urged by his friends, as he thinks them, but in reality the friends of Callimaco, when his marriage proves childless, to take his wife to the baths, he refuses, for he cannot face the upheaval in his life which a journey involves. "It vexes you," says Ligurio, "because you've never in your life been out of sight of the cupola of the Duomo." "Not at all! Not at all! I've been a great traveller in my youth! I've never missed going to the fair at Prato (less than two miles away) and there isn't a suburb of Florence I've not visited. And even more than that—I can tell you I have been to Pisa and Leghorn." "Good Heavens! have you seen the sea? Is it bigger than the river Arno?" "The Arno! Why, it's four or six, or seven times as big! Nothing to be seen, I tell you, but water, water, water!"

Urged to go by what the doctors say he answers: "Doctors! One says this, another says that; they don't know themselves what they mean!" There follows the scene with the false doctor, who is really Callimaco disguised, and who rouses in Nicias every feeling of delighted pride which is felt by M. Jourdain when he learns that he can "speak in prose." Nicias comes from a more cultured society, and he is won over by the use of Latin. The false doctor explains in a Latin which at least veils from Nicias part of the meaning of what he is saying, the reasons for his troubles. Finally, being, like men of his type, a snob, he is won over to agree to the *mandragola* scheme on hearing that it has been employed by the King of France and "all other monarchs in a similar predicament."

To Callimaco is given one speech which has a curious interest. He is meditating over his plot and says to himself: "You are mad! You know you will only be disillusioned, and your pleasure be followed by repentance! But what is the worst that can result? If I die, I shall go to hell. But as so many nice people have died and gone to hell, why should I mind going there?"

When Machiavelli himself came to die, a story sprang up, and found its way into his biographies, that he had declared he would rather go to hell, where the company would certainly be good, than to heaven, where he felt he would be bored. This was improved upon, and he was said to have had a vision in which he saw a crowd of gloomy half-starved people, who proved to be the souls of the blessed in paradise. He then beheld another crowd of learned men all discussing high matters and recognized amongst them the great philosophers of Greece and Rome. These were the souls of the damned— and given his choice he said: "I would rather be in hell and converse with great minds than live in paradise with that dull rabble." The 'dream of Machiavelli,' notorious as it became, probably derives entirely from the views of Callimaco in the play.

Mandragola was not meant to be taken seriously. It was a high-spirited comedy, full of wit and humour. Yet in the prologue Machiavelli reveals his own feelings as he penned the lines to amuse his audience:

> "Sensatelo, con questo, che s'ingegna
> Con questi vani pensieri
> Fare il suo temp più soave,
> Perche altrove non ave
> Dove voltare il visso
> Che gli è stato inciso
> Mostrar con altre imprese altre virtue
> Non sendo premio alle fatiche sue."

"And if this story is thought unworthy from its lightness, to be the work of one who would appear wise and grave, make the excuse for him, that he does but endeavour with these vain thoughts to make more pleasant the evil lot fallen upon him, since he can turn his face in no other direction, it being denied him to show forth his talents in any better way, his labours being valued by none."

The same note is struck in the shepherd's song, which is

part of the same prologue:

"Perchè la vita è breve
E molte son le pene
Che virendo e stentando agnum sostiene
Dietro alle votre voglie
Andiam passando e consumando gli anni
Chè chi il piacer si taglie
Per viver con angosce e con affanni
Non conosce gl' inganni
Del mondo, e da quai mali
E da che strani casi
Oppressi quasi sian tutti i mortali."

"Since life is short and sorrows are many, and every man must suffer grief, let the years flow past and be given up to satisfying our desires; he who is content to live out his days enduring sorrow and trouble knows not the deception which the world will practise upon him, nor by what ills and by what strange tricks of fortune nearly all mortals are oppressed."

He is trying to divert his sad thoughts by turning them away from hopeless ills, and this is taken to prove the date of the comedy, written clearly after 1512, when he was in disgrace. *Mandragola* proved an immense success. It was acted in Florence and so enthusiastically received that its fame spread to Rome. It was once believed that Leo X had it performed before him, but there is no evidence of this. It was printed in Florence, and again in 1524 in Rome. An early edition in the Magliabecchiana Collection in Florence shows, as its watermark, the famous Florentine lily.

His friend Nerli in a letter from Modena says: "In Lombardy the fame of your great doings has spread . . . I hear of the smooth lawn which made a setting for your comedy, and I hear of the audience . . . your fame has reached to all places, and I have not heard all this merely from friends, but from travellers who are spreading the news in all directions."

His other well-known play is *Clizia*, preferred by some to *Mandragola*. It is far less original, being largely copied from the *Casina* of Plautus, but it has in it a good deal of Machiavelli's wit, and is written in the same easy fluent style. It turns, as early plays so often do, upon the substitution of one person for another. In *Clizia* a servant lad is substituted for the lovely girl with whom Nicomaco is in love. The story is concerned with a father and son, both in love with Clizia, and both eager to possess her. The son, by substituting the servant boy, brings his father to ridicule, and so cures him of his infatuation. The merits of the play lie entirely in the scenes between the old husband and his wife, and between the servants. Here again we have the vivid rendering of low life which we are to find in the Elizabethans, and again touches which re-create the life of Florence. The wife, lamenting the change which has come over her husband, says: "He used to go to mass, attend the meetings of the magistrates, be sensible in all things. Now, since he has taken up with the girl he neglects his business, pays no attention to his farms, lets his trade go to rack and ruin. He is always in a state of bad temper, he fusses about the whole day and is never still, he has no idea of what he is doing half his time." At the end, when she hopes his discomfiture has brought him to his senses, she says: "I never wanted to make fun of you, it was you who wanted to make fun of your own son, and you have had the tables turned on you. How could you have planned anything so low as to marry a girl brought up in your own family to a serving-man just in order to make love to her after her marriage? Did you think you were dealing with blind folk, or people who would not spoil your disgraceful plans? Yes, I admit I helped on the plot against you, there was no other way of bringing you back to your proper sense. The only thing was to make you come a cropper before enough people to put you to shame, this was the only way to do it, and now you see yourself exactly as I wished. If you want to become once more the Nicomaco you used to be, we will all forget what is past. No one need know anything of what has happened and if any breath of it gets about, well, it is common enough for people to be foolish and later see the error of their ways."

Machiavelli wrote no other plays which can even be compared to *Mandragola* and *Clizia*. The *Prose Comedy* and the *Comedy in Verse* are usually attributed to him, but are very poor stuff compared with the earlier play. A jealous husband is the subject of the *Comedy in Verse*, and here and there we get flashes of humour such as in the description of the jealousy he shows "even for my parrot and my magpie," says the young wife, "and he had my little white dog drowned because he was jealous of it—and he won't allow any sort of pen or pencil to be in the house, for fear I should write love-letters; he won't allow a desk or a piece of paper; I can't even write out the washing-list."

He cross-examines the maid-servant as to his wife's behaviour in church: "Did anyone look at her?" "Someone did." "What did she do?" "She just was there." "You begin to equivocate—did she turn her eyes to him?" "I can't say." "You *won't* say." "You make me forget." "Did she spit anywhere?" "Yes." "Why?" "I suppose because she wanted to." "Was she pale or red?" "I am sure I don't know! I was thinking of my own affairs." "What affairs?" "Well really, sir, I was saying my prayers. Why else does one go to church?" "One goes for quite different reasons, nowadays . . ."

"What did she say to the ladies next her?" "What all women say—spiteful remarks." "In a whisper?" "Yes! A loud one, so that everyone could hear!"

But apart from a few scenes, the play is not good.

His other contribution to prose literature is the delightful *Story of the Marriage of the Arch-Devil Belphegor.*

"A certain devout person, being one day at his prayers, had a vision, in which he saw numbers of souls descending into hell, the greater number of whom complained they were sent there owing to their wives. At which Minos, Æacus, and Rhadamanthus, and the other infernal judges were not a little astonished, and at first looked upon it as a slander on married women." The complaints "growing more frequent every day," Pluto himself was called in, and a debate took place in hell, which ended in "it being resolved to send a devil to earth to find out the truth, but as none appeared to offer their services as volunteers, the affair was decided by lot, and the lot fell upon Belphegor."

Belphegor, most unwilling to leave hell, insisted on being provided with 100,000 ducats down, to equip him handsomely, and with which to set up as a married man on earth. He then "set out for the upper world, with a train of devils in guise of servants," and "made a magnificent entry into Florence, where he assumed the name of Don Rodrigo, and took a very fine house in the suburb of All Saints. Being assumed to be rich, "several of the nobility who had many daughters but small estate, courted his alliance." He marries a girl, Honesta Donati, "and celebrated his nuptials in the most splendid and ostentatious manner, being subject to vanity and all other human passions by the conditions imposed when he left the infernal regions." He falls deeply in love with his wife, who, unluckily for him, "brought such pride with her as her portion that Rodrigo, who was a competent judge, being well acquainted with both parties, thought she excelled Lucifer himself." Seeing the devotion of her husband, "she laid aside all manner of affection and would call him the most opprobrious names she could think of whenever he deprived her of anything, however unreasonable her request." Rodrigo indulges her, and lets her have new clothes, "in every fresh fashion that came up in a city where fashions change as often as the wind." She grows "so insupportable that neither man-servant nor maid-servant could bear to stay in the house above two or three days at most, and even the devils themselves whom he had brought with him deserted him and chose rather to return to hell than live upon earth in the service of such a vixen."

She runs away with so much money that Rodrigo comes to the end of his resources. "He borrowed money of the bankers and gave them notes and bonds, but as many of them were circulating in the city this transaction became publicly known." To avoid his creditors he flies the city, and is pursued by the bailiffs. He takes refuge with a farmer Matteo, who hides him in sheaves of straw. As a reward, Belphegor promises Matteo that he shall have the power to drive devils out of women possessed by them, which will make his fortune, such women being so plentiful and their relations so anxious for their cure.

A girl in the neighbourhood is shortly reported possessed of a devil, which indeed she was, and the devil was Rodrigo himself. Matteo, "having caused certain devout ceremonies to be gone through to give a good colour to the matter," whispers in the girl's ear and bids Rodrigo depart, which he does, only to enter into the daughter of the King of Naples. Matteo drives him out, much to Rodrigo's annoyance, who now goes to the King of France's daughter. Hearing of the cures wrought by Matteo, the King of France sends for him to heal the Princess, which he was unwilling to do, fearing to vex Rodrigo. However, he was obliged to go, and finding Rodrigo refused this time to obey him and leave the Princess, he hit on a plan of his own.

He desired the king to have a dais put up in the cathedral of Notre-Dame, with an altar upon it . . . persons were placed on one side with all sorts of musical instruments ready to strike up, and the clergy and nobility, richly habited, came in procession, leading the Princess. Rodrigo, seeing such a multitude and all the apparatus, began to wonder what was the matter, and muttered to himself, "What the plague is this scoundrel about? Does he think to fright me with a parcel of Bishops? Surely he must know I have seen all the pomp of heaven and heard all the noise of hell, and am not to be frightened out of my wits?" However, "the musicians striking up, the trumpets sounding, and the mob shouting . . . Rodrigo said to Matteo, 'What is the meaning of this?' 'Alas!' said Matteo, trembling like an aspen leaf, 'Your wife is coming!' " No sooner did Rodrigo hear the name of his wife than he lost all presence of mind, and without waiting to reflect that which Matteo said could not possibly be true, he quitted the Princess and ran away as fast as his legs could carry him, choosing rather to go back again and get some peace in hell rather than return to the thraldom of matrimony.

One other most curious little piece of prose-writing may be considered, the *Creed of the Wool-weaver*, one of the most violent and revolutionary pieces of writing Machiavelli ever penned.

It occurs in the *Histories of Florence*, and is in the form of a speech delivered by a workman to his fellows when the city is in revolt against the so-called "Duke of Athens," who ruled as tyrant.

"If we were to argue the question as to whether we should resort to arms, pillage the citizens' houses, sack the churches, I should agree with those who say we must think twice about that, and perhaps I should really agree with those who prefer poverty with safety to the mere chance of improvement, which involves taking a great risk. But as we have taken up arms, and the evil is already done, it seems to me we must consider whether we should lay down our arms and how we can secure ourselves against punishment for the ills we have already done. And I think here we must be guided by plain necessity. You all can see that the city is full of hatred and fury against us, the citizens have collected together, the Signory is in session with the Magistrates. They are getting the fetters ready for our limbs and collecting new forces to overthrow us. We must aim at two objects, first to avoid being punished for what we have done, and secondly to be able to live with more freedom and happiness than in the past. Now, I think if we are to be pardoned for our recent crimes, we must commit fresh ones, and worse, redoubling the ill we do, multiplying our crimes of pillaging and burning, and trying to involve as many as possible with us. For where many sin, few are punished; small crimes are dealt with, but very serious ones are compounded. When many are injured, few think of revenging themselves, for widespread injuries are borne more patiently than those suffered by the few. If we increase the damages we do, we shall be more readily pardoned and in that way we shall lay open the path to freedom.

"It seems to me we are on safe ground, for those who oppose us are divided amongst themselves, and they are rich. Their divisions will give us victory, and their riches will guarantee our position when we have seized them for ourselves.

"Do not be afraid of those who will blame you, talking about the claims of blood and station. All men have the same origin, all come from equally old families, nature has made them all alike. Strip them naked, you will see they are made like us. Take off their fine clothes and put ours on them, and it will be we who will look like nobles, and they will look like artisans. The only inequality is that between riches and poverty.

"I am sorry to see some of you regret, because your consciences smite you, the things you have done, and that you do not want to commit fresh atrocities. You are not the men I took you for, or no conscientious scruples could deter you. Those who win, no matter what methods they employed to secure their victory, are never disgraced thereby. We need not trouble about moral consequences, for where, as with us, we have to face starvation and imprisonment, we need not bother about a future hell. If you look at the way men behave you will see that all those who have won wealth and power have done so by force or fraud, and afterwards, to hide the methods they have used they talk of 'honourable gains.' Those who, through timidity or stupidity, will not use these means, always stagnate in poverty. Faithful servants are always servants. To escape from servitude one must be bold and treacherous, to escape from poverty one must be grasping and dishonest. Thus men devour each other, and their state simply changes for better or worse. One must use force when the chance comes."

This is the true theory of revolution, arising from despair. Machiavelli gives a brief and formal denunciation of these views, but the spirit he has put into them is the spirit which has always animated social revolutionaries.

The rest of his writings, chiefly verse, are again of very varying character and merit. *The Golden Ass*, which is unfinished, is a poem in terza rima and meant to be a satire on Italian politics.

The poet, wandering in a forest, meets an enchantress. She takes him to her house, and then shows him bears, a giraffe, bulls, dragons, boars, and so on. She tells him these are men, turned to beasts. When left to himself, after a truly amazing banquet, he meditates incongruously enough on the decline and fall of empires. "The daring St. Mark (Venice), believing she always has the wind with her, never hesitates to ruin her neighbours"—and so on through the fortunes of Florence, Athens, Sparta, the Empire. Machiavelli himself wearied of it and abandoned it unfinished after writing ten cantos. The *Decennali* are also uninteresting to us, being again political poems, rather in the style of a prize competition on a rhyming version of Florentine history.

Yet he had poetry in him, and his sonnets show that he was capable of writing lovely verse. The best of his poems are the *Capitoli*, or short poems on various subjects, on Fortune, on Ingratitude, on Opportunity, on Ambition. Of these *Opportunity* is the most attractive. The idea is not original, being taken from a classical epigram, but it shows, in the transposition to terza rima, the real beauty of Machiavelli's style, and the poetic feeling which was in him.

Capitolo del l'occasione.

a Filippo de' Nerli.

"Chi.sei tu, che non par donna mortale?
Di tanta grazia, il ciel t'adorna et dota!

"FORTUNA"
By Giovanni Bellini (in the Academia, Venice).

Perchè non posi? Perchè à piedi hai l'ale?"
"Io son l'occasion a pochi nota;
    E la cagion che sempre mi travagli
    E perch' io tengo un piè sopra una rota;

Volar non è che al mio correr s'agguagli;
    E però l'ale a' piedi mi mantengo,
    Acciò nel corso mio ciascun abbagli
Gli sparsi miei capei dinanzi io tengo
    Con essi mi ricopro il petto, il volto,
    Perch' un non mi conosca, quando vengo.
Dietro del capo ogni capel mi è tolto
    Onde in van s'affitica un, se gli avvienne
    Ch'io l'abbia trapassato, o s'io mi volto."

"Dimmi: chi è che teco viene?"
    "E penitenza; e pero nota e intendi
    Chi non sa prendermi, costei ritiene.
E tu mentre parlando il tempo spendi
    Occupato di molti pensier vani
    Già non t'avvedi lasso, e non comprendi
Comm' io ti son fuggita delle mani."

Opportunity

"Who art thou, who transcendest mortal things
    With heavenly grace that thou canst not conceal?
    Why pausest not? Why do thy feet have wings?"
"That I am Opportunity I reveal
    To few, and I move ever, day and night,
    Because I have my foot upon a wheel.

No speed can rival my eternal flight;
>   And by the wings that on my feet I bear
>   My passing dazzles every gazer's sight.
Upon my brow all loosened is my hair
>   Therewith to veil my bosom and my face
>   That none may recognize me anywhere.

Behind my head each lock is fixed in place,
>   That, once I pass——or if I should return—
>   Pursuers labour vainly in the chase."
"Who thy companion is, I fain would learn?"
>   "He is Repentance, and he is grasped (mark well)
>   By those who fail my presence to discern.
While thou art lingering, empty tales to tell,
>   And vainly striving much to understand,
>   Thou seest not, until thy clouds dispel,
That I have slipped already from thy hand."

*I owe this verse translation to the kindness of Lionel Stevenson, Professor of English at Arizona State College. In connection with this poem it seems clear that it is modelled on Ausonius, xix, xxxiii (Loeb ed., H. G. Evelyn White, vol. ii, p. 176), "For a Figure of Opportunity and Regret," which recalls Posidippus, Anthologia Graeca, Planudean, Appendix No. 275 (Loeb ed., W. R. Paton, vol. v, p. 324); see also Jacobs' edition of the Greek Anthology, 1794 (vol. ii, p. 49, and viii, p. 145), who refers to Politian (Misc. cxlix Wernsdorf. ad Himer. Eclog. xiv, p. 240). Politian, Professor of Latin and Greek eloquence, lived in Florence at the same time as Machiavelli and was sent by Lorenzo de' Medici at various times to collect rare MSS. and books from Venice and other places. Ausonius was printed at Venice in 1472, and the first printed edition of the Planudean Appendix appeared in 1484. For these details I am indebted to the kindness of Mr. T. F. Higham, Trinity College, Oxford.

CHAPTER IX

"THE PRINCE" : HIS POLITICAL THEORIES

"WHEN evening comes I return to the house, and I go into my study. Before I enter I take off my rough country dress, stained with mud; I put on my good robe, and thus fittingly attired I enter into the assembly of men of old time. Welcomed by them I feed upon that food which is my true nourishment, and which has made me what I am. I dare to talk with them, and ask them the reasons for their actions. Of their kindness they answer me, and for the space of four hours I suffer no more; I forget all my injuries, I no longer fear poverty or death, I forget myself in them.

"And as Dante had said, 'Knowledge consists of remembering what one has heard,' so I have noted down all that strikes me in their conversation, and from these notes I have composed a little work, *The Prince,* in which I have studied as best I can the whole subject."

In these well-known words Machiavelli tells us briefly how he came to write his famous book, and as he writes he conjures up for us the feeling of utter relief with which he could turn from the difficulties of his life to the world of books and imagination. He does not, however, there tell the entire story, and unless we realize fully the spirit of bitterness with which he was then filled, we cannot completely appreciate much of the tone which runs through *The Prince.*

If ever man wrote in misery and desperation, it was Machiavelli, in his silent little room at San Casciana in the year 1512. He had been the busy and successful Secretary of State, devoted to the Republic, enthusiastic over the troops he had trained in her defence. Now he was an outcast, sent into exile from the city, newly released from the prison of the Bargello, his hands still swollen from torture. He had lost his position, his work, and his money. He had not enough to maintain his wife and children. A few months later he wrote: "I shall have to cower among my rags, or retire to some out-of-the-way spot to teach children their letters, forsaking my own family as though I were dead," and again: "I am wearing out and cannot go on long in this fashion without being contemptible from sheer poverty."

In the little house which stood by the inn at San Casciano he led the strange existence which he describes in a letter to Vettori in Rome. "I am living in the country since my disgrace. I get up at dawn and I go to the little wood, where I see what work has been done since the day before. I stay there for a couple of hours, chatting to the wood-cutters, who tell me of all the local quarrels and gossip. . . . When I leave the wood I go to a little spring, and then to the top of the hill, carrying under my arm either a volume of Dante or Petrarch or one of the minor poets Tibullus or Ovid. I read their verses and think of their love affairs and of my own and for a moment I am happy in these thoughts. Then I go down to the inn which stands by the high-road. I talk to the passers-by, and ask the news. Dinner-time comes and I go home and share with my family whatever fare is provided by my poor patrimony. Then I go back to the inn, where I usually find the landlord and the butcher, the miller, and a couple of brick-layers. I spend the afternoon with these boors, playing cards or dice; we quarrel over farthings and our wrangling can be heard up at San Casciano. Yet in plunging into this degradation lies my sole chance of preventing my brains from rotting, and I mock at fortune being willing to let her trample me under foot only to see whether thereby she experiences any shame."

Then, as night drew down, Machiavelli could leave behind him this sordid wretched existence. His books called him into another world. He turned to the life of the mind, and instantly there sprang up in him the determination to write down the thoughts and ideas which thronged upon him. "I am accustomed to ponder over government and the constitution of a State . . . as I cannot discourse of the art of the making of silk or of wool, or of loss or gain, so fortune has decreed that I enjoy discussing the art of government."

Moreover, his mind was full of the downfall of the Republic and the return of the Medici. He had seen how the constitution in which he had believed had proved itself too weak to survive; he had seen his friend Soderini, the head of the State, forced to save himself by flight, and worst of all he had witnessed the horrors brought about at Prato by the sack following on the display of utter cowardice of his beloved militia. Every institution in which he had believed had shown itself a failure and with this he set to work to "discuss the nature of sovereignty, how it is to be maintained and why it is lost." If we bear in mind the genesis of the book, and this whole background which lies behind it, we shall find it easier to comprehend the flashes of cruelty, of scorn, almost of hatred of mankind, that give to it the pungent flavour which is one of its characteristics. It does not quite truly represent Machiavelli's political theories; they are more moderately expounded in the *Discourses* and his letters. Yet perhaps this book has acquired its swing and stimulus just because it was written with such a tumult of bitterness and disillusionment behind it.

Cynics have said that *The Prince* has been so widely read partly because it is so short. Certainly it can be glanced through in a couple of hours, and its clear style, its brevity and its arrangement make it easy to read. Probably many who look at it for the first time lay it down with a slight feeling of disappointment. Is this, indeed, one of the most well-known books ever written? Can it have been studied by kings and rulers of every country for over four hundred years? Is it to this day so important as to have been the subject chosen by Signor Mussolini for his thesis as candidate for a doctorate? Above all, is it really as wicked and perverting as tradition represents? True, it has passages which are both brutal and amusing: "anyone who acts up to a standard of goodness must be ruined amongst so many who are not good," "to be liberal with the property of others adds to your reputation," "men will sooner forget the murder of their father than the stealing of their patrimony."

Yet apart from this, does it contain any real depth of thought, any original or profound philosophy?

Well, in the first place we may doubt whether any book, written by an obscure official of a small fifteenth-century State, would have survived and have been translated into every language and read by countless people over so long a period of time, unless it had contained within it something of permanent value. Nor, once read, do we find that we either forget it or remain satisfied. Something is left in the mind which impels us to look again, and the more the book is studied, the more troubling it becomes. Machiavelli, writing for occupation, for distraction, 'a little book' which he hoped might bring him the chance of employment, has produced a work which not only brought him fame but to this day interests and disturbs mankind.

The main interest of *The Prince* is, of course, its political theory, and therefore it seems best to consider here that aspect of the book, and to leave for later consideration Machiavelli's expressed views on religion, and on the art of war, both of which enter into *The Prince*, but can be dealt with separately.

When we, therefore, take up *The Prince*, we begin at once to search out Machiavelli's political views, and almost immediately we come upon a stumbling-block. The book sets out to deal with the various forms of government, which are the best, and what are the rules which men have set up for their guidance in statecraft. As we read we are aware of a feeling of bewilderment at the multiplicity of analogies with which we are confronted, and this may merge into one of disappointment.

One of the superficial causes of disappointment in *The Prince* is the perpetual reference to classical antiquity. We are not really very much interested in knowing "how Agathocles came to be King of Syracuse," nor "why the Kingdom of Darius did not rebel against Alexander's successors." Those unfamiliar with Italy of the Renaissance must tire of references to Pope Alexander, to such men as Oliverotto, and to the mistakes of the King of France. But these references are all part of the methods which contemporary beliefs imposed upon the writer, and they are indications of the fundamental differences between his theories and ours. He had, of course, no faintest conception of the doctrine of evolution; he did not see history as the story of a progressive development. He held the then orthodox belief that history returned upon itself, that it was a cycle, and that in studying the past men would learn what was to come in the future. He was enquiring as to what was the destiny of a people, why did empires and kingdoms, as the study of antiquity proved, rise, flourish, and then decay? He based his arguments on Roman history and literature with which he was familiar, and not on the politics of Aristotle, known and studied by the Renaissance Italian in translation.

Another touch of strangeness is given by his belief in the great power of 'Fortune' or 'Destiny.' Here, perhaps, we have a trace of the belief in the stars and their influence on mankind, prevalent in the Italy of his day, when astrology was still practised at every court. "Fortune," he says, "is the mistress of one half our actions." But it should be noted that in the *Discourses* he does not stress this view, but puts far more weight on the importance of studying the past, "it appears from all history that men may assist their fortune, but cannot resist it; they may follow Destiny's designs, but not defeat them. However, they ought never to despair, for as her ways are dark and intricate, there is always ground for hope and whilst there is hope they should not be wanting to themselves in any vicissitudes of their affairs" (*Disc.* II. 29). He thought that stability was an illusion, life was a flux, nothing is eternal and all must change. Believing that the golden age lay behind, he also hoped for its return: "whoever wishes to see what will be, must look to what has been." He believed this view to be based on human nature: "for men, having always the same passions, will produce the same results." Therefore, if you studied antiquity you would learn how to act. As to the decline and fall of kingdoms, he thought that "good and ill vary in one place at one time," but power moved from one country to another. "The world has always been the same, and has always contained as much good as evil, although variously distributed according to the times. Thus 'virtue,' which one seemed fixed in Assyria, afterwards moved to Media, thence to Persia,

and thence to Rome" (*Disc.* Prol. to II.). He held that the
peoples of antiquity were specially to be praised and envied
because they were free, and not subject to foreigners. Hence
his insistence upon classical examples, most of which cease to
interest us to-day. Even his contemporaries objected to this
dwelling on the lessons of antiquity. Guicciardini, commenting on the *Discourses*, says: "How greatly do those
deceive themselves who always go to the Romans! If we are
to make comparisons by them it would be necessary for us to
have the same conditions as theirs."

Yet when we have put aside all the arguments from ancient
history, when we have realized that many of his statements
were only applicable to the Italy of his day, a very small
residue is left to us.

Where, then, lies the interest of the book and the source of its
influence? The answer is in the view which it presents of the
omnipotence of the State. And we have here to make a small
mental adjustment if we are to see why *The Prince* can have any
meaning to-day. Where Machiavelli speaks of *The Prince* we
need to think of him as representing simply sovereign power.
To the modern mind this means the 'State,' and with this we
can at once see that Machiavelli's arguments are truly of
universal application. The State is to be supreme, not bound
by the laws which regulate ordinary human intercourse.
Reasons of State are to override ordinary morality, and on the
attainment and exercise of sovereign power actions are
justifiable which in private persons are condemned. Here is
the theory which was endorsed by Frederick the Great, by
Christina of Sweden, by Metternich: "a ruler who desires to
maintain his position must learn how to be other than good,
and to use or not to use his goodness as necessity requires."

There can be no explaining away of this point of view.

[139]

Machiavelli knew as well as any other man what was good and what was evil. He deliberately states that in order to establish and maintain power a ruler may do what in other men is wrong. He believes this is justified by taking a long view of what is ultimately to the good of mankind. The man who aims at establishing a rule of law and order must not shrink from the price to be exacted. Thus "cruelties, we may say, are well employed if it be permitted to speak well of things evil, which are done once for all under the necessity of self-preservation, and are not afterwards persisted in, but so far as possible modified to the advantage of the governed . . . injuries must be inflicted at a stroke, and not renewed daily, that their ill savour being less lasting may the less offend." It is the plea brought forward in every case of a *coup d'état*, or of the use of violence when it is meant to teach a salutary lesson. Evil is not declared to be good, but it is declared to be necessary in order to prevent a greater evil. "The ruler need never hesitate to incur the reproach of those vices without which his authority can hardly be preserved, for he will find that there may be a line of conduct having the appearance of virtue, to follow which would be his ruin, and there may be another course, having the appearance of wickedness, by following which his safety and well-being are secured." . . . "A ruler should disregard the reproach of being thought cruel where it enables him to keep his country united and obedient. For he who quells disorder by a few signal examples will, in the end, be more merciful than he who, from leniency, permits things to take their course and so result in bloodshed, for these hurt the whole State while the severities of *The Prince* injure only individuals."

One modification may be noted. While he does not hesitate to justify cruelty Machiavelli elsewhere admits the efficacy of other methods. "I must also say what great things a good and wise man may do and of how much service he may be to his country when he has extinguished envy by his own merit and virtue," and again: "tenderness and humanity have sometimes a much greater effect upon the minds of men than any sort of violence which can possibly be used . . . and whole provinces have often been subdued by one act of compassion or generosity" (*Disc.* III. 20).

If the accusation of cruelty is not to be dreaded, neither is that of lack of faith. This is one of Machiavelli's most famous and most outspoken efforts. "Everyone understands how praiseworthy it is in a ruler to keep faith and live uprightly. Yet we see that Princes who have known how to overreach men by cunning have accomplished great things and in the end got the better of those who trusted to honest dealing. . . . A prudent ruler neither can nor ought to keep his word when to keep it is hurtful to him and the causes which led him to pledge it are removed. If all men were good, this would not be good advice, but since men are dishonest and do not keep faith with you, you in return need not keep faith with them . . . a ruler should know how to follow evil courses if he must . . . In the actions of all men we look to results. Wherefore, if a ruler succeeds in establishing and maintaining his authority, the means will always be adjudged honourable and be approved by everyone. For the vulgar are always taken by appearances and by results, and the world is made up of the vulgar, the few only finding room where the many have no longer ground to stand on."

Here we have the full flavour of bitterness, and one reason why *The Prince*, despite all our willing agreement with the common sense of its comments, yet does jar, and rouses us to reject its pronouncements. Machiavelli at this period dwelt on the baseness and fickleness of the mass of mankind. His other writings, calmer and more balanced, do not show this insistence, and in them we find the real patriotism and belief in better things which guided his own political life. But in *The Prince* he gave vent to the feelings which recent events in Florence and in Italy aroused in him. "For of men it may generally be affirmed that they are thankless, fickle, false, studious to avoid danger, greedy of gain, devoted to you while you are able to confer benefits upon them, but in the hour of need they turn against you."

Here is that belief in the evil of mankind which has been made to loom so large in the popular estimate of Machiavelli, and it is here that we may join issue with him. History and our own experience do not show that the nature of man is bad and his actions based on self-interest. On the contrary, they show repeatedly that man is an altruistic animal, ready to sacrifice himself for his family, his wife and children, capable and ready in time of catastrophe to lay down his life to save others. So much is this the case that it is rather instances of cowardice and shame which are the exceptions; we take for granted the bravery, not the cowardice, of men in battle; we expect a man to sacrifice himself for his country, we assume that men and women in all times and in all countries willingly prefer the good of their children to their own. Machiavelli allowed himself to underestimate the nobility of mankind and to ignore the basic fact that all society rests upon the assumption that men are to be trusted.

Yet even here, if we look below the surface we may catch a glimpse of the theory which, possibly unconsciously, he was establishing, and which has become an increasingly powerful influence in the world. He glorified the State, he emphasized the right of the State to the loyalty of the individual. Man, as an individual, has no rights against the State, or to put it from the opposite angle, man reaches his greatest height in subordinating himself to the community. These are the ideas which are implicit in *The Prince*, and it is because history, in showing the further development of the State and of the nation, has made all theories of a sovereign power of greater importance, that Machiavelli is still studied to-day. Indeed, it is a commonplace that the developments on the Continent in recent times, whether in the corporate State of Italy, or Germany, or Russia, are the full logical development of the supreme power treated of by Machiavelli.

At first sight we may not realize how these theories are to be traced in *The Prince*. But Machiavelli's *Discourses*, the contemporary comments of Guicciardini upon them, and his correspondence on political theories, both amplify his views and enable us to see that *The Prince*, compressed as it is, does contain the essence of his views.

Moreover, we have to bear in mind that *The Prince* was written with a very definite object in view. Machiavelli did not aim at being a theorist; he emphatically wished to see his ideas and recommendations put into practice. Hence he was primarily concerned to produce a 'handbook for rulers' of Renaissance Italy, and it is only gradually that we can see how, in dealing with a concrete situation, he formulated rules which have been given a more universal application. Dealing with his own day all Machiavelli's reading of history impressed him with this idea of a supreme governing power. As history to him was past experience, so he perpetually looked back to Rome, and saw in her the supremacy of the State. He perceived how utterly Italy had fallen away from that period of glory and that she was now broken in pieces and sunk from her high estate. He wanted to find if there were no remedy for her ills. *The Prince* was meant to be a practical book, showing what was wrong and how an attempt might be made to set things right. He saw that Rome had been sustained by an idea of the 'common good.' Now, clearly, Italy had no longer any 'common good' to unite her, and where could such a principle be found? Looking at her actual organization into States, he saw as a hopeless barrier across the Peninsula lay the Papal States, making union seem an impossibility. Yet, with the help of an individual, Machiavelli believed that a nucleus of union might be formed. He could hope for nothing from the Republics, neither Florence nor Venice had been able to withstand the combination of the Papacy and the foreign invader. A strong ruler might override faction, and in his urge-to-power might by force create a strong State. Machiavelli's career had impressed upon him once for all the potentialities which had lain in the career of Cesare Borgia. "I shall never cease to cite the example of Cesare Borgia and his actions. . . . I know not what lessons I could teach more useful than the example of his actions." And though Cesare had failed and was dead, Machiavelli may have been deluded by the sudden rise to renewed eminence of the Medici. Cardinal Giovanni de' Medici had now become Pope, and was all-powerful. There was the faint hope that here was the possibility of the formation of a new strong State. The last chapter of *The Prince* makes this clear. "Turning over in my mind all the matters which have been considered above, and debating within myself whether in Italy at the present time a fit opportunity offers for a leader to bring about changes beneficial to the whole Italian people, it seems to me that conditions combine to further such an enterprise, and there is no time so favourable to it as the present." He goes on to give the justification which he firmly believed existed for all actions, however cruel and ruthless, which should lead on to the consummation of such a State, namely the liberation of Italy from the foreigner.

"Our country, left almost without life, still waits for one to heal her bruises, to put an end to the devastation and plunder. We see how she prays God to send someone to rescue her from these barbarous cruelties and oppressions. . . . We see no one except your illustrious House who could undertake the part of a deliverer. . . . This barbarian tyranny stinks in all nostrils. Let your illustrious House therefore take upon itself this enterprise with all the courage and hope with which a just cause is undertaken."

Here he strikes another chord. Italy seemed ruined, but, paradoxically enough, Machiavelli, who on the one hand found man so base, yet when he gave rein to his theories, believed firmly in the capacity of man to act nobly. Italy was still full of vitality; she could revive, she could show her ancient bravery, if only the leader would stand up to inspire and lead her. "In Italy material is not wanting, and we see daily in single combats, or where but few are engaged, how superior are the strength and dexterity of Italians. But when it comes to armies those who are skilful in arms will not obey. . . . It is before all things necessary to be provided with national troops, since you can have no braver, truer, or more faithful soldiers, and that you may be able to defend yourself against the foreigner with Italian valour, the first step is to provide yourself with an army such as this."

He had again and again emphasized the evil of the mercenary troops, he had declared that money even was useless to a country if she had no troops, for wealth was sterile if no men were to be had. He is beating himself against a wall, for in truth Italy had gone so far on the path of military decay that for centuries to come she was to have no armies, and even in the far-distant future her liberation and her union were to be achieved largely by the instrumentality of a foreign king and foreign troops.

Yet though he wished for an individual to found the State, Machiavelli did not minimize the need for popular support. In one of the contradictory passages of *The Prince,* when he allowed himself to dwell more hopefully on human institutions, he says: "This is the sum of the matter, that it is essential for the ruler to be on a friendly footing with his people, since otherwise he will have no resource in adversity. . . . And what I affirm let no man controvert by citing the old saw, 'he who builds on the people builds on mire,' for that may be true of a private individual, but when he who relies on the people is a ruler capable of command, of a spirit not to be cast down by ill-fortune, who, while he animates the whole community by his courage and bearing, neglects no prudent precaution, he will not find himself betrayed by the people, but will be seen to have laid his foundations well. . . . A wise ruler should devise means that his people may feel the need of the State, and then they will always be faithful to him." This is in truth the doctrine which seems so opposed to the general trend of *The Prince.* "Will, not force, is the basis of the State." The people will cling to the State, because they desire to do so. The ruler who has not got the true support of the people behind him will fall in the hour of danger. The people may acquiesce in violence, agree to fraud, but the power of the State in reality rests on that acquiescence and agreement.

This argument may be traced here and there throughout the book. The ruler is to seek support as the prime necessity, and that support will be gained by observing certain rules. Thus: "The ruler must be discreet enough to avoid the infamy of vices that would deprive him of his government. . . . He must not concern himself if he be called miserly. Because in time it will be seen that through parsimony his revenues are sufficient, that he is able to defend himself against those who make war on him, that he can engage in enterprises against others *without burdening his subjects*." (Queen Elizabeth leaps to the mind as the standing example of the fulfilment of these precepts.) "It is better," he sums up, "to put up with the reputation of being miserly than to be obliged to incur the reproach of rapacity."

In a very famous passage, often misquoted, he says: "It may be said that we should wish to be both feared and loved, but since love and fear can hardly exist together, if we must choose between them, it is far safer to be feared than loved." But he goes on to say that by this he means it is useless to try to purchase love, "for the friendships which we buy with a price and do not gain by nobility and greatness of character, though they are fairly earned, are not made good, but fail us when we have occasion to use them." That is to say, the ruler must in the long run earn the loyalty and support of the people, and he will not do so by bribes. This same thread, that power ultimately is founded upon the support of the governed, may be illustrated from sayings scattered throughout the whole book. "A ruler must lay solid foundations, since otherwise he will be destroyed, and the main foundation of all States are good laws and good arms." "When the whole body of the people is provoked, the ruler can never be safe" (*Disc.* I. 16). "A Prince should be very careful so that to see and hear him we would think him the embodiment of mercy, humanity and religion . . . because men in general judge by the eye. Everyone sees what you seem, but few know what you are, and those few dare not oppose themselves to the opinion of the many." "A Prince is despised if he is seen to be fickle, pusillanimous, or irresolute; he must so bear himself that greatness, courage, wisdom and strength appear in his actions. The Prince who inspires such an opinion is greatly esteemed, and against one who is greatly esteemed conspiracy is difficult; nor, when he is known to be an excellent prince and held in reverence by his subjects, will it be easy to attack him." "The best fortress you can have is in being loved by your subjects. If they hate you, no fortress will save you." In fact, Machiavelli knew and expounded it as an axiom that any government, founded, as it might appear to be, by force and conquest, could really only be maintained by having the will of the people behind it.

As to his glossing over the possible crimes, whether of fraud or violence, which might be performed by the ruler in search of power—and we have only to think of Frederick the Great, amongst other students, who believed they did but put Machiavelli's theories into practice . . . let us note the passage in which he said: "Still, to slaughter fellow-citizens, to betray friends, to be devoid of honour, or pity, or religion, cannot be counted as merits, for these are the means which may lead to power, but confer no glory."

If, then, we admit that Machiavelli knew quite well that government, however founded, must rest upon consent, we have to face the problem, why does the general tendency of *The Prince* seem to be an exhortation to an individual to establish power by force?

We can find the explanation if once more we return to the fact that Machiavelli was a patriotic Italian, trying to deal with a country which had fallen into corruption and weakness.

Now we know that Machiavelli rated the intelligence of the Italian far above that of the Frenchman or Swiss or Spaniard;

he usually referred to them all alike as 'barbarians.' Yet he saw that, whereas other countries had strength and a national spirit, Italy had none. He thought he perceived that this was due to the devotion of the Italian to material ends, not to ideals such as the welfare of 'one's country.' He hoped, in the ideal ruler, to find an individual who would create the ideal of the 'common good.' His limited historical views made him believe that progress always started with the individual, the 'great man' whom he recognized in such persons as Moses, Cyrus, and Thesus. He was, in fact, a believer in what moderns call 'the leader.' In this he was animated by his feelings of patriotism.

But because he lived in a particular age, and saw that desperate remedies were needed for desperate diseases, it does not follow that his theories, justifiable when a State is faced with extinction and is fighting for its very existence, ought to guide other nations at other times. He put his theories boldly and crudely, and because the touch of savagery which the mode of life of his day rendered inevitable offends our modern susceptibilities, we try to disguise it. We admit that he advocates a 'reason of State' which he allows in special circumstances to override the moral law. This is the true 'Machiavellianism' which has gained such ill repute. We feel we ought to stand up for a 'moral' view, and because the English feel this especially strongly they try in political action to provide a 'moral' reason for their policy, and thereby have for long gained for themselves in the eyes of other nations the reputation for hypocrisy. The theories attributed to Machiavelli really aim at the goal all patriots set before themselves; they are meant to advance the good of the country.

Machiavelli whole-heartedly took that as his object, but he was an opportunist, dealing with special conditions, and it is pressing his views too far to take them as pure theory. He objected just as strongly as we would to the political conditions of his day, and condemned them partly on the grounds that they were morally wrong, but he saw no alternative but to use any means to attain his end. Mankind always revolts from the theory of the divorce between State and morals, and is reluctant to commit itself to the doctrine that an end is *morally* justified if, in order to obtain it, one must knowingly do wrong. But Machiavelli had his views forced upon him by the conditions under which he lived.

Now in this very theory that man could will both end and means, he came into conflict with the philosophical ideas of his century. The ideas of the Greek philosophers, as interpreted by the Renaissance, considered that man was not free to *do* good, but only to *wish* to do good. That is to say, his intentions were to be good. Machiavelli said that man's actions depended on the internal will. He saw man free to wish, and to do, to influence events in the direction he wished to assume. True that in dealing with 'fortune and 'free-will' in *The Prince* he declared 'fortune' decided one-half of life and 'free-will' only the other half, but this he abandons in the more considered *Discourses*. The 'virtue' which he so constantly praises was for him human free-will in action. He did not accept the fatalistic—

"The lucky have good fate, the wise bear all fate bravely";

he thought that "desires which can never be completely attained are the motive force, and desire, fulfilling its impulse in action, is the freedom of man, his sense of liberty" (*Disc.* I. 37). To be 'virtuous' means not only to wish a 'good end,' but to act so as to make it a reality. Man can transform his situation. Circumstances will decide, not the end but the

PORTRAIT MEDAL OF CESARE BORGIA
"Fortuna" on the reverse.
(From Rodocanachi's Histoire de Rome—une cour princière
pendant la Renaissance). *By kind permission of the Executors.*

SIGNATURE OF MACHIAVELLI
(From one of his letters).

means whereby the action can change the situation. "He who does not choose the path of good, chooses to take the path of evil" (*Disc.* I.). Here we have no awarding of pre-eminence to destiny, but a plain assertion of freedom and of choice, and he continues: "some do not choose good, nor dare they choose evil and therefore they never harness their desires to their lives."

This freedom to act cannot be moral, for it is purely utilitarian. Man means to act so as to benefit himself. Humanity divides itself into those who wish to do good and will do so at all costs, those who wish to do evil, and the great mass of those who are neither good nor bad (*Disc.* I. 27).

Yet, when even those who seek only for benefit to themselves work towards an end which is greater than the benefit it brings to the individual, then we have reached a 'universal' or 'common' good. Thus what Machiavelli calls *virtù maloagia* is that of an individual who attempts to attain an end which is good for him but bad for the community. *Virtù buona* is that which, desiring an end necessary to the common good, will do all that is necessary to attain that end. The character of the State will depend on the number of individuals in it who wish for good or bad, though even the good State will always contain certain bad men who will work against good, and the bad State will always contain men who will live and die for their good ideals. The value of the moral code will make itself felt in that men will not carry out their evil wishes, because they are restrained by a moral code.

The good will prevail in the State and through the State, because man as an individual is selfish, as a member of the State he is unselfish. The State will raise man from his conception of an individual good to the higher one of a common good. "True glory," he says, "belongs to the man who acts in the best interests of the community," and again:

"no good man will ever wish to do anything save strive to defend his country in all possible ways" (*Storie*, V. 8).

As we study his later writings we see that towards the end of his life Machiavelli became more and more interested in these aspects of the relations between the State and the individual. His ideas are expressed more fully in some of the most interesting letters he ever wrote. Towards the latter part of his life he had made a friend, the young Francesco Guicciardini, who was rising to fame in Florence in the very posts Machiavelli had once occupied. The older man, now poor and a failure, showed no envy of the younger and more successful, and the correspondence between them is one of the most attractive episodes in Machiavelli's life. One little point brings out their relative positions. Guicciardini, as formerly a credited representative of the Republic in Rome, was naturally the disgraced Machiavelli's superior in station, and as such Machiavelli begins the correspondence by addressing him as 'Excellency,' but at once the younger man begs him to abandon this form of address, and to write to him as one friend to another. Machiavelli later shows his own feelings where he says that gradually, as he continued the correspondence, he was beginning to be better thought of by all who knew him, by reason of his intimacy with the young ambassador. These letters are of importance, for Guicciardini was both acute and critical, and he brought against Machiavelli's theories the very objections which we ourselves feel.

Machiavelli wrote these letters with his eyes constantly fixed on the increasingly deplorable state of Italy. He believed that reformation was possible, but he did not shrink from announcing that whoever set out to rebuild Italy must be prepared for harsh and savage methods. Here he was completely ruthless, and his classical instances are only flimsy veils thrown over his genuine convictions. Thus he says in the *Discourses*: "There is no more potent, nor more valid, nor healthier remedy than to murder the sons of Brutus," by which he means the State is justified in removing dangerous persons by any means which it chooses to employ. And again he says: "No ruler will ever be censured for taking extraordinary measures to constitute a kingdom or found a Republic." "Even when his deeds accuse him he shall be justified by their results. . . . He who commits violence for purposes of destruction does verily deserve censure, but not he who commits violence in order to establish security." "If the ruler has to get rid of possible rivals he must endeavour to rid himself of them by any means whatsoever, for this must be done before anything else can be effected" (*Disc*. III. 30). He objected to half-measures, because he believed them to be ineffectual: "he who will not follow the way of righteousness must for his own safety enter on the way of evil, and ever eschew those middle courses which without rendering him virtuous are not profitable either to him or others." We can perhaps see the scope of this argument if we think of some of the incidents of history where a leader, faced with a decision, has "entered on the way of evil," as did Clive when he forged Watson's signature in order to deceive Omichund. Here again we strike one of Machiavelli's statements which simply sum up the universal practice of men and States, namely, that "it is not necessary to keep faith with deceivers." Or, that it is not necessary, indeed it is useless and dangerous, to behave with honour, or observe the moral law in dealing with people who have no honour, and who are outside the pale of society. It is a question which perpetually vexes mankind. Voltaire dealt with it in his own style when, in arguing as to how the good were to treat the brutal, he inquires whether they were to resist or were to set an example of gentleness? and his famous dictum is: "*Que messieurs les assassins commencent.*" He was, in fact, in agreement with Machiavelli that we are not bound to obey the higher law in dealing with individuals who reject it. Yet to many, Christians and others, this way of dealing with evil offers no hope. Idealists have always wished to stick to their high code, no matter with whom they deal. Dostoievsky has embodied this ideal in his novel *The Idiot*, whose theme is the effect produced on depraved and corrupt people by one who simply treats them as good brethren. It is a problem to which the saint will always offer one solution and the statesman the other.

Now Guicciardini, in his arguments on these points with Machiavelli, often puts himself in the position of the saint's advocate, while Machiavelli sums up the view called 'statecraft.' Both men were intent on the welfare of Italy, both looked at the situation as it was, and both wished to reform it. Guicciardini, like Machiavelli, recognized that the State did not follow the moral law of individuals, but in pursuit of the common good would take measures and perform acts justified by the wider view. "It is expedient that one man should die for the people." Both desired civil liberty for each individual to go about his business, protected by the law. Machiavelli always stresses the need for the people to be secure and free to carry on their daily life. Both, in addition, believed that political liberty was possible only under a Republic. "Although it is most proper that one man alone should form the first model" (of the State), writes Machiavelli, "yet any government he shall establish will be but of short duration if it devolves upon a single person, but if it be transferred to many it will be much better, because many will be interested in the maintenance of it" (*Disc.* I. 10). He believed that in the long run a popular government would survive better than a dictatorship, as we would call it, "for Republican governments have more resources in times of distress and flourish longer because they can better accommodate themselves to the necessities of different times . . . for a ruler, having been long accustomed to act according to one particular manner, cannot tell how to alter when the times change and it becomes absolutely necessary to vary his measures" (*Disc.* III. 9).

He also believed that "The multitude are wiser and more constant in general than a ruler," and says: "I must take leave to differ from the common opinion that the people are more changeable than a ruler" . . . "it is a very difficult matter to persuade them to advance a man of bad character, and in the choice of officials they are more judicious. When all the good and ill qualities are duly stated betwixt a ruler and a popular government, it will plainly appear that the balance will be greatly in favour of the latter, especially in point of probity and true glory" (*Disc.* I. 58).

Both men thought that political liberty depended on the level of intelligence of the masses and that justice should be the basis of the State. Guicciardini says: "I desire to see these things before I die, our city governed by a Republic, Italy freed from the barbarians, and the world freed from the tyranny of priests." When they came to discuss the human element on which governments were founded, a profound cleavage became apparent and the two men represent the two opposing schools of thought, those who believe in the 'sinfulness' and those who believe in the 'perfectibility' of mankind. Machiavelli held to the belief that "Men are always bad," though he agreed that in certain circumstances they would behave well, chiefly, he thought, when forced to do so by law or the conventions of religion, and in this he saw the chief use of religion.

Guicciardini thought that man's nature was in essence good, and that men voluntarily tried to become better. "He who wishes to do evil is not a man, but a beast, for he lacks that [instinct for good] which is natural to all mankind." When they approached the moral effect produced by the State on the individual, both agreed that the 'civil life' of the State was necessary for the moral life of the individual. Machiavelli saw in it an institution which would restrain mankind from its evil tendencies. Here he anticipated Hobbes' "The life of man is hasty, brutish and short," and the function of the State is to raise man from that level. Guicciardini thought that it was rather to uphold and strengthen the good tendencies innate in man.

For Machiavelli 'good' was the complete subordination of the individual to the common good. For Guicciardini it was the right balance between the interest of the individual and the interest of the community as representing the sum of individuals. That is to say, Guicciardini would not admit the complete supremacy of the State; he stood for the maintenance of the right of the individual so long as the pursuit of individual ends did not infringe on the liberties of others. "The law of well-doing," he writes, "is never to injure anyone, and to give happiness as far as is possible to all." He considered the 'moral law' to be the due balance between egoisms, Machiavelli believed rather in the overriding of egoism by the State. This is a 'hard saying,' for few will wish to sacrifice themselves so completely to the community. Individualism is too deeply implanted in some races, and where it has been fostered by representative institutions the individual still is loath to accept the supremacy of even a representative government.

As to the imposition of the will of the State upon the individual, Machiavelli did not scruple to return to his former argument that it must be imposed by force—nor did he hesitate to say that measures of great inhumanity might be employed in the interest of the State. "Touching the advice I gave as to the massacre of the Pisans, I did so not because I spoke according to the Christian religion, but I spoke according to reasons of State." And lest we may be tempted to feel no great importance attaches to the distant fate of the Pisans, we may recollect that Napoleon used identical arguments when he ordered the massacre of his prisoners at Jaffa. Guicciardini did not believe this was necessary, for he held that men go through the world anxious, it is true, to advance their own interest, but also wishful to advance the common good. They will work for themselves, but will also wish to help on others, and to the truth of this view the whole social development of the modern State lends support.

Finally Guicciardini joined issue directly with Machiavelli over *The Prince* and its insistence on self-advancement. He held that the individual must never aim at or use power solely for self-advancement, but that it must be directed and used for the general good. He refused to accept a 'ruler' who, absorbed in consolidating power, would not hesitate over means and would commit crimes and murder. He insisted that the individual must set limits to the means he employed.

"It is legitimate to discuss these matters between ourselves, but we cannot use these measures against others, nor should anyone do so." To which Machiavelli could only reply: "It is hard to live in the world, and to act according to the rule of God, and he who wishes to act according to God will not be able to fit in with the customs of the world."

This is the core of the difference between the two men and the schools of thought which they represent, and Machiavelli has won his pre-eminence not from any originality in his views but from the force and brevity with which he has summed up 'the customs of the world,' and the arguments which, from time immemorial, men have used in their justification.

CHAPTER X

MACHIAVELLI AND RELIGION

IT is natural, when we see how profoundly interested Machiavelli was in the ethics of government and their reaction on the individual, for us to inquire whether he held any definite views on religion, and whether we can gather what were those views. Scattered through all his writings there are many indications of his attitude towards religion, and here again we have to recognize the boldness with which he set out ideas and conclusions which he might have known were likely to rouse prejudice. Here too, as elsewhere, we find the subordination of all else to the State, and a clear indication that to Machiavelli religion was of most importance in reinforcing the political power of authority.

He declares this to be his standpoint in the very heading he gives to one of his chapters in the *Discourses*: "of what importance it is for the preservation of a State to pay due veneration to religion, and how much the neglect of it, occasioned by the Church of Rome, has contributed to the ruin of Italy."

His thesis is that "there is no surer prognostic of impending ruin in any State than to see divine worship neglected or despised. . . . The religion of all nations is founded upon some principles . . . all rulers and commonwealths ought to have a special regard to the fundamental principles of the religion of their country, for whilst they are kept inviolate it will be an easy matter to maintain devotion and consequently good order and union amongst the people." This is, to Machiavelli, his *idée fixe*, "good order and union," and he valued religion in proportion as it assisted in attaining these things.

Thus his objection to the principles of Christianity, as revealed in the second book of *The Art of War*, turns on the belief he held that the virtues inculcated by Christianity were not those which would promote his political ideas. "I ask myself," he writes, "why the peoples of antiquity enjoyed greater liberty than we do, and I find my answer in the fact that men to-day are feeble, and I believe the reason is to be found in the difference between our religion and that of antiquity. For one thing, our religion by showing us the one true way makes us think less of earthly prosperity. The ancients, seeking their good only in this world, were more active in their pursuit of it. . . . Their religion, moreover, glorified men full of earthly renown such as great generals or republican leaders. Our religion rather glorifies men who are 'meek and lowly of heart,' and exalts the contemplative over the man of action. Moreover, it praises all those who are humble and submissive, and it teaches contempt for worldly grandeur, whereas the pagan religion praised a high spirit and a strong body and all that is calculated to make men brave. If our religion does urge one to be courageous, it is the courage to bear suffering which she advocates, not the courage to act boldly." And as if to show that he does not shrink from pushing his ideas to their logical conclusion he adds: "To-day it is rare for soldiers to kill their prisoners; indeed, as a rule men are only imprisoned for short periods, and are often readily released. Rebellious cities are no longer destroyed, men are left in possession of their goods, so that often the very worst they have to fear is nothing more than

attacks upon their property." This passage probably refers
to the surrender of Pisa, where Machiavelli wished the most
severe punishment to be meted out to the city, all prisoners
to be slain, and the city pillaged, and he greatly resented the
overruling of his advice. Like so many before and after, he
believed in the salutary effects of a bloody example; he thought
humanitarianism only led in the end to further bloodshed.

Of course, much of his hostility to religion was due to the
unfortunate times in which he lived. All his life he never saw
the Papacy occupied by one man of even ordinary goodness
and decency. Sixtus IV was one of the most scandalous of
Popes, corrupt and treacherous. He did not even hesitate
to encourage the Pazzi in their plot to kill the two Medici in
the Duomo of Florence during mass, the signal to be the
elevation of the Host. When even the hardened condottiere
Montesecco refused, Sixtus urged on the conspirators.
Innocent VIII was equally bad, and Alexander Borgia
specially incurred Machiavelli's hatred by his political actions.
Even Julius II, though less lax in sexual matters, was a violent
and bloodthirsty man filled with secular and warlike ambitions
and who donned armour to fight in person at the head of his
troops. It is unnecessary to labour the point. All Christendom
knew the state of Rome, and Guicciardini did but represent
the view commonly held when he wrote to Machiavelli:
"Were it not for the respect I have had for the two
Medicean Popes I should love Martin Luther more than
myself, for I should hope that he and his followers might
ruin or at least clip the wings of the wicked tyranny of
priests . . . it is not possible to speak more evil of the Roman
court than it deserves, for it is an abode of infamy, an example
of all that is most vile and shameful in the world."

In addition to the low moral level of the Papal court,

Machiavelli found his bitterness of feeling aroused by the temporal power. His desire for the union of Italy against the foreigner has been sufficiently emphasized, and he hated the temporal power because he saw in it the obstacle to the realization of his aims. "The Popes, at first by virtue of their power to excommunicate, and later both by this and force of arms, together with indulgences, inspired fear and veneration; but from having abused the one and the other, the first they have now wholly lost, and in the second they remain at the discretion of others." Again and more strongly: "Nor can we have surer proof of the decay of religion than in seeing how these peoples that are nearest to the Roman Church, the head of our religion, are the least religious. . . . Through the evil example of that court the country has lost all piety and faith . . . we Italians owe this first debt to the Church and the priests, that we have become irreligious and wicked; yet we owe them a greater, which is the cause of our ruin, this is, that the Church has ever kept, and keeps, our country divided. For in truth no country was ever united and prosperous that did not yield obedience to some one ruler or Republic, as has been the case with France and Spain. And the sole cause why Italy is in a different position, being governed by no one ruler or Republic, is the Church, which, although she here exerts her temporal authority, has never yet been strong or courageous enough to seize upon the entire country and make herself its ruler. And, on the other hand, she has never been so weak as when in fear of losing her temporal dominion, not to be able to call in some foreign potentate to defend her." Guicciardini agreed with him over the temporal power. "I have naturally always desired the destruction of the Ecclesiastical State," he wrote— but he did not go so far as Machiavelli, because he did not believe the union of Italy was possible even if the temporal power were destroyed.

Machiavelli therefore blamed the Church because its policy was definitely detrimental to Italy. He blamed it, too, because it had brought religion into disrepute and he thought religion was useful to the State. "The religion of the Romans was one of the chief sources of their greatness, inasmuch as it caused the laws to be respected and morality preserved. The wise politician will always respect religion, *even if he have no belief in it*, since there have been frequent proofs that, through inculcating it, even by craft, much valour has been aroused for the defence of the country . . . the Romans, either in good faith or by calculation, always enforced respect for religion, and found their profit therein" (*Disc.* I. 2).

Yet he shows one indication that he realized religion ought not to be condemned simply because of the state of the Roman Church. He writes: "Had the Christian religion been maintained as it was instituted by its founder, things would have gone differently, and man would have been greatly happier." He very often praises the "founders of religions," as he calls them, and says: "infamous and detestable are the destroyers of religion . . . and though it may appear that the world has grown feeble, yet this assuredly is caused by the baseness of those who have interpreted our religion to accord with sloth and not with valour. For were they to remember that religion permits the exaltation and the defence of our country, they would see that it is our duty to love and honour it, and to strive that we may be fitted to defend it."

His views on ecclesiastical institutions are therefore abundantly clear. For the Papacy as a political force he had nothing but hatred and contempt, and he saw it only as a political force; its religious aspect was so buried beneath the

[163]

temporal power and the low moral standard of the individual Popes of his day. The priesthood was almost as abhorrent to him. He and his friend Guicciardini agreed in this. "I do not know," writes Guicciardini to his friend, "what man could dislike more than the ambition, avarice and laxity of the priests, both because each of these vices is in itself hateful, and because each and all together are most unseemly in those who profess to live a life in the service of God." Monks and friars he did not respect, and his wonderful sketch of Fra Timoteo in the *Mandragola* shows on what he based his opinion. In fact, he was in the position of many at that time: he could not respect the institution which he saw so greatly abused, and he had not the spiritual instinct to make him look further.

As to his own personal beliefs, as distinct from his perception that religion might be a useful adjunct to the State, we can infer a good deal from the utterances he occasionally allowed to escape him. He shows little belief in the supernatural side of religion and says of Savonarola's claims to have received revelations from God: "Whether this were so I do not take it upon me to pronounce . . . but very many believed him without having any real grounds for their belief." He does not fail to point out how a belief in the miraculous can be fostered. "All rulers must carefully attend to all circumstances and events, however false or frivolous they may appear to them, that seem conducive to maintain devotion, and the wiser and better acquainted they are with the natural course of things, the more they will avail themselves of such a system. This method, utilized by prudent rulers, produced in the past the opinion of miracles, many of which have been pretended to be wrought even in nations under the influence of false religion . . . many of these

miracles might be instanced from history" (*Disc.* I, 12).
Yet he could not altogether shake himself free from a belief
that these were manifestations not capable of explanation in
a materialistic sense. In the *Discourses* he has a chapter "that
when great calamities are about to befall, signs come to
presage them," and gives such instances as the thunderbolts
which fell in Florence twice during his lifetime: once when
Lorenzo died, and once when the Gonfalonier Soderini took
flight on the return of the Medici. Of these he says: "The
causes of such manifestations ought, I think, to be studied
and interpreted by someone who has a knowledge, which I
have not, of material and supernatural things. It may be,
as some wise men hold, that the air is filled with beings, to
whom it is given to forecast human events and who, taking
pity upon men, warn them with omens, that they may prepare
for their defence. Be that as it may, these things occur, and
are always followed by new and strange disasters."

He did not believe that God directly ordered the affairs
of men. "It cannot be said that God has helped one man
because he is good and another has suffered misfortune
because he was wicked, for very often the contrary is the case,"
wrote Guicciardini, and Machiavelli agreed with him. In
his poem, *The Golden Ass*, he writes:

"Creder che senza te per te contraste
    Dio, stanoti ozioso e ginocchioni,
    Ha molti regeri e molti stati guasti."

That is, 'the belief that by kneeling idly upon thy knees thou
canst leave all to God, has brought many kingdoms and
States to ruin'; and goes on:

"Ma non sia alcun di si poco cervello
Che creda, se la sua casa roveria,
Che Dio da salvi senz' altro puntello."

'Let no man be so senseless as to think that if his house fall he can leave it to God to save him.' In short, Machiavelli believed in an impersonal non-interfering Deity.

In *The Prince* he shows by his bitter irony in dealing with 'ecclesiastical princedoms' that he did not believe they were founded by God. " 'Ecclesiastical princedoms' are acquired by merit or good fortune, but are maintained without either . . . these princedoms alone are secure and happy. But inasmuch as they are sustained by agencies of a higher nature than the mind of man can reach, I forbear to speak of them, for since they are set up and supported by God Himself, he would be a rash and presumptuous man who would venture to discuss them," and then proceeds to discuss and criticize them most vehemently.

Later he comes more to grips with the question of Divine dispensation as opposed to free-will. "In order not to deprive us of our free-will and such share of glory as belongs to us, God will not do everything Himself." Here he began to involve himself in his doctrine of fortune or destiny. "We see every day things happen contrary to all human expectations, and that our free-will be not wholly set aside, I think it may be the case that Fortune is the ordainer of one-half of our actions." Fortune, it is to be noted, and not God, here controls the fate of mankind. He thought, in fact, that judging from appearances God did not intervene in directing the destinies of individuals, but that men could work out their own salvation, subject to the incalculable laws of chance, fate, opportunity, call it what you will, which clearly sometimes undid all the efforts of man. Perhaps in this he let himself be unduly, if unconsciously, influenced by the tricks fortune had played him, and by the unfair situation in which he clearly felt himself thrown, while others whom he knew continued to flourish. He also believed that at times events seemed to pass beyond human control. "These times are too much for human wits," he writes, when the French first came into Italy. In this connection he thought men suffered because they could not adapt themselves. "The times and human affairs are constantly changing, but men do not alter their ideas and so it comes about a man will have good fortune at one time and at another bad . . . as to why men cannot change, two reasons may be given. One is that we cannot act contrary to the bent of our characters; the other, that when a man has greatly prospered through following one line of action, it is hard for him to be brought to see that he would do well to alter, and hence a man's fortune changes because the times change, but he himself does not change his ways."

He dimly sees that destiny obeys a law of mutability. "Countries change because nature does not permit human affairs to be stationary, and when countries have attained their greatest height, they begin to decline; and when they have sunk to the bottom they begin to rise once more. Thus States always move from prosperity to adversity, and from adversity to prosperity." It is the idea of the cycle of perpetual rise and fall, and of one part of the community being at the top of the wheel, while others of necessity are whirled to the bottom. He gives this doctrine a tinge of a more religious tone in *The Golden Ass* when he says: "Thus the power that governs us ordains that nothing under the sun is stable, or ever will be. Thus it is, and was, and shall be to all eternity, ordained that evil succeeds good, good succeeds evil, and the one is always the cause of the other."

He concludes that the duty laid on man is to fight, never to give in, never to be dismayed even when fortune turns her back. "Men must never lose heart, since not knowing what is Fortune's goal, and moving towards it by uncharted paths, they have always ground for hope. They must not give up, whatever befalls, and in whatever straits they may find themselves."

His own strongly marked characteristic of courage comes into play here. Just as he longed to see Italians fighting to liberate their country, just as he made it the whole object of his life to train Florentines to fight for their city-State, so he preached that men must return to the old Roman spirit and show valour in every sphere of life. It was not even enough to learn to take up arms for the defence of his land; every man must likewise learn to fight and to struggle against misfortune. He wanted to see Roman courage and fortitude once more displayed by the inheritors of a great tradition.

Beyond this desire to reanimate Italians with love of country and bravery towards personal fate, Machiavelli clearly had no belief in the spiritual life. His energies found their inspiration in the practical task he set himself. Men who live at a time when their nation is in a state of decadence seem, if they love their country, to perceive nothing beyond the need to revive and reform her. They become entirely absorbed in that one aspect of life and they neither see nor desire any other. In their pursuit of power for their country and the restoration of national energy and self-respect, they can value no other claims. A strong national spirit in them drives out all thought of humanity as a whole. Naturally enough, a religion which stresses, not the rights of peoples but the common humanity of mankind, makes no appeal to them. They neither appreciate that aspect of Christianity nor the virtues it tries to call forth. Love, gentleness, long-suffering are for them sources of weakness. They desire courage, and the ruthless pursuit of the advantage of their own nation. Hence they turn their back on that side of man's idealistic nature, and, like Machiavelli, see in religion a force which, if controlled by the State and used to reinforce its authority, will be useful, and nothing more.

CHAPTER XI

MACHIAVELLI AND THE ART OF WAR

ONE of the paradoxes of Machiavelli's nature is that while himself a writer, and a civil servant, one of his chief preoccupations was the art of war, and for him has even been claimed the honour of having written 'the first of modern classics on military subjects.' Owing to the Florentine system, the Ten of Balìa, of which he was the Secretary or Chancellor, had in its hands the conduct of the military operations of all kinds undertaken by the Republic. The Ten, of course, sat in Florence, and held its meetings in the Palazzo Pubblico, but they sent out commissaries to the actual seat of operations, to supervise and report upon the activities of the military. This is the system later adopted by the French Revolutionary Government in the great crisis of its war against Europe in 1792. In the case of Florence this system of sending out commissaries was rendered absolutely necessary in view of the fact that the troops she employed were hired mercenaries, led by a condottiere who was not a Florentine. The hired captains were anxious, if possible, to save casualties amongst their trained bands, which they had laboriously recruited themselves, and were never too wishful to bring their operations to a speedy conclusion and so throw themselves out of employment. Moreover, as they were in every sense of the word mercenaries, one of their main objects was to secure as much money for themselves as possible. In consequence they were always open and ready to consider other offers for their services, and the fact that they were in the pay of one State never precluded them from accepting a better offer now and then. To counteract this tendency, and to keep an eye on the conduct of the leaders of the army, civilians were sent by the Ten to supervise and report.

Usually these commissioners were appointed by the Eighty, or as it may be called the Senate, being balloted for in that Council, the names coming from a select list, usually of ten names previously sent in for the ballot by the Ten of war. Once elected by the Eighty, the Ten then had power to extend the period of the commissioners' office. Further, if they considered a special emergency had arisen, the Ten would appoint an additional commissioner for the period of fifteen days, who could be sent at once to any place, and whose election as a permanent commissioner could be subsequently ratified by the Ten alone, without further reference to anybody. This system led to great abuse, and the Ten in 1496 were the subject of much attack, being accused of giving unnecessary commissions to friends and adherents. So loud was the outcry against "the Ten Squanderers," that when an election had to be held, their opponents rallied the people with the slogan, "*Nè Dieci nè danari*," which may be translated "Down with the Ten and the Taxes," and as not enough members attended the Great Council to form a quorum, no elections could take place. No Ten being elected, the Signoria had to nominate to that office themselves, and to carry on all the supervision of the war direct.

One of the first acts of this Signoria, acting themselves as conductors of the operations, was to place Machiavelli in charge of all the negotiations now carried on with various condottieri in order to secure their services in the war against Pisa. He was sent to Jacopo da Appiano, and hired him, "giving him the same pay as that received by Messer Rinuccio." Some idea of the methods of the condottieri and of the difficulties encountered by all who employed them may be seen in the fact that this agreement becoming known, another captain, Paolo Vitelli, at once demanded that his pay be raised to the same level, "each being resolved to receive as much as the other." Usually a man bargained for the sum he was to receive, on the principle of 'to him that hath shall be given.' Thus when Florence wished to conciliate Caterina Sforza, she had to offer to Ottaviano, Caterina's son, the sum of 10,000 ducats, while later Cesare Borgia, knowing Florence dared not refuse him, asked for, and obtained, no less than 120,000 ducats.

Having dealt with the pay of the captains, Machiavelli was next entrusted by the Signoria with the task of communicating with the leader hired to act as commander-in-chief the well-known Paolo Vitelli. Here Machiavelli gained his first practical experience of warfare, and of the methods of the condottieri, and we can see how from the very outset he was horrified at the wasteful extravagance and poor results achieved by the system. He writes back to the Signoria at Florence: "Having expended up to this time over 64,000 ducats on this enterprise these men demand yet further expenditure, and if it be not supplied we must renounce all hope of victory . . . it would be impossible for half Italy to supply all that is demanded." In spite of the money voted, and supplies sent from Florence, he has to report that no progress is being made; Paolo Vitelli would not press the attack upon the city. The Signoria wrote to Vitelli, pointing out: "Because of the deep affection we bear towards your excellency . . . and when we reflect upon your great virtues and how fortunate we are in having secured your services, we

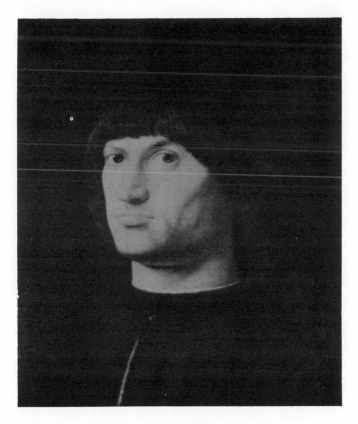

CONDOTTIERE
by Antonello da Messina (Louvre).

do not for a moment doubt that you are taking all steps to secure victory . . . yet as delay will both diminish the lustre which attends your excellency and our own satisfaction, and as we have equally at heart the advancement of your glory and our preservation and, since we have granted you the fullest powers over our forces, we beg you to crown your victorious career by assaulting the city, so that you may win not only the admiration of Italy but of the whole world." Vitelli, however, was not moved so much by this flattering hope of glory as by the secret offers of money he was receiving from the Venetians. The next letter he received, five days later, from the Signoria was, therefore, in a very different tone: "We have heard with the very greatest displeasure which we have ever felt at any time that we can no longer expect any results from you . . . we have given you all the supplies you asked for . . . but we see that you throw away all your advantages and do but waste our substance, and all our pains are of no avail . . . both your idleness and dilatoriness waste time and ruin the morale of our troops and our own reputation " The money sent from Florence, and being paid out to the soldiers these incontinently ceased all active operations in order to spend their money, "and the citizens of Florence no longer feel inclined to empty their purses when they see nothing is accomplished in return." They continue: "We wish to speak plainly and to give you clearly to understand that we insist upon the matter being carried on according to our instructions," and a marginal note records, "These are threatening words." Vitelli seems to have acted in the belief that hard words break no bones. He paid no attention to the Signoria, and when the troops, reinforced by some enthusiastic volunteers from Florence, did assault Pisa and breached the wall, he and his brother Vitelozzo "rushed amongst them and drove them back

[173]

from the breach with blows." The Signoria, rightly convinced that Vitelli was betraying them, decided on his arrest, and Machiavelli wrote to the commissars in the camp before Pisa: "Proceed with energy against this traitor . . . but be circumspect, and be not misled by too much zeal and do more than is necessary." The arrest, trial, and execution of Vitelli followed, and Machiavelli summed up his impressions of the whole affair in the *Discourse made to the Ten over Pisa.* In this he declares that it is hopeless to expect Pisa to surrender, and therefore all efforts to conciliate her are vain; force, and force alone, will succeed, and ruthless prosecution of the war is the only method to be advocated.

This first insight into the actual conduct of the war was reinforced by his further experiences. In the next year (1500) he was himself sent to the camp as secretary to the two commissars, Albizzi and Ridolfi. They had to march with the army of foreign troops now provided by the French, both in order to check, if possible, the violence of the foreign troops, and to arrange for their billeting and the provision of food for them en route. Ridolfi almost at once returned to Florence, terrified at the indiscipline of the foreign soldiery. Albizzi and Machiavelli remained, Albizzi saying, "Let cowards return to Florence, I stay with the army." Machiavelli's letters exist, showing what courage was shown by Albizzi, and incidentally by the secretary himself, who might equally well have followed Ridolfi's example of flight. The mutinous French and Swiss, having extorted their pay by threats of personal violence, deserted. The Pisans made a successful sortie, and the campaign ended in Florence withdrawing her commission while the army went into winter quarters.

Machiavelli evidently became, through these experiences, much bitten with military ideas. From this date he began to interest himself especially in all military matters, and gradually to consider himself as something of an expert. He began to write upon military affairs, and his enthusiasm was evidently well known, and gave rise to some amusement amongst his friends. Thus Bandello, in a prelude to one of his *Novelle*, says that he once found himself in camp at Milan with the celebrated condottiere, Giovanni delle Bande Nere, and Machiavelli. Machiavelli wished to demonstrate one of the manœuvres about which he had written, and endeavouring to do so, kept three thousand men out in the blazing sun for over three hours, and at the end of that time had still not achieved his desired demonstration. Giovanni delle Bande Nere at length lost patience, for the dinner hour was long since past, and, pushing Machiavelli aside, took command and at once manœuvred the troops exactly as he desired. Machiavelli was then condemned by his companions to recompense them for what his inexpertness had caused them to suffer, by doing that in which all recognized he really was a master, and relate to them one of the "stories" for which he was renowned.

For the next few years after the failure of the attack on Pisa Machiavelli was employed in the various embassies—to France to Cesare Borgia, and to the Emperor. These, though often concerned with the raising of armies and granting of *condotta*, took him away from the scene of operations itself. In 1504, however, he once more took part in the actual conduct of the war. He was now one of the chief instigators in the famous attempt to divert the Arno, which, as we have seen, ended in total failure. The project was too ambitious, and the engineers too optimistic. The failure of the attempt spurred on Florence to another great effort. It was decided to try to take Pisa by storm, and once more Machiavelli was selected as the special bearer of instructions to the commissaries. He was the person who now raised the fresh troops required, hiring men in Bologna and Romagna, and even sending to Rome to buy off a body of Spaniards, who were threatening to take service with the Pisans. The troops, however, when assembled for the assault, showed utter cowardice and their complete failure obliged Florence once more to withdraw.

It was this experience which inspired in Machiavelli the determination to organize his militia, and his zeal and competence being recognized by the Signoria, he was given permission to do what he could. The formation of the militia and its immediate success against Pisa and the very large part Machiavelli played in the final attack have already been noted. Here it is only necessary to say that in all this military scheme Machiavelli was not acting as an inexperienced theorist; he was a man who had been charged with the administration of the war office, who had frequently been to the front, and who had definite practical knowledge of the methods of the condottieri.

It is this, of course, which lends such fire and fury to his denunciations of the mercenaries. It was useless for people to urge that a commercial city was wise to devote her energies to creating wealth, whereby she could hire other men to fight her battles. Machiavelli's onslaught on the system is too well known to need elaboration. He stressed two aspects: one that the men who were hired were untrustworthy, expensive and accomplished little; the other, that money, in whatever quantities it might be collected, was really useless in national emergencies. In *The Prince* he deals with the first aspect. The chapters "Of Mercenaries" and "Of Auxiliary, Mixed, and National Arms" say all that can be said, with the utmost clarity, and with that beautiful style which has helped to popularize his works. "Captains of mercenaries are either able men or they are not. If they are, you cannot trust them, since they will always seek their own aggrandizement, either by overthrowing you who are their master or by the overthrow of others contrary to your desire. On the other hand, if your captain be not an able man, the chances are you will be ruined." As to the men, "such troops are ambitious, factious, insubordinate, treacherous, cowardly. Whenever they are attacked, defeat follows, so that in peace you are plundered by them, in war by your enemies. And this because they have no tie or motive to keep them in the field beyond their paltry pay, in return for which it would be too much to expect them to give their lives." He elaborates this in the *Discourses*, where he says: "Soldiers whose hearts are not warmly affected in the cause and interests of those for whom they fight will make but a very feeble resistance if vigorously attacked." To those who said all troops showed these characteristics, Machiavelli retorted: "If it be said that whoever has arms in his hands will act in the same way, whether he be mercenary or no, I answer that both kings and Republics when they depend on their own arms have the greatest success." He sums up the decay which the use of mercenaries had brought upon warfare thus: "Moreover, they, the condottieri, spared no endeavour to relieve themselves and their men from fatigue and danger, not killing one another in battle, but making prisoners who were afterwards released without ransoms. They would attack no town by night; those in towns would make no sortie by night against a besieging army. Their camps were without rampart or trench. They had no winter campaigns. All which arrangements were sanctioned by their military rulers, contrived by them to escape fatigue and danger."

He went on to point out that even worse than the hiring of paid mercenaries was the enlistment of allies. For such allies, if victorious, speedily made themselves masters of the land. This point needed no emphasis in an Italy where the Spaniards, enlisted by Pope Julius, had made themselves arbiters of the fate of the country. He saw, indeed, no hope for Italy but in the creation of patriotic national armies, and much of his bitter disillusionment comes from the fact that having laboured so long and so whole-heartedly in the creation of his famous militia, he saw them, by their cowardice and flight, bring about the ghastly horrors of the sack of Prato and the immediate downfall of the Republic.

The *Art of War* is chiefly based upon these theories, re-inforced, as was Machiavelli's wont, by endless citations of the behaviour of Romans, Medes and Jews, and cast in the, to us, unattractive form of a dialogue between 'Fabrizio' and 'Cosimo' and others of his friends. He gives full details as to how he would create his national army, how train it, and how equip it. He did not believe in artillery, he thought the foot soldier or infantry was all-important and that victories were won by valour and discipline of the foot-soldier in hand-to-hand fighting. "As to the theory that hand-to-hand fighting is out of date," he writes in the *Discourses*, "and that now war-fare depends on the use of artillery, I say that this opinion is quite wrong, and whoever wishes to create a good army should, through manœuvres and exercises, accustom his men to attack the enemy by the use of the sword . . . and one should rely more on infantry than cavalry. When one bases one's operations on the infantry in this way, artillery becomes use-less, for in attacking the enemy it is easier to avoid the cannon balls than it was in the old days to avoid the elephants used by the Romans. It will also be easy to evolve some counter-measures to protect the troops against the artillery . . . and I conclude by saying artillery is useful in an army when that army is courageous, but that without that spirit of courage it is of no use." One of Machiavelli's most ardent supporters maintains that here he was showing "that he foretold the importance of cold steel and the advent of the bayonet," but we need hardly go so far as that. He lived before artillery was fully developed and could not be expected to see its true importance. What he did see, quite correctly, was the importance of coherence and spirit amongst the troops. This has never been lessened, even by the advent of modern warfare. The capacity of troops to stand bombardment by artillery demonstrated by the raw French levies at Valmy has shown itself again and again from that day down to modern times to be a decisive factor in all engagements.

This is the same point which he makes in his argument, "that money is not the sinews of war, as it is commonly thought to be." He says that no country can be defended "where there are not proper forces to defend it, and as for abundance of money, instead of securing a State, it often exposes it to great danger, by tempting others to invade it. I say that good soldiers and not money are the sinews of war, for money alone is not sufficient to provide a good army, but a good army will always provide itself with money. . . . Money is necessary, to be sure, but money can neither make nor procure *good* soldiers."

As to his preference of infantry to cavalry, he says: "Cavalry cannot go everywhere as do the infantry; they are less mobile when the order of battle has to be changed, slower to obey when an order to retreat is given, or to set off when they have been dismounted. Cavalry once thrown into confusion by some unexpected check only re-form with difficulty . . . and all experience shows us that a nucleus of infantry is always stronger in defence and more invincible than cavalry." This superiority of infantry over cavalry was one of his favourite theories. He mentions it in all his writings on warfare, and in *The Art of War* many pages are devoted to proving his thesis. Here again military history has upheld him and it must be credited to him that in this he was in opposition to all his contemporaries.

In his remarks on the health of an army Machiavelli also shows himself thoroughly progressive. He says that great attention should be paid to health, especially in selecting the site for camps. "Marshes, ground exposed to cold winds, ought to be avoided," words which evoke at once the memories of the bad sites selected in the Crimean war. The appearance of the men, their colour, "whether unduly pale or not," the fact that they cough a great deal, all ought to be studied. Sheltered spots "where the men can sleep soundly, and where they have plenty of wood for their fires," ought to be selected in bad weather, and especially when snow has fallen great attention should be paid in setting out for the provision of kindling for fires when the men come to halt. Drunkenness ought to be treated seriously, as impairing efficiency, and it should be impressed on all commanders that if men are over-fatigued with long marches and worn out they will not be able either to be on the alert against surprise or to fight well when called upon to do so.

His views on fortresses have become celebrated, for in this, too, ahead of his times, he condemned them. He thought a general should not shut up his troops in fortresses, and waste his army in too many garrisons. He really envisaged war as the defence by a people of its own territory against invasion; he did not treat of wars of aggression, and thus his whole object was to animate the minds of those with whom he came in contact and to spur them on to valour. He did not wish to encourage them in passive shutting of themselves up in castles. He knew that Italy could not be defended by the fortifying of her cities, and his whole doctrine is therefore one of attack in the field against foreign armies, whom he considered could be driven out by a trained army of patriotic troops. The best justification for his military theories is to be found in the armies of revolutionary France. Those armies were composed of the patriots whom Machiavelli had longed to find in Italy; they were troops at first quite raw and untrained, who yet were able to stand firm against artillery fire at Valmy, who rushed to defend their country, and being pitted against less patriotic armies went on from one victory to another. Carnot, the 'organizer' of victory, the man who decreed the *levée en masse*, or a people in arms, is the embodiment of Machiavelli's military theories, and his methods made possible the victories of Napoleon, in whom it is perhaps unnecessary to point out we may see the incarnation of Machiavelli's Prince.

The theories of a writer who lived so long ago, and so far removed from modern conditions, clearly cannot interest us as they did his contemporaries. At the time *The Art of War* was an immense success, and Machiavelli won much praise and much renown for it. Yet his opinions on these matters are of real interest, because in them he does make clear what was at the bottom of Italy's utter collapse before both French and Spanish invaders. Charles VIII would not "have conquered Italy with a piece of chalk," merely marking up his reckoning of expenditure as he passed from town to town, as a man marks up his reckoning in an inn, had Italy possessed any system of military defence. The verdict of one of her most acute observers that all her misfortunes came from her military weakness cannot be disregarded. The further interest in this branch of his writings comes from the fact that it was here he allowed his true spirit to show itself. All his cynicism, his bitterness, and even his coldness fall away. In his military schemes, and in the tireless energy with which he tried to translate them into action, in his project for the militia, the long years of unremitting work he put into the organization of that force, and in the rather pathetic way in which throughout his disgrace he never ceased, when opportunity offered, to press for its revival, we see the inner secret flame which warmed him into life. In a life which contained much that is ironical perhaps the most ironical reflection is that he never lived to know that Florence in her last desperate effort did revive his militia, and that militia did do something to justify its creator in the courage it showed in the final struggle.

CHAPTER XII

(1) *Taxation*

ECONOMIC history gives a very accurate, and at the same time a very vivid picture of the level of civilization attained by any people at a given time. We may know from artistic and literary sources what was the culture of a nation, and yet not realize fully how that culture finds its counterpart in the material side of daily life. We are perfectly familiar with the heights reached by Renaissance Italy in the world of art. We know that the Florence of Lorenzo de' Medici and of Machiavelli was a city full of beauty in every shape. We know that it abounded in glorious buildings, pictures, statues; that its citizens had magnificent palaces, and wore sumptuous clothes of brocade and silk; that they lived well and had great learning and great wealth. Yet when we turn from this aspect to the more prosaic side of their lives, we seem to touch something which brings to us an almost sharper sense of reality. For example, when we find that the men who lived in those beautiful surroundings were business men, familiar with all the processes of banking, credit, bills of exchange; that they speculated in stocks and shares; that they practised marine insurance, and if they did not take out policies to insure an education for their sons, they took out policies for dowries for their daughters; that they knew all about limited liability; that they chafed against income-tax and tried to

[183]

evade it by false assessments, then perhaps we realize once more how close the past can come to the present, if we do but study it.

Italy was the pioneer of Europe in financial matters, and Florence was in many respects the most advanced State in Italy. This was due largely to her geographical position. She had no port, and she had no very extensive territory. Her vast wealth came to her through the fact that she lay where the great roads from across the Alps converged on Rome and were crossed by the road running from Pisa on one coast to Ancona on the other. She made herself a great centre of industry, and early realizing the importance of money, she developed the art of banking, leading to her command of international credit. In dealing with this side of her life, it seems best to take first her system of taxation, and to deal afterwards with her commercial and financial development.

Florence may claim to be the first State to produce and publish a 'Budget,' which she called the 'Bilancio,' that is to say, a statement of her revenue and expenditure. Her first recorded budget appeared in 1336, and the series continued from then on. An early budget shows a highly satisfactory balance, for Florence, owing to her system of not paying most of her officials, but getting them to perform public duties voluntarily, had no expensive administration, and as most of our modern items of expenditure were actually unknown to her, the debit side of her balance-sheet was not formidable. With a revenue of 300,000 gold florins, an income greater than that of contemporary England, her expenditure was only 120,000.

The expenses include:

		Gold florins
Salary of the Podestàs (chief judges and always foreigners)		50,000
Salary of the executioner		4,500
Salaries of gaolers		2,000
Payment for fireworks		1,900
Payment for trumpeters		1,500
Salaries of ambassadors (the only paid officials of this date)		15,000
Payments to spies		1,000
Guards of fortresses		12,000
Food of Priors in their term of office		3,600

The chief sources of revenue were:

			Gold florins
Gabelle at the gates (charges on goods entering the city)			90,000
Gabelle on	wine		59,000
„ „	meat		15,000
„ „	salt		14,000
„ „	usurers		3,000
„ „	contracts on sale of lands		11,000
„ „	rents		4,000
Profit on the mint			2,000
Fines received in law courts			20,000
Household tax			5,000

No payments appear for soldiers, since Florence hired mercenaries, and this was reckoned as an extraordinary expense and, as such, did not appear in the annual budget. The upkeep of roads was borne by the local communes, as was that of canals. Bridges were usually owned by individuals, who kept them up out of tolls charged. This system was not satisfactory in some respects. Machiavelli says in one of his official letters: "We should wish to press on the construction of canals and roads, as they do so much to benefit the country, but we cannot, because so many communes are devastated owing to the war [with Pisa] and cannot afford the expense and in others the harvest has failed. Do not, therefore, be too severe on them for not carrying out these works" (*Lett.* X).

"All systems of taxation," it has been said, "bear traces of where they were made." The Florentine system shows the theories of a Republic, anxious to avoid the creation of either a bureaucracy or an oligarchy. Thus her paid judges are foreigners, she has no standing army, no navy, and she aimed at placing the chief burden of taxation on the rich, and this she attained by a graduated tax on wealth. By the time of Machiavelli she had systematized both direct and indirect taxation and we find the democrats continually pressing for lower customs and for an increase in direct taxation.

All laws and regulations concerning taxation were brought before the Signoria, and they had to be passed by a majority of two-thirds, in a quorum of two-thirds. They also had to pass through the College and the Senate, and when Savonarola instituted the Grand Council, it was given the right to introduce and pass money bills.

Direct taxation at first took the form of a tax on land: one florin for as much land as was cultivated by two oxen, half a florin on as much land as was cultivated by one ox, and one florin for every lira of rent on those lands where no plough was worked. This last was transformed into a tax of ten denarii for every lira of rent. The proportion in both cases to income was estimated at 4.16 per cent. There was also the *arbitrio*, or tax on professional incomes. In times of emergency taxes were imposed, usually in the shape of forced loans. These were called *decima*, as representing one-tenth on all real property, and when assessed on income worked out at 6.5 per cent in the case of a loan of this description enforced in 1292. The 'loans' though 'forced,' were true to name, in so far as interest was paid on them by the State, that is to say, taxes paid were credited to the payee at the *Monte* and bore interest. Guicciardini pointed out that forced loans always created great discontent, and were the cause of much grumbling and confusion, and advocated the raising of real floating loans in their stead. Though these were more expensive, as a higher rate of interest was paid, yet as they roused less resentment and created less trouble, they did less harm to the city, which did not realize the greater burden placed upon it. We may recognize here in a different guise the familiar arguments as to the respective merits of direct and indirect taxation. A special board existed, the *Credenza*, to enforce the payment of taxes. A simple and efficacious way to secure this was found in the enactment that if a citizen "showed delay" in paying his taxes, he could not sue in any court in any action until he had discharged his debt to the State.

Individuals, then as now, tried to evade the payment of taxes by making false returns in their assessments. When Machiavelli was rumoured to have won a lottery ticket of 3,000 ducats, his friend Nerli wrote to him: ' Do not let your luck be known in the city, for if it gets out you will have the tax-collectors down on you, and your luck will vanish in their extortions" (*Lett. fam.* 58).

A register was set up in 1427, the *Catasto*, with lists of individuals and their estates assessments to tax based on them. These were drawn up on statements made under oath by the proprietor in the case of real property, and the professional man and the merchant in the case of earned income and profits. In 1427 the government believed that the valuation did not correspond to the city's real wealth, and Giovanni de' Medici had a fresh valuation made. All property, real and personal, was now assessed, and an allowance given for houses and repairs and a special rebate of 200 ducats for each member of the family. Every seven florins of rent was reckoned to represent a capital of 100 ducats and the tax was, in 1427, half per cent on this estimated capital. The result of this new assessment was a rise in taxation paid, and it was estimated that "those who had only paid twenty ducats before, now paid 300," a state of affairs usually repeated in every reassessment of property when the purpose is taxation. In 1457 a law was passed ordering new assessments to be made every five years, and each time complaints arose. Thus Piero Vespucci complained to Lorenzo de' Medici after a fresh assessment was made in 1471 that his *catasto* on an income of 400 ducats had been four ducats, and had now been raised to nine and says: "It is enough to make a man burst with rage." Naturally the richer citizens complained bitterly, while the poorer rejoiced. Machiavelli, commenting on it in his *History* (Vol. IV), says: "This proceeding weighed heavily on the rich, who were now not able to oppress the poor . . . the people also wished to recover arrears . . . and the rich in their turn declared the tax unjust, especially in that it taxed movables many times over, as such things change hands repeatedly."

Lorenzo, pressed for money and with great influence over the government, had in his day carried the principle of taxing 'superabundance' to unheard-of lengths. He put the main burden of taxation upon land and raised the amount to be paid, and his tax, the *decima scalata*, was very sharply graduated. The scale rose from seven per cent on landed

property worth less than fifty florins to twenty-two per cent on
that worth over 400 florins. As this did not bring in enough, a
further tax, which brought upon itself the name of *dis-
piacente sgravato*, was added, taxing movables and possessions. These taxes were so arranged that the citizen paid
monthly instalments, and the old idea was retained of treating
them in the technical sense as loans. That is to say, the sums
were paid to the *Monte* (Public Debt Office), entered in the
citizen's name, and interest was paid on them, which in turn
could be used towards the instalments of tax as they fell due.
So heavy was the burden of taxation under Lorenzo that one
of the first reforms of Savonarola's government was to abolish
these taxes, and revert to the old land-tax with the *arbitrio*.
When Soderini was in power in 1503 he had to meet a great
financial crisis, and the speech which he made to the Great
Council on this occasion is represented by Machiavelli's
Discourse on Taxation. The wealthy citizens had already been
obliged, besides the ordinary taxes, to lend 400,000 florins to
the Republic, 18,000 of which had been lent by Soderini. He,
anxious to recover his capital, pressed for measures which
would enable the State to repay these loans. He first proposed
a general tax, to be borne by the poorer classes as well as the
rich. He was met by a furious outburst on the part of the
majority of the Council, composed of the poorer citizens, who
declared the Gonfalonier wanted to benefit the rich at the
expense of the poor; and in face of this he agreed to *decima*, or
tenths, being levied on all real property, and a slight increase
made in the *arbitrio*, or tax on the professional classes.
Machiavelli seized the opportunity in this *Discourse* to point
his favourite moral, that it was no good for the State to heap up
money if she could not use it to obtain trustworthy troops.
Reading the 'speech' one cannot but think that it contains

little to help a practical financier struggling against a deficit.

Machiavelli had strong views on taxation; indeed, to-day he would in this respect find himself very much on the Left Wing. He believed in taxation in order to equalize wealth and went so far as to say: "The State should be rich and the citizens poor and the best laws are those which keep the citizens poor." For he believed "poverty is more useful than wealth, in that it encourages effort" (*Disc.* I. 37). "As to idleness," he writes, "the laws ought to oblige everyone to work," and again: "The enemies of the State are all those who live without doing anything, and exist on the interest of their money, who neither practise agriculture nor any trade nor profession." The nobility, he thought, would be better destroyed, for they were both wealthy and idle.

Here he is in accord with all that stream of thought which believed in the virtues of poverty, and which had sought to express its higher aspirations in the Franciscan doctrine of poverty. He always preaches moderation in public expenditure, and opposes heavy taxation—"a military victory costs too dear if the State is thereby forced to impose new taxes and duties" (*Hist.* 6), and "a prince who taxes his people heavily will lose all credit and risk the loss of his State."

He also added his individual touch to the theory of the positive value of wealth, in his arguments as to the importance of money in warfare. Contrary to the ideas held by his contemporaries that "money is the sinews of war," Machiavelli declared: "It is not gold, but men who win victories"—and tried in his *Art of War* to emphasize the fact that in times of crisis no amount of treasure would save the State if no soldiers existed to be hired by her money. In this one respect he differs from other theorists of those times who, like our own Thomas Mun, emphasized the need for a

THE HOUSE OF VANOZZA IN ROME
WHERE THE BORGIAS WERE BORN
(From Rodocanachi. *By kind permission*).

State to amass treasure in order to pay troops.

He was more orthodox in his attitude towards a policy of tariffs on imports. He believed that the State must be self-sufficient and develop its own resources. For this reason, amongst others, he believed in strong government. "Security." he writes, "must be guaranteed by the ruler, so that the people may not be driven to neglecting their property for fear of its being confiscated if they improve it or to neglect trade from fear of arbitrary duties being levied. Public safety is the basis of agriculture and commerce, hence the ruler must help his subject to develop their resources in security" (*Disc.* II).

He also thought that export trade was of supreme importance, in that it brought more bullion into the country. Believing, as did his contemporaries, that money was wealth, he could not see that complete self-sufficiency must, by restricting the import of foreign goods, check the hope of selling to foreigners. On his visit to the Emperor Maximilian Machiavelli wrote praising the inhabitants of Austria, "because as they live so simply their money never leaves the country, and they buy no luxuries; on the contrary they bring money in by the sale of their own products."

Yet in his own Republic Machiavelli could have seen an excellent example of the fact that an imported semi-manufactured article might form the raw material of another industry. Florence was the great centre of the cloth trade; her fine, beautifully dyed and finished goods were sold all over Europe. Out of a population of 120,000, she had no less than 200 cloth manufacturers, employing 30,000 workpeople. One whole branch of this vast industry was the 'Calimata.' This was the trade which brought in English woollens, heavy, coarse, and dark, and, by treating them, transformed them into light, soft, gay-coloured stuffs. Florence and England both gained by this commerce, but it dwindled away as the English began to work up their own cloths and ceased to export.

Florentine budgets show clearly how high was the tariff wall she drew around herself. That the customs officials did their work thoroughly may be discovered from Machiavelli's official letters, many of which deal with the complaints that the customs had been too zealous. Thus, in 1510 a Portuguese merchant lodged an official complaint that his personal table-silver had been charged with duty at the *douane*, and when he refused to pay, it was confiscated. Machiavelli ordered that the silver shall be restored, as it should not properly have come under the duty. Again in the following year a Pisan merchant who had moved back to Pisa from Rome complained that fifteen pounds of salt, an expensive commodity in those days, had been heavily taxed when discovered in his baggage. He declared that it had been put there "by inadvertence," "being put amongst other kitchen necessaries by his friend's wife, who had been very exact in sending everything that might be of the least use in his housekeeping," and apparently Machiavelli believed his plea, for he ordered the refund of the amount charged.

The absorption of the Florentines in trade did not react very favourably upon agriculture. Thus, in the interests of the manufacturers, regulations were sometimes made compelling the cultivator to produce certain crops, such as, for example, mulberry trees required for the silk-worms. The land was still burdened with many feudal dues, *corvées* and other local impositions. In addition the high return to capital invested in trade had a bad effect on agriculture, from which the return was lower and which, in consequence, could not attract the capital it needed. Taxes were levied on a piece of land on the basis that each unit ploughed by an ox-team was to pay a certain amount. This meant that in bad times land could be abandoned, as not earning the tax levied on its cultivation. The price of corn was not left free, but was fixed by the commune, and in times of scarcity its export was forbidden. In short, Florence with her vast town population thought more of the town dweller than of the country cultivator, and as political power rested with the city folk, her policy was shaped in their interests.

Florence was unwilling also to dispose of her own goods to the neighbouring States, who might resell to more distant countries. She preferred to send her goods across to her neighbours' territories, paying the duties they charged, and then securing her profit by direct sale to her distant customers. A special "Six of Commerce" formed one branch of the administration of the Republic, whose function it was to carry out the laws relating to mercantile affairs. They negotiated commercial treaties, which under the universal tariff policy became most important. Thus, in Tunis, duties on Florentine goods were heavier by eleven per cent than those on Venetian and Genoese, until Florence was able to bargain for better treatment. In 1511 a commercial treaty was negotiated by Machiavelli himself with Monaco, whereby Monaco was to guarantee Florentine merchants against incessant tolls and vexatious opening of goods in transit through Monaco, and both parties undertook to allow ships to use their ports as free-ports, Florence by now having acquired Pisa. Most important of all was the political consequence of her economic need for a treaty with France. So much Florentine money passed through French hands, so great was the volume of trade, that she was bound to seek terms from the French. Florence, until she conquered Pisa, having no port, had sent her goods overland, and the great trade with England thus passed through France. The need for commercial concessions was imperative, and when Charles VIII planned to invade Italy, he bought the friendship of Florence by offering that "the citizens of the Republic shall trade in France with the same rights" as his own subjects.

When, by the conquest of Pisa, Florence at length obtained a port of her own, she carried out her 'mercantilist' policy by a series of what we should call 'Navigation Acts,' ordering that Florentine goods should be carried in Florentine ships. The fall of the Republic, though it did not produce any modification in this policy, by depriving Machiavelli of office, deprives us too of his views upon this branch of policy.

While developing this system of restricting imports, Florence was occasionally driven into checking exports. Thus in 1511 Machiavelli, in his capacity of Second Secretary, issued an order forbidding the export of tan, of which there was a shortage, and which was required by the great leather industry. Another year (1510) he dealt with the grain trade. "We order you to prevent grain from leaving the territory under any pretext," he writes and again: "No one, on pain of most severe penalties, is to export grain." Here he was dealing with shortage, due to bad harvest and the devastation of the countryside in the Pisan war, and the government actions aimed at protecting the consumer.

(2) *Public Debt*

Besides that side of public finance which dealt with taxation, the State had the management of all the operations concerned with the public debt. Florence, together with other Italian States, was by the fifteenth century perfectly familiar with all the processes of floating and funding loans. Originally she had managed her finances by the help of floating loans. That is to say, known recurring expenditure, such as salaries and pensions, was met by loans secured on known sources of revenue. Then her debt, swollen by the extraordinary expenses of war, became very large, and at length it was consolidated, or funded, and the famous *Monte Commune* was founded in 1345. This simply represented the national indebtedness; every citizen was assessed, and definite blocks of shares were allocated to each individual in proportion to his assessed wealth. Interest was paid quarterly and secured on the customs. The rate varied, sometimes being only three per cent, sometimes political manœuvres pushed it as high as twenty-five per cent. It was, however, stabilized in the fifteenth century at six per cent. The funds of depositors could not be seized, and were negotiable. The price of the bonds naturally varied with the prosperity of the city. Thus in 1432 the price dropped from sixty to forty-two and a half and in 1458, when Cosimo de' Medici's policy had brought about a *coup d'état*, they actually fell to twenty. In the first years of Lorenzo's rule they touched bottom at eleven, but after that rose to more normal levels. Actually, as might have been expected, the public debt was really concentrated in the hands of the capitalist class, who bought up large blocks of the bonds. When the interest was reduced, as, for example, in one year it was from fifteen per cent to five per cent, speculators bought up the stock, and naturally made great profits when the rate later rose. It was to check this form of speculation, which was most bitterly resented by the poorer citizens, that the stabilization of the rate of interest was carried through. Controversies arose as to whether speculating in the shares was justifiable, the Dominicans asserting that it was lawful to buy below the face value, the Minorites denying this. Speculation was carried on, just as more ordinary dealings were, at the equivalent of the modern Bourse or Stock Exchange, which was held in the *Mercato Nuovo*, the centre of the banking and exchange district.

In Florence the *Monte* remained a financial institution, but in Genoa the famous Bank of St. George, which was founded on the same lines, acquired such a hold on the revenues that it ended by taking over the administration and became "a State within a State." Florence, however, managed her finances better; she never let her debt become too swollen, and she retained the management of the revenue in her own hands, and in consequence the *Monte* remained what it was intended to be, a department raising loans and guaranteeing the investor a safe but not very high rate of interest on his money. The officials of the *Monte* were, in theory, elected by the Signoria, but if, as under the various Medicean periods of rule, a *Balìa* was created, that committee invariably took as one of its functions the control of appointments. Thus when Machiavelli lost his post on the return of the Medici in 1512, his misfortune was shared by the officials of the *Monte*. The 'spoils' system, giving office to the political supporters of the new government, was enforced, and Pope Leo, writing to his nephew Lorenzo de' Medici, says: "Take special heed to the elections to the offices of the *Monte*. It is highly important to choose keen-witted, secret, and trusty men, entirely devoted to thee, since the *Monte* is the heart of the city."

(3) *Banking*

The management of the public debt shows us how advanced Florence was in the financial sphere, and this brings us to the consideration of that branch of finance in which she was pre-eminent, namely, banking and the financing, through her great banking houses, of international loans.

Money in the Middle Ages was comparatively scarce, many payments and much revenue being made and received in kind. In an age of incessant warfare, the demand for money was great. Kings, such as those of England and France, were in perpetual need of cash, and their credit was not especially good. They were obliged to borrow, and at high rates of interest. The bankers of Italy, and notably of Florence, were their most important creditors. Florence lent vast sums to Edward III to finance him in the Hundred Years War, and when he repudiated payment, the Frescobaldi, who had been his bankers, were ruined. In 1360 Florence already possessed thirty-two banks which by 1400 had increased to eighty. These were mostly owned by the great houses such as the Medici, Pazzi, Peruzzi, Acciauoli and others. Each had branches all over the world; in the Levant, where Florence had great trading interests, in Morocco, Tunis, Rhodes, Avignon, Sicily, Paris, Lyons, Bruges, England. By the time of Lorenzo de' Medici, his family had become the most important in the city. It had for some time been the bankers of the Curia, and that involved the handling of large sums of ready money, since the Papacy derived a great revenue from the pilgrims who flocked to Rome. Lorenzo's quarrel with the Pope, when he refused to advance the money for Sixtus IV to purchase Imola for his nephew, led the Pope to transfer his account to the rival bankers, the Pazzi. This, as has been mentioned elsewhere, in turn led to the conspiracy of the Pazzi, which culminated in the murder of Giuliano de' Medici in the Duomo and so nearly accomplished the murder of Lorenzo as well. Later, under Innocent VIII, Lorenzo got back the Papal account. The Strozzi specialized in Neapolitan affairs, all the Angevin Kings of Naples banked with the Strozzi branch in Naples. Their object really was to leave their cash in safe keeping; no interest was paid on their deposits, but they were used, though very cautiously, by the bankers in credit operations.

Showing the way to later financiers, the Medici knew how to reap their profit by lending to both parties in a war. Thus Lorenzo lent money to the King of England in 1462, and to Burgundy in 1470. Other Florentine bankers supplied Charles the Bold with the 50,000 crowns he lent to Edward IV when he wished to regain his lost kingdom. Though Edward succeeded, he was very reluctant to pay his debts and the Florentines had a hard struggle before they recovered their money.

Lorenzo is not considered to have been a good banker; his great house did not flourish under his regime. He was not sufficiently cautious and took too great risks. Thus the reputation of the Emperor Maximilian as a debtor was known to be of the worst. He was the sovereign who, possessing some of the finest crown jewels in Europe, never saw them, for they were perpetually in pawn. Yet Lorenzo, through his Bruges house, supplied Maximilian and his wife Mary of Burgundy with such large sums that when, as might have been anticipated from Maximilian's record, no repayment was forthcoming, Lorenzo was obliged to close the branch at Bruges.

France, however, was the favourite client of the Florentines. One of the most powerful and richest of European countries, she was also one of the most warlike, and enormous sums were lent by all the Florentine bankers. France in those days had a system of taxation which brought her King in a larger revenue

than most of his contempories could collect. The *'taille'*
was a direct tax, and in addition the gabelle and customs were
very profitable. Thus creditors of France had better security
for their loans than they could reckon on in the case of England and the Empire. Even so, the rates they charged were
fairly high. Philip IV, whose credit was comparatively good,
had to pay Florence interest at fifteen per cent on the large
sums he borrowed.

As time passed, the financial bonds between France and the
Republic became even closer, until at the very end of the
struggle of the Republic for its independence, this inter-action
of financial and political interests showed its fatal effect.
Florence was bound to France, and thereby forced into
opposition to Pope and Emperor. When they, in 1526, for
political reasons, combined against her, she was in desperate
need of money to organize her defence. Florentines in all
parts of Europe were called upon, and sent what sums they
could spare. The Republic sent to the King of France,
begging him to repay a part of the money he owed, for her
safety was at stake. Francis I, who the year before had
borrowed no less than one million and a quarter crowns in
order to ransom his sons from Spain, would not, and possibly
could not, send a penny, and Florence was left without the
money to hire troops for her defence.

Here we come upon a foreshadowing of a situation which
seems familiar enough to us. High finance must, from its very
importance, play a great part in deciding peace and war and the
fate of a State. The Florentine magnates had used their money
in financing the wars between other countries, and had made
much profit in so doing. Their prosperity cannot be attributed
solely to commercial loans; clearly it derived in large measure
from their international loans, which in turn were called for by

the wars between the kings and princes who were their customers. These financial connections led on to political considerations, and Florentine politics, influenced by the power of the banks, were involved. Economics here affords an excellent example of its profound repercussion upon history.

(4) *Exchange and Insurance*

The magnitude of these operations shows us how greatly the banking art in Florence had prospered. Nor were her financial magnates behindhand in other branches of their profession. Trade in the Middle Ages had centred round the great fairs, and at those fairs, naturally enough, had grown up the system of exchange of bills. The dangers and cost of moving bullion about in these times were so clear that inevitably people meeting at the fairs exchanged the bills due amongst each other. For example, merchants from all countries meeting in all the great fairs in Champagne would cancel their respective indebtedness. From this the bankers developed the whole system of bills of exchange. Thus, in 1405, a Florentine company, having money at Venice, wished to send to England goods bought in France. Another house had funds deposited at Lyons, and wished to import Italian goods to that place. The two houses exchanged bills of exchange, the one on Lyons, the other on Venice. As soon as they heard the goods had been sold they instructed their agents to take up bills, and "thus they could dispose of the value of their goods long before the money was really at hand." They realized, of course, that if a bill were proffered by a customer in another country they must know if that person's credit were good. This they achieved through their system of agents and consuls, established in every important town. They also knew when money was likely to be plentiful, or in demand, and in what places, having full information as to crops, and such factors as the 'tightness' of money due to the demands of soldiers for pay.

Pegalotti, who in the fourteenth century wrote the *Manual of a Merchant*, says that in accepting bills or sending bullion the rate of exchange between countries must be considered. Money may have a higher value in other places, and "it is useless to send money where there is a great deal." Pegalotti and Antonio da Uzzano, his contemporary, both wrote treatises dealing with currency, rates of exchange, and insurance. Bills, credit, and clearing-houses were all thoroughly understood by the fourteenth-century Italian banker. The trade in bills led to trade in capital, and how wide were the ramifications may be seen when the Sienese banker, Tolomei, wrote to his agent in France that he had sold bills in Siena, as this was the best way of raising money, it being not profitable at the moment to borrow, presumably on long-term basis in Siena, the rate being twelve per cent or fifteen per cent 'between merchants' and double that for other persons, while the sale of bills in England was not so good as the sale of bills in France.

Another branch of business understood and undertaken by the Florentine financiers was the whole business of insurance. In one aspect, this arose out of the mediæval prohibition of usury. The Church utterly forbade usury, as being contrary to the direct precepts of Christ. It was left to the Jews, who in consequence charged exorbitant rates. The sight of such fortunes going elsewhere was too much for the Christian, and naturally wits were set to work to evade the prohibition. This was done through the establishment of the principle of 'annuities.' It was wrong to lend money at usury, but it was not wrong to obtain interest if one never asked for the return of the capital. This theory enabled the State to develop the *Monte*, where the shares were irredeemable, and it also enabled it to set up the famous *Monte delle Fanciulle*, or *Monte delle Doti*, the Dowry Insurance office. A Florentine of those days had to provide a dowry for his daughters, otherwise they could never marry. What to the rich man was easy, to the middle-class was difficult and to the poor impossible. Thus the State organized this institution, in which any individual could invest money, and at the end of a specific term receive his 'annuity' or dowry. Machiavelli had but the one daughter, and in 1523 we find him negotiating, as a good father, for a policy in the *Monte delle Fanciulle* to ensure her a dowry. The system was for the father or relation of the girl to make an annual payment to the State, and this accumulated at a high rate of interest, usually seven per cent. If the girl were to die, or enter a convent, before the dowry was due to be paid, the father would recover half the sum he would otherwise have received. In the assessment for income-tax the dowry was originally included, but it was found that this reduction in the sum received led to a decrease in marriages. Accordingly, in the *Catasto* fifty per cent of the dowry was not to be taxed. Under Lorenzo de' Medici, when the finances of the Republic were not flourishing, it was decided that the dowry should no longer be paid down in a capital sum. A new system was inaugurated and the dowry had to remain in the *Monte*, the interest on it only being paid, not the capital. Evidently, ambitious young men, then as now, liked to have capital to handle, for immediately on the promulgation of this law there followed a heavy slump in the marriage rate. The Italian of the day attached the utmost importance to this question. No young man would marry a girl without a dowry; a marriage was regarded as indispensable to the girl. 'Spinsters' might be said to be unknown to Florence; a girl must marry or go into a convent, and the endowment provided by the *Monte delle Fanciulle* was regarded by the Florentine not simply as a provision for his daughter in life, but as a safeguard against dishonour. Lorenzo's manipulations of the Dowry Fund, it has been said, did more to discredit him in the eyes of the citizens than any other action of his life.

Besides this policy of family endowment, Florence practised what we call marine insurance. This grew quite naturally out of the heavy risks attending voyages in those days, not only of storms, but from the corsairs who infested the Mediterranean. At first the banker, lending to the small capitalist who wished to embark on a venture, would add an extra charge to cover the interest on the loan, and would take over the whole risks of the enterprise, paying the shipper the costs of transport and taking the profits which might accrue at the end of the transaction. Most capitalists like the system of *commenda* or *societàs*, which gave them a share in the eventual profits. The rate of interest charged on the capital lent varied with the route taken, a higher rate naturally obtaining where the route was known to be dangerous. Usually bills were given, and the money was paid at the port of destination. If the goods never arrived, the capitalist lost his money. Gradually the idea was introduced into bills of freightage, which came to contain a clause with a stipulation that the 'risk' must be covered by a special supplement. If the ship were wrecked, or attacked by pirates, the shipper did not get his freight, and had to pay the cost of lost, damaged, or stolen goods.

By the fourteenth century persons had begun to combine to share the risks, and by contracts of 'security' (*asciuzare*) several individuals would join in sharing the risks of an enterprise. Even reinsurance now appears, and risks by sea were differentiated from risks by land and formed a separate branch of business.

At first the capitalist would provide two-thirds of the capital needed, the trader would provide the remaining third, and undertake all the work of the transaction. This was altered by the *commenda* of the late fourteenth century when the capitalist would give a trader either goods to sell or a sum of money, and the trader would simply provide the labour. The profits were divided in the proportion of three-fourths to capital and one quarter to labour. In the *societàs* the capitalist gave two-thirds of the capital and received two-thirds of the three-quarters share due to capital. The trader, who supplied his share of capital and the labour, got his usual quarter on profits as the reward of his labour, and one-third of the three-quarters share allotted to capital.

As the great trading companies developed, the man with small capital began to hand it over to a company in whose stability he believed. He could ask for a fixed rate of interest, but as the feeling against usury was still strong, he more often preferred a share in the profits.

A minor development was the practice, adopted by the small investor, of agreeing to take a smaller share in the profits, in return for being freed of any payment if his goods never arrived at their destination.

Finally, men came to prefer to pay a fixed charge to cover the risk of loss, and thus insurance was developed. Rates varied from six per cent to fifteen per cent, in proportion to the distance covered and the locality, some being far more hazardous than others. Special rates were naturally charged for the transport of bullion. Where credit was not very extensive, the movement of bullion was more frequent. The competition between commercial houses affected the rate charged for carriage. A special duty of the various agents of the great companies was to notify their head offices of local circumstances which might obviate the necessity for sending bullion. Thus arrival of various consignments from different parts of the world in one town might, through the exchange of bills at a local fair, render it unneccessary for gold to be sent from the Florentine house. In deciding questions of this sort, moreover, weather conditions, prevailing winds which affected the arrival of ships, or conditions in the deserts traversed by the Levantine and African trade caravans, were all taken into consideration.

As might be expected, where all money transactions were so highly developed, the laws regarding debt received attention. All commercial firms kept properly audited books, which in legal cases were admitted as evidence. Debtors had to pay their debts within a certain time, and insolvents paid so much in the pound. If a man could pay nothing, then his creditor had the legal right to claim his person, an enactment which, though probably fallen into disuse by the time of Machiavelli, possibly finds its faint reflection in Shylock's claim to his 'pound of flesh.' Syndicates were formed to take over insolvencies, and if they could come to an agreement with creditors holding three-quarters of the debt, the remaining creditors were compelled to agree to the terms fixed.

(5)   *Organization of Trade*

Turning now to the organization of commerce, from which also much of the wealth of Florence was derived, we find ourselves in a world where the government of the State was based on the organization of her industry. The constitution of Florence took its peculiar form from the guilds, or as she called them, the Arts, into which the trade of the city was systematized. Originally there were the Greater Arts and the Lesser. The Greater were seven in number and included the lawyers, the doctors, the bankers, the merchants of the 'Calimata,' or foreign cloth, the wool merchants, the silk merchants, and the skinners and furriers. The Lesser numbered fourteen and included the butchers, the bakers, the black-smiths, shoemakers, stone-masons and wood-carvers, the linen merchants, the wine-dealers, the inn-keepers, the tanners, the sadlers, the oil-sellers, the locksmiths, the carpenters and the armourers. Each guild had its own officials, notaries, and statutes. All demanded entrance-fees, and caution money, and certificates of respectability and solvency, these in the case of the *Arte del Cambio*, which included banking and exchange, being very high. Though, as every-where in Europe, the guilds gradually declined, they continued in Florence to provide the 'Priors' of the Arts, who formed part of the highest body in the government. In the economic sphere, they were replaced by the great companies, whose development marked the fourteenth century. Florentine merchants proved themselves so progressive, that very early on they organized themselves into companies, the most well known to later days being that of the Medici, which even in the days of the Magnifico had for its title 'Lorenzo and Giuliano de' Medici and Company,' while another firm was 'Jacopo Peruzzi and Nephew.' These were great family affairs, where the shares were held either solely by the family or a few chosen friends. Other less celebrated and smaller companies were the *Accomondite*, or associations where the liability of shareholders was unlimited, while that of depositors was limited to deposits; for many of the companies combined the functions of dealing in commodities with those we properly associate with banking. It was a connection dating from the period when cash was relatively scarce, and many transactions had to be conducted through exchange of goods. The Medici were thus, strictly speaking, dealers in wool, and officially remained as such, and out of those activities developed the great bank which bore their name.

All commercial transactions were written down and recorded in *libri maestro*, books of accounts which, like our most up-to-date literature, were written without capitals or punctuation. It may also be noted that, as books had to be produced when taxes were assessed, merchants sometimes kept two sets, one showed their real transactions, but others, produced before the tax-assessors, did not.

To sum up, this sketch of the organization of the business life of Florence serves to show us both the material level of civilization and also the type of man with whom Machiavelli was associated in his public life. For this great mercantile State, with its complete financial system, was also a Republic, and its business men had, in addition to their profession, to carry on the work of governing the State.

CHAPTER XIII

THE CONSTITUTION OF FLORENCE AND MACHIAVELLI'S PLAN FOR
ITS REFORM

(1) *The Florentine Constitution*

THE Florentine constitution has been a stumbling-block to many, and yet it is of great interest. Its study presents a real mental exercise, and may raise in our estimation the men of the Renaissance who took its complexities in their stride. It is, moreover, an extremely good example of the difficulty of constructing a non-democratic form of government where there is a high level of intelligence and civilization on the part of the governed. The rulers of Florence did not wish to give power to the people, and yet the people themselves were too clever and quick-witted to be merely passive members of the body corporate. Those who tried their hands at constitution-making were at once faced with the problem of how to combine a strong executive, having an element of permanence, with the desire of the body of voters who were not organized in any assembly to control that executive. It has taken us several centuries and much experience before we have evolved our doctrine of an executive forming part of an elected legislature and responsible to it. Any such system was, of course, unthinkable to the Renaissance Florentine. Yet this was at the root of their trouble.

Moreover, we must find interest in the very persons who tried to grapple with those problems. Lorenzo de' Medici himself, Savonarola, Machiavelli, all attempted the reform of the constitution, and each one presents an approach from a different angle. Lorenzo was the great merchant prince, and as we might conceive it, a millionaire with vast business and political interests; Savonarola was the disinterested moralist, thinking of the good of the people; and Machiavelli was the expert in political theory, helped by actual experience in working the government machine as an official. Each in turn has left the record of his theories, and in the case of Lorenzo and Savonarola their constitutions were actually put into practice, yet none of them succeeded in the task they attempted. Their efforts show how, when men of a very high order of intelligence and with much practical experience consciously trying to find a good form of government, yet fail, the stumbling-blocks must be very formidable and the difficulties of the task very great.

There is an additional touch of novelty in the fact that the Florentine constitution, as it existed before and during these experiments, represents the form of government created by what we might call 'business men.' It was the work of a class of people whose whole life and training should have made them specially apt at dealing with problems in a practical way. The system which they evolved was built up by a State in which power was concentrated in the hands of a ruling class, composed not of nobles, but of merchants, traders, and above all bankers and financiers. The nobles were not allowed to be members of any of the 'Arts,' and were thus debarred from trade or business. They were deliberately excluded from any share in the government, and so in practice were the 'plebs' or artisans. The theorists and school-men kept to their books, and affairs of State were entirely in the hands of the merchant and business classes. The various Florentine constitutions do, therefore, represent the form of government which the 'business man' drew up, untrammelled by any theorists or politicians, and unhampered by any need to conciliate a powerful democracy.

That constitution, reduced to its simplest terms, was one where the business of governing was carried on by a few strong committees. These committees were, to some degree, helped by consultative councils, but the main feature was government by the executive. The people as a whole did not take part, for there was no national or elected assembly. The contests which took place in Florence were concerned with the best way of selecting the executive, and it was on this vital point that Lorenzo and his opponents exercised their ingenuity. How the executive was to be appointed, whether by nomination, or election, or by lot, was the first point at issue. Take this as a clue, and the vast tangle of councils and committees may be unravelled. One source of difficulty to us lies in the terrible Florentine idiosyncrasy of calling all governmental bodies by numerals, instead of by names. We do not have a ministry for war, we have 'the Ten of War and Peace'; we have the 'Eight of Watch and Ward,' instead of a ministry for home affairs; we have 'the Sixteen,' the 'Twelve,' the 'Eight of Balìa,' or commission to reform, and even the 'Eight of Pratica,' which simply means 'Committee of Eight.' Quite satisfied with his shortened, but to us unilluminating, title 'Eight,' 'Ten,' or 'Nine,' the Florentine went gaily on to impose the same nomenclature on his electoral councils, and we have the 'Eighty' or the 'Seventy,' the 'Hundred,' the 'Two Hundred,' and even the 'Hundred-and-Thirty-One,' whose functions we have to memorize laboriously, though presumably to the Florentine they were familiar and simplicity itself.

Yet complex as the system appears to be, and to us need-lessly so, we have need to remember that the fourteenth-century Florentine was a remarkably intelligent man. If he created this net-work of councils and committees, he had some reason, clear to him if not to us. Though some of his councils seem to us redundant, to him they fulfilled a useful purpose. For the Republic had struggled throughout her history with faction, and she had emerged with some lessons firmly imprinted on her memory. First, at all costs, she must prevent any in-dividual from acquiring too much power, and hence her insistence on short terms of office, on election by drawing of lots, and of an elaborate system of checks. Second, she must aim at enlisting the support of as great a number of persons as possible. Florentines seem to have had a regular mania for holding office, whether in an important or in an ornamental capacity. By multiplying committees and councils, many of which performed purely nominal functions, she was able to satisfy their aspirations and to give comparative nonentities the happiness of acting as State officials without thereby in any way endangering the State. On this point Machiavelli is enlightening when he says: "Councils were invented to flatter, and to dispose of offices of no value."

Further, the Republic of Florence did not resemble any modern State in the functions it was called upon to fulfil. It was a city-State, with no very great territory. It had no standing army, no navy, and of course none of the parapher-nalia known to us as 'social services.' The duty of poor-relief lay not with the State, but with the Church and individuals. Education was likewise a private, not a public obligation. For 'forms of government' her citizens did not even have a very great respect, but the corner-stone of their system is to be found in their efforts to ensure sound administration; "whate'r is best administered is best," would win their hearty commendation.

In this connection, too, we can see how difficult it was for the Renaissance to work out a balance between legislature and executive. Florence had her laws, and she did, of course, add to or alter them from time to time. But the legislature was not to her the most important part of the constitution. We in the twentieth century need to realize that fact very clearly. We are so accustomed to begin our constitution-building with a representative assembly, that it is necessary to remind ourselves how alien such a conception would be to the fourteenth-century Florentine. Nor can those who have had centuries of experience behind them realize how difficult it was for the men of those days to see how they could reconcile a strong executive with a legislative assembly. Naturally, they had no conception of such a doctrine as cabinet responsibility to a Parliament, which, growing up in England by slow and almost unrealized stages, has helped to solve our problem. They tried to solve theirs by making their strong executive frequently apply for election, to the electorate, which thus retained its hold and control over officials, and here lies the explanation and the justification of their very curious system.

(2) *The Constitution under the Medici*

To come now to the constitution as it was established under the Medici, before the democratic changes introduced by Savonarola set up the form of government under which Machiavelli was to carry on his work as a public official.

The most important body in Florence may be said to be the Signoria. This was the chief executive body. It consisted of the Gonfalonier of justice, the acting head of the State, and of eight Priors. They were unpaid, as were all Florentine councillors and committee-men, but the Signoria during their term of office lived in the Palazzo Pubblico, and had their board and lodging provided for them. In the formation of the Signoria we have the survival of the old Guild organization. The Priors were drawn two from each quarter of the city. They were originally elected by the Arts, and they were still members of them and were drawn in the proportion of six from the Greater Arts and two from the Lesser, and the Gonfalonier, too, had to be a member of the Greater Arts. The Arts, it will be remembered, represent what in England we call Guilds. The Greater Arts were seven in number and included the cloth merchants, woollen merchants, silk merchants, skinners and furriers, and the doctors, bankers, and lawyers. The Lesser Arts numbered fourteen, and included the butchers, bakers, blacksmiths, shoemakers, linen workers, stone-masons, wood-carvers, wine-dealers, the inn-keepers, tanners, saddlers, oil-dealers, locksmiths, armourers and carpenters. Outside these organizations were the nobles, who could not become members of a guild, and the *ciompi*, or artisan class, who were not qualified, and who had no representatives.

The extra numbers in the Signoria and in all the committees drawn from the Greater Arts were meant to weight the government in favour of the wealthier classes. This policy is followed throughout; the Greater Arts are always given a preponderance of three to one over the Lesser, a further indication of the strongly mercantile bent of the city. Here was no democracy, giving equal power to the masses, or even to the lower middle classes. Power and office were firmly concentrated in the hands of the well-to-do. The Priors sat with the Gonfalonier in council, each took it in turn to preside, along with the Gonfalonier, for three days, and any one of them could put a measure to the vote if the Gonfalonier refused, this right being called the *proposto*.

Only certain classes were eligible for this, the highest office, or magistracy as the Florentines called it, in the State; no noble, no plebeian, or any person not enrolled in one of the Guilds, and no person inhabiting the country area as distinct from the city, was eligible; nor was any person who had been *ammonito* or 'warned' for any political offence. This qualification was, of course, capable of great abuse, and by denouncing an individual the party in power could effectually disqualify its political opponents. Any person who had not paid his taxes was likewise disqualified, the technical term being *moroso di specchio*, and any person who paid up was declared *netto di specchio*, or freed from this disqualification. Finally, even if any individual fulfilled all these conditions, he could still be declared unable to sit if he or any relation had recently held office, and he was then declared *veduto ma non seduto*, or, as we might phrase it, "eligible but not elected." The task of deciding whether persons passed all these tests was carried out by a special board, the board of Scrutiny or *Squittino*, and here again political influence, by deciding the composition of that board, could ensure the retention of power in the hands of a party. It was by the manipulation of the elections through these channels that the Medici secured their predominance. They had, indeed, complete mastery of the art of influencing elections without openly contravening any law or regulation, or bringing about an open revolution.

When the names of those eligible for office had thus been tabulated or registered, there remained the further process of election of the required number. Names were put in *borse*, originally 'purses,' which later, in point of fact, became boxes. The names of those standing for the Signoria were done up in fifty sets of eight, each set was enclosed in a wax ball, and these were put in a special box. Then the whole eight Priors were elected at once, by the drawing out of one of the wax balls. Three days before the Signoria went out of office a youth, dressed in white and rose, took the *borse*, or boxes, to the Council of the People, where the whole Signoria, *Collegi* and the *Podestà* were assembled. There the boxes were opened and the new names drawn and announced. When elected, the members held office only for two months, and at the end of that time another ball would be drawn. The function of "drawing out" was performed by a friar, who was presumed to be an impartial person. Naturally, as the end of an electoral period drew near, it could be roughly estimated from those who had already held office, who amongst the few left would get in, and we find that this was often turned to advantage by charlatans who deceived the ignorant by their apparent power of foretelling the future.

Though the officials were changed every two months, this did not involve a new 'scrutiny,' for the electoral lists were made once in five years in normal circumstances, and the *borse*, or boxes, filled up with enough names to last during the elections required for the next five years. If, in the interval, there was a minor revolution, the party seizing power might order a special *Balìa* or committee, one of whose duties would be to empty the boxes and refill them with new names, obviously thus eliminating any opponents. The disadvantages of allowing high officials to sit for only two months were just as apparent to the Florentines as they are to us. They were perfectly aware of the lack of continuity which the plan involved, but, terrified by the past with its bloody record of faction, and by the ever-present fear of the establishment of a tyranny, they deliberately held that it was better to bear with the disadvantages rather than run the risk which permanence in office might involve. They also believed that in the permanent paid subordinates was to be found some check on the disadvantage of frequent elections. These subordinates, though few in number, were of importance. Machiavelli himself, as Second Secretary, was one of the chief officials of the Republic, and as such, though he might attend debates, could neither speak nor vote. The respect and importance attached to these high officials are exemplified in the words of Nardi, who wrote: "We owe a great debt to the first Secretary of the Chancery, who carries on the work of administration with each of the magistrates successively. In the mind of this man is contained the thread and continuity of the management of the Republic."

The functions of the Signoria were to initiate all legislature (they alone could propose laws) and to carry out all the supreme powers of the executive. In this they were assisted by various other bodies, and to them we must now turn.

Immediately beneath the Signoria came a kind of Privy Council, called the *Collegi,* usually translated 'colleges,' but a term which gives a more exact rendering is, perhaps, 'colleagues.' These were the Twelve *Buonuomini,* and the Sixteen Gonfaloniers, usually known, for short, as the "Twelve" and the "Sixteen," and the nine assessors of the Priors. Besides the special inclination which the Florentine showed for these numerical titles, they add to our confusion by carelessly allowing the name to remain when often the committee or council no longer consisted of its original number. Thus Lorenzo's famous Seventy never really consisted of that number. In the case of the Twelve, these *buonuomini* were again representatives of the Arts, nine from the Greater and three from the Lesser. The Sixteen were the 'gonfaloniers' or 'banner-bearers' of the very ancient militia companies, drawn four from each quarter of the city. Both bodies acted really as checks on hasty action by the Signoria, bills having to be brought before them on successive days, and passed in each by a two-thirds majority. This provision was not altogether an idle form, for lists still exist showing substantial minorities, and proposals must quite frequently have failed to obtain the requisite number of votes.

The laws, when at length passed, were entered in the public records called the *Riformagioni*. The whole body, Twelve, Sixteen, and Nine, formed the three greater magistracies. The rules of their election followed those of the Signoria. The qualifications were the same. The only difference lay in the fact that names were drawn from the boxes separately, not in the 'balls of eight' used for the Signoria. The Twelve held office for three months, the Sixteen for four. They thus had slightly longer terms of office than the Signoria, as being of less importance and therefore not requiring so stern a check.

Below these greater magistracies, who, it must be repeated, were the real executive and holders of power, came two very ancient councils. These, to a very limited extent, may be said to represent the legislative function. They were the councils of the People (*del Popolo*) and of the Commune. The Council of the People consisted of 300 members, again drawn from the Arts, and renewed every four months, and the Council of the Commune of 390 persons, including judges and legal officials. In this last council, and in this alone, the nobles could hold office, for as they were entitled to be judges or law officers they could enter the Council of the

Commune. The officials of the greater magistracies sat in both. Any law, proposed by the Signoria, which alone possessed the right of initiating legislation, came first before the 'Colleagues,' and then before the Council of the People and the Council of the Commune. In every case it had to obtain a two-thirds majority. Voting was by ballot, black and white beans being placed in an urn. Black beans meant 'Yes,' white beans meant 'No.' In the Signoria a two-thirds majority—six beans—was called *l'autorità dei sei fave.*

One striking feature was that no debates proper were allowed. Those in favour of any proposal were allowed to speak, but those against must not reply; they must keep silent and show their feelings only by their votes. Nor might any proposal occupy more than one day. It must be voted on at the end of that day, though if rejected its supporters were at liberty to try their luck again on a subsequent day, and to continue to do so until either they tired or their opponents were worn down.

Now it will be clear that as Florence rose in the world and emerged into a political sphere where State warred and intrigued against State, it became necessary for her to develop both her foreign policy and her war ministry. Hence we get the creation of her two famous Committees, the Ten of War, first appointed in 1423, and the Eight of Watch and Ward, or Justice. At first the Ten of War sufficed, dealing both with questions of war and peace and, as intimately bound up with them, all foreign affairs. They, in process of time, called in two councils to assist them, the duties of which were to consider all bills relating to foreign affairs before they were presented to the Great Council of State. These two—the Two Hundred and the Hundred-and-Thirty-One—seem to fulfil Machiavelli's attributed function: 'of no value to the

State, they were no guarantees of the popular will, and were invented only to flatter.' The Eight of Watch and Ward may be said roughly to represent Home Affairs, for it was their duty to deal with all offences against the State and its safety.

This was what may be called the regular structure of government. At its head the Signoria, then the Colleagues, the Councils, and the great Committees. We may see that in them Florence thought she had provided a competent administration, a rather elaborate method of checking legislative proposals, and a separation of function through committees to deal with the new developments necessitated by her rise to the position of an international power.

She found, however, that this framework, though adequate for everyday purposes, would not suffice when extraordinary crises arose. Or, to put it differently, when certain elements, such as the Medici, forced their way to the front, or when popular feeling, as under Savonarola, rose to fever height, something was needed to bring the ordinary routine into harmony with the prevailing spirit. Two possibilities were known to the Florentine in these emergencies. Under very ancient custom, in time of crisis, the Signoria might call a 'Parlamento' or meeting of the whole city. The great bell of the Palazzo would toll, the crowd would rush to the Piazza, the Signoria would step out on to the platform before the Palazzo Pubblico, and would ask the assembly its will. This took the form of inquiry whether the assembled people would have recourse to the other expedient known to the constitution, namely, the appointment of a *balìa*, or committee, to reform whatever was wrong, and remove whatever were the grievances complained of. In theory this might be regarded as a true plebiscite, the supreme will of the people asserting

[219]

itself in times of crisis. In practice it was an astute misuse of the forms of democracy to strengthen the hold of a party. For a Parlamento was the easiest thing in the world to manipulate. In the first place it was summoned by the Signoria, who in consequence could take measures beforehand as to its composition. Men-at-arms could be stationed at the narrow approaches to the Piazza, and only those whom the Signoria favoured need be allowed to gain access to the wide open space before the Palazzo. Furthermore, paid adherents could always be provided, who at the first clang of the great bell would swarm out and take up their stations. When the crowd had collected, out would come the Signoria, and one of the Priors would ask :"Is two-thirds of the people here present? Do you wish for the appointment of a *balia*? Do you agree to the nomination of the following persons?" Provided a clique near the platform shouted sufficiently loudly, the Signoria could declare itself satisfied and withdraw to appoint its nominated and packed committee. So farcical did the Parlamento become, that once abolished under Savonarola, it was never revived. He, as an ardent democrat, saw in the Parlamento such an instrument of oligarchy that he bade his followers, "when the great bell sounds, let you hack to pieces the first Prior to set foot upon the platform," and the law which annulled the calling of a Parlamento decreed that, should any Prior attempt it, his house should be put to sack by the gonfaloniers of militia.

Though the Parlamento could cease, the use of *balia* remained, and it was here that innovator and restorer of the power of the Medici alike turned when they wished not to destroy, but to manipulate the constitution. A *balia* was simply a special *ad hoc* committee. Its members were nominated, not drawn by lot. It could appoint *Accopiatori*.

who nominated to all councils and committees, thus abrogating election and ballot. Or, *it could empty and refill the 'borse,'* and thus ensure the composition of the government for a period of years. It could order a Scrutiny, and so disfranchise its opponents. It offered the eternal opportunity of maintaining the form while altering the spirit.

(3) *The changes made by Lorenzo de' Medici.*

In 1480 Lorenzo de' Medici was determined to obtain control of the constitution. He did not apparently wish to destroy its framework, but he, in characteristic Florentine manner, wished to control the appointment of the executive, and to this end to manipulate the electorate.

His foreign policy suffered from the delays and uncertainties imposed upon it by the endless elections to the committees which dealt with public affairs. He wished both to consolidate his influence and to expedite and strengthen the process of administration. Accordingly he obtained, this time without a Parlamento, the appointment of a *balìa* of reform. This *balìa* brought about the momentous change known as the appointment of the Council of Seventy and the Eight of *Pratica*. The Council of Seventy was not elected; herein lay one source of its importance: it was appointed by the Signoria of that day, which Lorenzo controlled, and vacancies were to be filled up by co-option by the Council itself from anyone who had held the office of Gonfalonier. This both secured the permanence of Medicean influence on the Council and confined its membership to a very limited class.

The function of this council was to appoint to all the chief magistracies, who were no longer to be elected. It was divided into two bodies of thirty-five, each acting for six elections, which, occurring every two months, occupied exactly one year. It could draft rules for the qualifications of candidates for the Signoria, and could fix the number of names to be placed in the boxes. The decision as to what names should be allowed to enter the boxes must be made two days before the actual election took place. This was intended to prevent any aspirant to office changing his views if he found he was not on the favoured list, for two days gave insufficient time to convince the examiners of a thorough change of heart. Thus no known opponent of the party in power could really hope to get his name into the electoral box. In this way popular control was lost, and power handed over to the clique who controlled the first members of the new council. The only sop to public opinion was the rule that the first council must contain ten representatives of the Lesser Arts. But as the Medici in reality had none but their nominees on the original Council, and as that Council would in future appoint to Signoria, *Collegi* and Councils, the ruling family had, indeed, attained control of the governmental machine, and, as it seemed, in perpetuity.

The other task of the Seventy was to select two Committees, the well-known Eight of *Pratica*, who were to control foreign policy, and the Twelve of Debt and Trade, or, as we should say, Finance. These Committees took the place of the old Ten of War, and really represent a development of the plan of working through standing committees. The members were, of course, nominated by the Seventy and sat for six months. Their position was consolidated by the proviso that every measure, including money bills, initiated by the Signoria, must now come before the Eight and the Twelve, in addition to its usual perambulation through the more ancient Councils. Lorenzo hoped in these rather more permanent Committees to provide a less shifting executive; he meant them to perform really important functions, and he intended them to act as a link with the more ornamental magistracies. In 1490 he went a step further. The Seventy delegated some of its functions to a smaller committee, the so-called Seventeen, of which Lorenzo himself was a member. To this little inner ring was given the power to nominate *accopiatori,* that is to say, persons who were selected *a mano,* in distinction to the old election by ballot, to all the offices of State. This measure both tightened Lorenzo's hold, made it easier for him to control every member of the small body, and led on to the measure he was undoubtedly contemplating, namely, his appointment as Gonfalonier for life. He died before he could achieve that, but it would have been only the final outward sign of the possession of a power he had long wielded, as in fact the nominator to every post, and to every committee and council, in the constitution.

Florence had agreed to these enactments, forced or induced to do so by the pressure of Medicean influence. Yet she had been restless and dissatisfied. With the death of Lorenzo and the misfortunes which threatened her, hidden feelings broke out, and in the revolution which expelled the Medici and called for a reform of its constitution we get a swing towards democracy. This is emphasized in the changes brought about by Savonarola, and known to posterity as Savonarola's government.

(4) *Savonarola's Constitution.*

When the departure of the French in 1494 and the flight of Piero de' Medici left Florence free to make a new start, the great bell tolled, the Parlamento met, and the *balia* was appointed. Its first act was to abolish Lorenzo's Council of Seventy, and the *Otto di Pratica*. Various schemes were put forward and Savonarola, as one of the foremost men in the city, was called upon to declare his views. In his sermons he said that monarchy might be an ideal form of rule, but it was not suited to the Florentines, and he called upon all the magistracies to produce their plans, so that the city might select the best. The Sixteen Gonfaloniers, the Twelve *Buonuomini*, the Twenty, the Eight, and the Ten of War, each produced a scheme, and of all these that of the Ten of War put forward by Soderini and backed by Savonarola was chosen.

The most striking and novel feature of this much debated scheme was the creation of a Great Council, or national assembly. This was a true effort to give a more democratic tinge to the constitution. A large body of people were to be enlisted as members of the governing body, and to them wide powers were entrusted.

Thus the Great Council was to be composed of all those who had either been themselves eligible for any of the three greater magistracies (Signoria and Colleges), or whose father, or grandfathers, or great-grandfathers had been. This it was estimated would produce a number of about 3000 persons. The total population of Florence was then 120,000, so the enfranchised represent no great number. Until a great hall could be built, to hold all those eligible, this 3000 was to be divided into three, and one of these divisions was to form the Council for six months, and then be replaced by the others in turn. Each year a small number of additional members, but not more than twenty-eight, might be elected if two-thirds of the Council voted for them. Actually it was found that very few did receive the necessary majority. For the whole Council members must have reached the age of twenty-nine and have paid their taxes.

As to the functions of this great assembly, they were in the main electoral. Florentines must have been extremely fond of elections, for they never jibbed at endless proceedings calling for election of persons to nominate others, who again might elect others. Thus the Great Council decided on two methods of electing, one adopted for the major offices, the other for the minor. For the major offices, Signoria, Twelve and Sixteen, the electors were first drawn by lot, and these then nominated candidates, who had to go to the poll. For the minor offices the Council was content to have only one process, and names were simply drawn by lot.

Refreshed by these efforts, the next work of the Council was to choose a Senate. This was another innovation, and consisted of eighty members—hence its usual name, the Eighty—who had to be forty years of age and who sat for six months. It was an advisory body, assisting the Signoria when asked to do so, and electing ambassadors and commissioners to the army. To us this may seem a redundant body, but perhaps its age qualification, noticeably high for the period, shows that it was meant to conciliate the older citizens, who may have disliked the innovation of the Great Council.

Besides all this work of election, the Great Council had two other functions. Its consent was necessary for the passing of legislation. Every law was, as before, first brought before the Signoria, then went to the *Collegi*, then to the Eighty, and then to the Great Council. The usual Florentine rule as to debate obtained, only those in favour of a measure might speak, those against could only vote and might not speak. Members did not vote by name, but simply in *pancate,* that is to say, the number of the seats, or benches, into which the great hall was divided.

But as it is clear that the Great Council really involved a widening of the basis of power, and an extension of political influence, so we find that the Florentines, anxious to improve their legislation, did avail themselves of another instrument for discussing plans and enactments. They adopted the practice of appointing a *pratica,* or special standing committee, to consider proposals. A *pratica* was not bound by the laws of the other Councils; its members could debate and discuss. An adverse point of view could be expressed. The *pratica* was usually drawn from the Senate (the Eighty), but specially qualified persons could be summoned to sit upon it, such as leading lawyers or any citizens held to have special qualifications.

Finally, experience having shown that Lorenzo's special committees were invaluable parts of the machinery of government, the Ten of Liberty were created to do the work and take the place of the Eight of *Pratica,* and to manage all home affairs. The *Mercanzia* was restored to deal with trade, and the Ten of War also reappeared.

The councils of the *Popolo* and Commune ceased to exist, and thereby the nobles lost their one contact with office, for membership of all the councils now necessitated being a member of one of the Arts.

For most of this constitution Savonarola, who warmly upheld it, has been praised, and even Machiavelli found in it much that was good, as he showed when he, in his turn, was asked to draw up a model form of government. But in one respect it was much blamed. Hitherto there had been no court of appeal in Florence for political offences. A man once condemned by a vote of two-thirds of the Signoria, or the Eight, or even 'warned,' had no redress and clearly the Signoria could be used as a weapon of political vengeance. To remedy this, because party feeling often produced grave injustices, an appeal was now allowed to the Great Council itself, and was known as the "appeal from the six beans." This referred to the six beans cast by either Signoria or Eight in giving their decision based on a two-thirds majority. Clearly this was not a good choice, for an assembly of 1500 to 3000 persons could not usefully act as a court of appeal. Savonarola himself did not like the idea, but he could not win support for any lesser body, and, *faute de mieux*, accepted it. Later this was made one of the chief counts against him, yet he did but emphasize the right of the people to be regarded as the sovereign authority having power to pardon.

For the next eighteen years Florence lived under this system. Savonarola himself died on the gibbet, but his constitution survived. Machiavelli's name was put before the Eighty as candidate for the post of Secretary to the Ten of War and Peace, and having passed that body went on and was approved by the Great Council. Florence struggled along trying to keep herself safe and free in the great storm of war which the French and Spanish invasions brought upon her. In 1502 the position was so threatening she tried one last expedient to strengthen her position. Venice had been held to have the best government in Italy. Florence had mistakenly believed that the strength of the rival Republic lay in her Great Council, and thought that in copying that body she was ensuring her own stability. Actually the source of Venetian stability lay in her Senate and her strong Council of Ten. Finding that the Great Council did not seem to be doing all that was hoped, Florence decided to try the experiment of appointing a Gonfalonier for life. She rightly thought that a permanent official would add continuity and experience, she did not see that one man alone, in a shifting world of officials and councils, was insufficient. She elected Soderini, and experience showed she had done nothing to better her state. Soderini himself was weak, and his appointment created a host of enemies, jealous of this elevation. When the Medici, allied now with the Emperor and backed by the Papacy, advanced on Florence in 1512, they at once demanded Soderini's abdication. On the fall of Prato, when resistance was at an end, Soderini solved the question by flight, and once more Florence returned to her domination by the great family of Medici.

(5) *Machiavelli's Constitutional Proposals.*

The restored Medici acted with great moderation, partly, no doubt, because with the departure of the Spanish troops they had to be careful to consolidate their supporters and not rouse up too much antagonism. They observed all due forms. The inevitable *balia* was created, and naturally enough at once swept away the Great Council and restored all Lorenzo's councils. Actually the chief offices were entirely filled by nominees of the two Medici, Cardinal Giovanni and his nephew Lorenzo. When Giovanni became Pope Leo X he was induced by his cousin Cardinal Giulio, who ruled Florence in his name, to ask Machiavelli to draw him up a report on the government of Florence. In doing so he was asking the advice of one whom he knew to be an acute and experienced student of this very subject, the best form of government. Machiavelli in his preface to his then unpublished *Prince* had written: "If the Medici read my book they will see how I have spent all my working life in studying politics.

Anyone ought to be glad to employ a man who has gained so much experience."

We would indeed expect much from such an expert, and we are perhaps correspondingly surprised to read Machiavelli's discourse on Florentine government and realize that he had nothing new to offer.

He did stand firm by his old principles, and urged on the Pope the re-establishment of the Republican forms of government. He was content that during their lifetimes Leo X and his cousin Giulio, later Clement VII, should exercise control over the appointment of the State bodies. "You," he wrote, "will be lord of all, you nominate the chief magistrates, the Gonfalonier and the Signoria . . . everything depends on your will." They were the last surviving descendants of the great Cosimo, and with them the elder branch would end, since as clerics neither had legitimate descendants. He declares that all the instability of government in Florence was due to the strife of parties, that Italy herself was unstable owing to foreign rulers having obtained a footing in the land. He pointed out that in Florence the old tradition of liberty was so deeply implanted that the city would never rest content without her Republican forms. One original touch comes in his division of Florentines into three categories: those really wanting to command and lead, those asking only for a share in the work of government, and the great mass who wanted neither to lead nor to share in government, but only asked for 'liberty and justice.

He wished to sweep away the old complicated system of Councils of One Hundred, or One Hundred and Thirty-One, of Seventy, and of Seventeen, reintroduced by the restored Medici.

Instead he advocated the Great Council of Savonarola,

and then proceeded to set forth his most peculiar attempt to give the stability which he so clearly recognized as essential to the State.

Difficult as are his proposals, they are worth attention as showing how a man who called himself practical, who was extremely experienced, and who had now seen two revolutions and two new constitutions, could fall into the very same mistakes made by his predecessors.

He wished to see an element of permanency introduced into the councils and accordingly he suggested that sixty-five citizens, aged over forty-five, should be elected for life, one of whom was to be Gonfalonier for at least three years, possibly for life. Of these sixty-five councillors (now, to be accurate, reduced by the appointment of the Gonfalonier to sixty-four), one-half were to form an advisory Council, holding office for one year. At the end of that time they were to be replaced by the other half, and were to alternate thus in perpetuity. Then, of this Council of Thirty-four, groups of eight were to be divided off, and each group, in turn, was to constitute the Signoria, holding office for three months.

Having thus, as he hoped, created an executive which, once selected, sat for life in rotation, he added a Senate of Two Hundred, and, still keeping the standing committees for specialized work, retained the Eight of *Balìa* for home affairs, the Eight of *Pratica* for the militia.

Finally he declared: "The mass of the people must be satisfied, and to this end it is necessary to reopen the hall of the Great Council . . . without satisfying the masses, no stable Republic has ever been established . . . it is requisite to reopen this hall and to restore this privilege to the masses." The membership, however, was to be confined to 1000, or 600 citizens. All 'eligible' under the old rules could sit in turn. As soon as the two Medici were dead this Council was to resume its old function of electing to the magistracies and thus he concluded in a burst of eloquence: "During your life this government does not differ from a monarchy, but at your death you will bequeath to your country a genuine free Republic that will owe its existence to you . . . The greatest good that can be accomplished is that which is done through our country. No men win so much praise as those who have reformed republics . . . therefore Heaven can grant no greater gift to mortal man, nor point out to him a more glorious path than this, and the greatest benefit God has bestowed upon your House is this of giving you strength and purpose to earn immortality."

Machiavelli's life was full of irony. We cannot think that Florence would ever have accepted his scheme. Councillors for life, Signoria chosen from life-members over forty-five years old, permanent Gonfaloniers, would all have been abhorrent to her. Yet, asked for his views, Machiavelli had been honest and sincere. He had shown that he thought power belonged to the people and should be given back to them. He showed, too, that he had come to believe whole-heartedly in his former enemy, Savonarola's democratic Great Council. Naturally his scheme did not find favour with the Medici. They neither sought to win the "praise given to those who reform Republics . . . the greatest good that can be accomplished," nor did they take the author into their services. All that the pamphlet achieved was to make strong Republicans feel that, in writing for the Pope, Machiavelli had fallen from grace. Seven years later came the sack of Rome, and the instant revolt of Florence from the yoke of the Medici. The constitution of Savonarola was again proclaimed, but Machiavelli himself was given no post in the new government. His scheme for a constitution, disregarded by the Pope, for whom it was written, was contemptuously dismissed by his fellow-citizens as "of a kind unusual to that city, and wholly extravagant." He, the expert, had failed more completely than any of his predecessors in the art of creating a government.

CHAPTER XIV

MACHIAVELLI'S LETTERS: OFFICIAL AND PERSONAL

To complete our picture of the man, we need to read some of Machiavelli's letters, for, as in the case of most diaries and private letters, here we get a first-hand impression of the life he was living. Indeed with Machiavelli it is only through his correspondence that we can seize that many-sidedness, and really understand the diverse elements in his character, which tore his life to pieces. We can see the excellence of his official work, his lapses into dissipation, and catch just a glimpse of the affectionate man whom his family knew.

I. OFFICIAL LETTERS.

1. *Ruin caused by floods.*

"To the Consuls of the Marine. August, 1511.

"We understand that this august Republic, having some years ago taken a resolution to divert the course of the river Arno in such a manner as to overflow the territories of Pisa, the work was actually begun and ditches cut for that purpose. So that ever since the river began to take a new course, it appears that all the lands belonging to the community of Fagiana have been so flooded and covered with mud, that no signs of any former boundaries or landmarks are now to be discovered, but all meadows are disguised with roots of trees, mire and sand to such a degree that it is impossible for any man to distinguish his own from that of his neighbour. Now the owners of the said lands being desirous to recover them, and to turn them to some account when every man knows his own, some of the most considerable amongst them have been before us and petitioned that you may take all necessary and proper measures to have those lands surveyed in such a manner that every man may have his own property restored to him.

"We therefore command you to take the matter in hand immediately and to search narrowly into every man's claim, and then assign them such portion of ground as they had before, taking care to distinguish the several pieces by proper names, landmarks and boundaries, and to have them specified and recorded in writing. And if anyone of the proprietors shall think himself aggrieved by this division, he shall have free appeal to our august Signoria.

"Now you know our pleasure, take care to act with prudence and justice. Farewell."

2. *A heretic doctor.*

"To the Chief Magistrate of Pisa. December 22, 1510.

"We find by your last letters to the Council of Ten that a certain Portuguese physician, and some others of that nation, are come to Pisa, under a safe-conduct, but that they are thought to be either heretics or infidels, upon which account you say you are resolved to send them elsewhere about their business. But for many reasons, and particularly because they come to Pisa under the sanction of the government, as well because it is a very difficult matter to form a true judgement of men in points of religious faith, and that we are desirous to have your city as well filled with inhabitants as possible, it is our pleasure that you suffer the said physician and his countrymen to stay amongst you for three or four months, during which time you will be able to guess pretty truly at their principles, and if you find at the end of that term that their further stay will be of prejudice to the community, you may then dismiss them. Farewell."

3. Taxation of ruined peasants

"To Francisco de' Caponsacchi, of St. John's. October 5, 1510.

"A deputation from the community of Lannolina has been with us and represented to us that all their corn, grapes and chestnuts have been destroyed this season by a dreadful storm, in such a manner that they cannot tell how to support themselves the rest of the year. Upon which account they have humbly besought us to have pity upon them, for if they are sent to prison for the taxes due upon their crops and lands they must inevitably perish from hunger. And as it is our duty to have compassion upon the poor and miserable, you are hereby required to inquire into the matter, and if you find they have actually sustained these losses, you are to favour them in such a manner in remitting the aforesaid taxes as your discretion shall think necessary in so grievous a calamity. You are a prudent man, and know our disposition in this respect, you will behave yourself, we make no question, so as to deserve our approbation. Farewell."

4. Evil behaviour of a lawyer.

"To the Chief Magistrate of Burgi.

"An information hath been laid before us that Jacopo Venuto, Doctor of Law, in your town, about four years ago married Madonna Giacopa, daughter of the late Christopher Picchi, a lady of good reputation and family. But that he keeps another woman in the house, under the very eyes of his wife, whom he has abused in such a manner that she has been forced to quit the house and return to her relations, while he and his mistress are spending her fortune. Now this being a matter of very bad example and highly culpable, we have been petitioned to take cognizance of it, upon which account it is our pleasure that on receipt of this you cite the said Jacopo Venuto to appear before you together with his wife, that you may know the truth of the matter.

"If you shall find it is as hath been represented to us, you are to reprimand the said Jacopo in a proper manner, giving him to understand that such conduct very ill becomes a member of his profession, and that if he persists in it, the Signoria will take such a course with him as shall not fail to reclaim him.

"In the meantime you are to take steps to see that he provide his wife with food, clothes and all other conveniences proper to her rank, and that he return her fortune immediately.

"These are our positive orders, act with your usual prudence in their execution, and endeavour to reduce this man to reason, but if you find him obstinate and incorrigible let us have a detailed account of his behaviour, for we are determined to redress the poor lady's grievances in a proper manner. Farewell."

5. *Myrtle for tanning.*

"To the Chief Magistrate of Pisa, and the Vicar of Lari, the Vicar of Vico Pisano, the Chief Magistrate of Campiglia. Feb. 25, 1510.

"We are informed that great quantities of myrtle and other materials made use of in tanning and dressing leather have been transported out of our dominions by your people, by which we are likely to suffer much inconvenience, as we shall not have a sufficient quantity of such materials left in our parts for the use of our own tanners and leather-dressers. In order therefore to repair this loss and to prevent foreigners being supplied with these things to your own prejudice, we command you, upon receipt of this, to cause proclamation to be made that if any person shall presume, either himself or by the help of others, to transport, or cause to be transported, either by land or water, any such materials, he shall forfeit not only the material but the carts and beasts that draw them, or the vessel in which they are freighted.

"You must be sensible yourselves how much we should suffer from the continuance of such practice. Exert therefore your interest, activity and diligence, and let it be your principal endeavour to prevent them. Farewell."

6. *Rudeness of a Marquis.*

"To the Chief Magistrate of Fiviziani. Sept. 18, 1511.

"It hath been represented to our Signoria that the Marquis Giovanni Lorenzo da Trespie not only behaves with great rudeness and insolence to the Marquis of Morello, his near relative, but actually disturbs him by force and violence in the possession of his estate, which certainly is acting in a manner that little becomes a man of quality and a near relation. We command you therefore to go in person to the said Marquis Giovanni Lorenzo (taking care at the same time to keep up your dignity in a proper manner) and give him to understand that it is the pleasure of this august Signoria that he should desist from all further violence and rudeness to his kinsman. If he persists we shall take the Marquis of Morello under our immediate protection, as he hath been well recommended to our care. If you find he is inclined to be peaceable, let him sue for justice in the ordinary way, for no private man ought to be permitted to right himself when he thinks he has suffered wrong. Farewell."

7. *Shortage of bread.*

"To the Chief Magistrate of Pistoia. July 8, 1511.

"We have been informed, to our great displeasure, that on the second of this month people could not have bread for their money in your city, at which we cannot help being much surprised, since there has been so fine a harvest this year that there can be no want of corn. We are still more surprised that you have not acquainted us with the matter before now, so that we might immediately have provided you with a proper supply. It is our pleasure therefore that after due consultation you cause a speedy and diligent inquiry to be made whether there be really a sufficient quantity of corn in the city, and if you find there is, that you force those that have it to bring it to market and sell it at a fair and reasonable price, as we should think they would naturally do in their own interest, after so plentiful a harvest.

"But if you find there is a real scarcity, you are to let us know directly, so that we can provide accordingly, for it is a shameful thing that people cannot have bread for their money in such a city and that you should have suffered it to be sold at the rate of 40 soldi a bushel, since it will not fetch that price, or anything like it, either in our city or any other part of our dominions. See that these orders be executed without fail, and farewell."

8. *Corrupt election of officials.*

"To the Vicar of Piscia.

"We are informed that the community of Monte Catini

are desirous to have a reform made in their Magistracy, now
that the time of choosing new officials is at hand. For which
purpose some individuals have been with us from that place,
acting in their own names and those of many others, who wish
to have the government altered for the better. They complain
that their community, which consists of about 500 inhabitants,
is entirely governed by 30 or 40 persons, who never go
out of office, but are succeeded by their sons, or brothers, or
near relations. So that they always control the same administration. In this manner, these say, a few persons share all
the honours amongst them as well as the public revenues,
which annually amount to 4000 ducats, and that though the
expenses of the community never exceed 2000, yet they
constantly make up accounts at the end of the year by which
they bring their fellow-townsmen in their debt. For which
reason a little circle of officials choose each other in such a
manner that when one goes out of power, another comes in,
a course of administration so iniquitous that they think they
cannot be worse off.

"It is our will therefore that either you yourself or your
chief justice should repair at once to Monte Catini, and not
only inform yourselves, but take care that the magistrates and
council who are to nominate a committee of Reform may not
appoint any relative of their own even in the fourth degree,
and that none of the old circle (that is, of those who have
been so long in office) may be elected, that so other people
may have their turn in the administration and the reform
proceed with impartiality. . . . And if the representatives
of the community shall feel themselves aggrieved by the
manner of proceeding we prescribe, they are at liberty
to apply to our most august Signoria. Farewell."

[239]

9. *Dissolute monks.*

"To the Chief Magistrate of Pistoia. July 20, 1511.

"The reverend father Agostino Filippo, Provincial Vicar of the Order of Servites in our city, hath been before us, and says they have a convent of the same order at Pistoia, in which there are some dissolute brethren who refuse to pay obedience to him and the established rules of the Society, with whose names he will acquaint you.

"And though he is desirous to reduce them to reason and obedience, as the duty of his office and the discipline of the convent require, he has not sufficient power to effect it and correct them in a proper manner. Upon which account he has petitioned the assistance of the secular magistrature. It is our pleasure, therefore, that when the said Provincial Vicar shall show you our sufficient licence and authority from their superior to correct those monks and reduce them to obedience, you shall give him all manner of proper assistance, as often as he shall require it, for the above-mentioned purposes. Take great care, however, to prevent all frays and tumults and scandal that may arise upon this occasion. You are a discreet man and know how we would have you behave in the affair. Act therefore in such a manner as may deserve our commendation, by reducing the said brethren to their duty, considering above all things that the honour of Almighty God is here immediately concerned. Farewell."

10. *The interdict.*

"To the Vicar of Pisa. Oct. 1, 1511.

"We suppose you and all your people have heard of the Interdict which His Holiness the Pope [Julius II] hath thundered out against us, though both we ourselves and almost all the city look upon it as vain and insignificant for many reasons. Especially because His Holiness having been cited to appear before a general Council, could not publish such an Interdict according to the Canons of the Church without leaving us at liberty to appeal to the said Council, for such an appeal is to be considered as self-defence and that being allowed by the laws of nature cannot be refused to any man. We might add that this Interdict has been published by His Holiness without ever citing us to appear before him, whereas a citation should always precede condemnation and punishment.

"That we may live like Christians therefore and have Mass and other divine services duly celebrated, we oblige such conventuals of our city to officiate as are always used to perform, namely the Servites, the Order of S. Maria Novella, and Santa Croce, and the Carmelites. As to the other orders and the seculars, we have given them leave to observe the Interdict if they please, lest they should be deprived of their benefices and revenues. Farewell."

11. *The interdict.*

"2nd Letter to same. Oct. 1, 1511.

"There is no occasion for any further answer to yours of the 30th than that you are to understand we do not look upon the present Interdict (as it is called) to be valid. In the first place because the Pope has been cited some months ago to appear before a general council, in the second because we have appealed to the council ourselves, thirdly because we have had no citation from his Holiness as is always usual upon such occasions, and for many other reasons which are not necessary to be mentioned at present. We have therefore caused the Conventuals, who have no benefices to lose and have always been accustomed to celebrate Mass in our Palace, to perform the same duties as usual, for the satisfaction and consolation of our city. But for the rest of our clergy who are beneficed, we would not expose them to any inconvenience, because the Conventuals are at present sufficient to perform all the necessary duties, and we hope in God the matter will blow over in a few days.

"Now you know how we act here upon this occasion, and we would have you conduct yourself accordingly and with discretion. Farewell."

II. Personal Letters.

The letters to Vettori are unpleasant reading, and yet they show an aspect of Machiavelli's life which cannot be ignored if he is to be understood. Most of them are written while he was Secretary of the Chancery, and some date from the period in 1512 when, with a kind of bravado, he wrote to the more successful man who had kept his post, and tried to show he could still enjoy life.

The following letter is one of the most notorious, and has often been quoted as an instance of Machiavelli's depravity.

"Verona. 1509.

" . . . A few days after I got here I met the old dame who washes my shirts. She lives in the basement where the only light comes from the door. One day as I was passing she called to me and asked me to go in, she had some very nice shirts to show me, if I wanted to buy any. I was quite taken in, and went in, and there in the shadows I saw a woman with a shawl over her head. The old crone took my hand and said: 'There's the shirt I want to sell you.' I went with the woman to the back of the room . . . when I was

PORTRAIT OF MACHIAVELLI
(In the Uffizi).

leaving the light chanced to fall upon her and I saw her . . . and I assure you I was so filled with repulsion I turned aside and was sick . . . and I swear to you by Heaven I will never wish to go there again, and hope I shall never have another such experience."

Written after his disgrace.

"To Vettori. 1512.

"Our little gang is now scattered, and all our former chiefs seem to have gone slightly mad. Tommaso has become very eccentric, crazy and boring, indeed he is so changed you would not recognize him. I will tell you what he did the other day. Last week he bought 6 lbs of veal, and then finding he had spent too much, and wanting to get people to share the expense, he came round to us all begging us to share the dinner. As I was sorry for him I went along with two others I collected. We dined, and when we got the bill it came to 14 sous each, and I only had ten on me. I borrowed the four from him, and he has pestered me for them each day, and yesterday he stopped me in the Ponte Vecchio . . . every now and then we go off and spend an hour with some girls, and I have just been watching the procession from one of their windows . . . if I do laugh and shout, it is only because I have no other way to conceal my misery."

Again: "Don't ever be surprised at anything that happens to you. All my life I have behaved as I chose in love-affairs. I let love do as it likes with me, I have followed it over hill and over vale, through fields, through woods, and after all I think I have done better than if I had avoided it. Throw the reins loose and say: 'Go ahead, Love! Take me where you want, if things turn out well, you shall have the credit and if otherwise you will take the blame. I am your slave,

[243]

you will gain nothing by destroying me, you will only destroy what belongs to you. If you take this line, you will placate love. So, my master, live dangerously!' "

"1514.

"Last night Ludovico Alamanini and I went to supper with Barbara (an actress), where we talked about *Mandragola*. She offered to bring a chorus, with her own singers, during the *entr'acte*, and in return I offered to write some dialogue for her . . . let me know if I shall bring her along to Mantua."

Again: "Barbara is downstairs, and I tell you my head is much more taken up with her than with the Emperor."

Written after his disgrace.

"1512.

"When I go to Florence, I spend my time between Donato del Corno's shop and La Riccia [a prostitute], and I think I am beginning to bore them both. The one says I crowd up his shop, the other I crowd up her house. However, with the one and the other I try to pass as a sensible person, and up to now with so much success that Donato lets me warm myself at his fire, and the other sometimes lets me snatch a kiss. I don't think this happy state of affairs will last, because I have given them both some good advice which they don't like. To-day La Riccia said to her maid—really talking at me: 'Oh! these clever people, these clever people! I don't know what the idea is! It seems to me they just twist everything round.' So you see, most noble ambassador, in what a hole I am—and yet I want to keep in with them both."

Vettori does not appear to advantage in this correspondence. His letters are all on the same lines, boasting of his love affairs, showing all the vulgarity and crudeness which can be called out by this kind of correspondence. Yet both of them clearly enjoyed these would-be dashing letters, for a great number of them passed, and most of them are unprintable in English.

Quite different are the later letters to Guicciardini, the young man who was rising to fortune as Machiavelli declined.

"To Francesco Guicciardini. 1521.

"Most excellent Lord,—

"I am obliged to be idle because I cannot conclude my mission . . . if I carry it through successfully I shall owe a great deal to your advice and help. If you were to send a horseman with dispatches, pretty often, as you have done to-day, it would help me, because I need to know what you think should be done. Also it makes the people here think more of me when they once more see dispatches being brought to the house. I must tell you that when your messenger arrived, bowing to the ground, and said he had been sent express, everyone began to stand round and ask me for news and show great respect. I said, in order to add to my reputation, that you were waiting for the Emperor at Trent, and that the Swiss had called a Diet, and that the King of France was trying to come to terms with Spain, so that they all stood round gaping, with their hats in their hands. When I sat down to write, they all stood in a circle round me, and seeing me write at great length they were more and more impressed. So as to impress them more, every now and then I laid down my pen and seemed to reflect deeply, which impressed them terribly—and if only they knew what I really was writing to you, they would be much more astonished."

Guicciardini replied:

"When I look at the list of the offices you have held, and when I think how you acted as envoy to dukes, kings, and emperors, you remind me of Lysander, who after all his victories was given the post of distributing food to the troops, and I tell myself that men change their outward appearances, but nothing really changes . . . I think you ought in your own interest to take any commissions you can and let no chance slip."

It was Guicciardini, indeed, who secured for Machiavelli the patronage of the Pope, and so provided him with occupation and the hope of regaining his position. As the two men became intimate, they began to discuss their political theories, and it was through Guicciardini that Machiavelli came, as we have seen, to develop his best political thought.

*   *   *   *   *

Finally here are letters to and from his son, giving a picture of the domestic side of his life. These letters were written less than six weeks before his death, when he was on the very fatiguing journey which helped to exhaust him and bring on his illness. We cannot help but notice the little daughter, longing for the present her father had promised, and for his return with it.

"Imola. April 2, 1527.

"Guido, my dearest Son,—

"I received a letter from you, which I enjoyed very much, especially as you told me you were now recovered. I could have no better news. You see, if God grants you life, and me too, I reckon to help you to do well, if you on your side will do your duty, because besides the great friends I have already, I have just got to know Cardinal Cibo, and he has taken such a fancy to me I am quite taken aback. You shall gain by this, but you must take pains. And since now you are no longer kept back by ill-health, do work hard, learn music and study literature, because you see what a help to me my gifts, such as they are, have been. So, my boy, if you want to please me, and help yourself, behave well and work hard. If you help yourself, everyone will help you.

"Since the little mule is mad, she must be dealt with, but in the opposite way to human madmen. They are tied up, but she must be let loose. Tell Vangelo, and tell him too to take her to Montepulciano, and there he is to take off her bridle and rope and let her run wild, and then her madness will go off, the meadows are big, and the beast is small, and she can be caught again when she is cured. As to the horses, do what Ludovico told you. I am glad to hear he has recovered and that he has sold the horses, because he must have done well over it as he handed you some money, but I am surprised and vexed that he has not written to me.

"Greet Madonna Marietta [his wife] and tell her that I have been expecting to leave here any day, I have never been so delayed in setting off before, but I can't help it. Tell her that whatever rumours she hears she must not worry, and that I shall be back before anything goes wrong. Kiss Baccina [his little girl], Piero and Totto, I shall be very glad to know if Totto's eyes have recovered.

"Enjoy yourselves, spend as little as you can, and tell Bernardo I rely on him to look after things. I wrote to him a fortnight ago, and have had no answer.

"God bless you.

"Niccolò Machiavelli."

From his son Guido:

"April 17, 1527.

"Most honoured Father,—

"In answer to your letter dated April 4th, we are delighted to hear you are well, for which God be thanked, and may it please Him to keep you so.

"Totto cannot write to you himself, since his eyes are not yet well, but he says they are much better, and I hope they will soon be quite all right. The mule has not been sent up to Monte Pulciano yet, as the grass has not yet grown enough, but as soon as the time has come we will send her somehow.

"I read your letter to Madonna Marietta, and she asks if you have bought Baccina the little chain you promised her. Baccina does nothing but talk about the chain and she prays God for you and that He will send you back quickly.

"We are not worrying over your delay, because you promised you would come as soon as you could, and Madonna Marietta is not worrying over it.

"We are all well, I am in the best of health, and this Easter, as soon as Baccina is better, we three will begin to sing part songs. I have begun the first metamorphoses of Ovid in Latin, and when you come back hope to say it all to you by heart. Madonna Marietta sends you two shirts, two night-shirts, two caps, three pairs of breeches, and four pairs of socks. She hopes you will soon come home—and so do we all.

"Your son,

"Guido."

Letter from his son Ludovico:

"Ancona. May 22, 1527.

"Honoured Father,—

"I last wrote to you from Pera, and have not written since as nothing had happened. Now I am here, having arrived

[248]

two days ago, and to-day I have an attack of fever. Please let me know if my horses have been sold, because I have bought some beauties here, only they cost 110 ducats, which I cannot yet pay. And tell whoever you send not to delay anywhere. I do not write more now, as I have not much time, and I don't feel well. We came from Ranga in thirty hours, and there people are lying dead in the streets from the plague. It was horribly frightening. May God help me! I always send you my best respects. May God keep you safe. Remember me to Madonna Marietta and tell her to pray God for me, and kiss all the family.

"Your son,

"Ludovico Machiavelli."

This is the wild son who was such a trouble to his father, yet we see he writes on terms of affection and respect. He sounds as if he were afraid he had caught the plague, but he had not. He was killed in the defence of Florence, which Machiavelli was then helping to organize. Both father and son were dead before the year was out.

CHAPTER XV

SUMMARY:

IMPORTANCE OF MACHIAVELLI'S POLITICAL THEORIES

WE come, then, to consider what impression of Machiavelli we have derived from this study of his life and times. In so far as a man can become clear to us, he emerges from the mists of bygone days and stands before us; we have his letters, his papers, his writings and we know the details of his life and career. We know how he lived, how much he earned, on what amusements he spent his money. We know of his affection for his children and for his friends. We know what sort of books he liked to read, and the kind of plays and poems he wrote. The knowledge thus derived makes up the portrait of a man, very gay and lively, always eager for fun and company, ready to find his pleasure either with men of education and standing, or if they were not available, to go down and dice with yokels in a village inn. This was Machiavelli in his hours of ease. At work in his office, transacting the multifarious business of State, he becomes quite another. Now he is conscientious, hard-working, intensely practical. Often, even as an official, he shows sympathy for those who have been unlucky, whether it is for the merchant who has been unfairly taxed by the customs or for the peasants who have suffered from a bad harvest. His official letters are never stiff or obscure; indeed, they are models of what letters should be. And then we have that totally different side, the side he reveals only in his serious writings. Here he is the thinker, setting out his ideas coldly, lucidly, never shrinking from anything, ready to face and admit the consequence of all he writes. Here he reveals what lay underneath everything else, a burning indignation at the state of Italy and the decadence of Italians, and a hard ruthless determination to point to the only remedies in which he believed.

It was the hidden force of his nature which reveals itself in *The Prince*, and in the immortality of the book we can measure the true greatness of the man.

Certain facts in his story stand out. He was, if dissolute in his private life, a man without stain in his public office. When he was dismissed in disgrace, imprisoned and put to the torture, it was only for his political opinions. No one ever charged him with dishonesty, his papers were found to be in perfect order, he was completely above reproach, in everything belonging to his work.

He was also a man who made and kept his friends. Very sociable and gay, in his prosperity he had a large and admiring circle, but in his disasters they did not abandon him. He made new friends, even after he had fallen from office, and they, in turn, did all they could to help him.

He always showed great courage, in every sense of the word. He was not afraid to stick by Albizzi in the midst of the mutinous Swiss soldiers, threatening to kill with their lances and swords when Ridolfi had long since fled. He did not break down under the torture, but bore it, and emerged from prison with his spirit unbroken. He did not let himself sink for good when utter poverty and ruin fell upon him, he struggled upwards, and at least attained to some measure of dignity. He was not too proud to accept, in his retirement, any employment that offered. He went on a dull little mission to the Friars at Carpi and undertook work for the woollen guild of Lucca. He was magnanimous enough to become the real friend, esteemed and loved, of the young ambassador Guicciardini, not just a poor hanger-on, trying to restore his fortunes.

Yet he could have had little happiness once he had lost his work. He became, and remained, terribly poor. His son, after his death, wrote: "You know that my father died in the utmost poverty." His family, though he clearly loved them, were an anxiety. He had great difficulty in earning enough to provide for them, and his sons did not turn out very well. Guido, the youngest, was the best. He was gentle and sweet in his disposition, and turned for his career to the Church, which Niccolò himself so greatly despised. The eldest son, Bernardo, was a violent turbulent youth, and the very year before his father's death, when he was twenty-two, he was summoned for "blasphemy at the gambling table," and a little later "for outraging a young girl," and he was fined a florin in the same year for "thrashing a notary." He died in Constantinople a few years later. The other grown-up son, Ludovico, was equally turbulent. He was several times fined by the Eight for rioting in the streets and was involved in quarrels over a woman of bad character. He would have atoned, in his father's eyes, however, for all his misdoings, since when in 1527 Florence tried to fight her last battle against the Medici, he enlisted in the militia and was killed in defending the city.

The family survived through the descendants of the only daughter, Baccina, or Bartolommea. She married Giovanni Ricci, and her daughter, Hippolyta, married into the Serristori family, and until recent times that family survived, and still owned the little house and property at San Casciano, once the house of Niccolò and where his works were all written.

We have to note one or two things about his death. He had long suffered from some sort of digestive trouble, and had been in the habit of taking some special pills, which he was fond of recommending to his friends. The prescription for these pills was preserved, and runs as follows: Aloes, one and one-half drachm; cardamon, one drachm; saffron, one-half drachm; myrrh, one-half drachm; bettany, one-half drachm; pimpernel, one-half drachm; smooth paste to bind all together, one-half drachm.

This has been said by doctors to be a simple digestive remedy, and no other use need be attributed to it. One story ran that, disappointed at not being reappointed to his old post as Second Secretary, he took an overdose. But further research disproves this. His son, writing to his relations regarding his father's last illness, simply says that he had a very bad attack of pain, that recourse to his pills brought no relief, and he knew himself to be dying. His wife and children were with him, and he sent for a friar, to hear his confession. Fra Matteo came, and gave him the last rites of the Church, and stayed with him till the end. He had never attacked the Christian faith, though he had attacked priests and friars, and he died now in accordance with the rites of the Church of which he was a member.

He left very little money. Though he had inherited his father's estate, he must have mortgaged it, or had to realize property to pay off the debts contracted while he was living in style as envoy and Secretary of State. The little house and property at San Casciano we know continued in the family. The whole of his property was divided amongst his sons. His wife presumably had the dowry secured to her, for no Florentine girl married without that being arranged, and nothing was left to her in his will, though he spoke of her with affection and left her executrix of his will and guardian of the younger children. It should be noted that his first will spoke of various jewels; in his second, made in 1522, those have disappeared, presumably sold to provide funds.

Here is the letter his son wrote to his nephew: "Dear Francesco,—I cannot keep back my tears, because I have to tell you that on the 22nd of this month my father died, from internal troubles. He confessed his sins to Friar Matteo, who helped him to the last. He has died in utter poverty, as you know. Being very hurried I can wait to tell you no more——"

We cannot minimize his faults, though they were those of his age and country. His low standard of morality where women were concerned, his bouts of dissipation, his extravagance, were typical of the men of the Renaissance. He had few to inspire him to any higher standard, and where all adopted the belief that pleasure could be obtained in any form, that no obligation rested on men to do other than satisfying every impulse, he saw no reason to differ from his fellows. He went with the crowd, he flung himself into every sort of amusement, and he told friends later that he did not regret it; he had enjoyed himself.

He did not always do himself justice. The famous prologue to the *Discourses* gives us the truth: "I go to my books, and from there draw the nourishment which *alone* is mine, and which has made me what I am." He scarcely perhaps realized the full implications of this. We forget the playwright, the poet, the man who lived so gaily, and who worked so hard and struggled so valiantly for his city. We remember instead the political philosopher, who pored over the history of the past, who flung himself into the making of the history of his own times, and whose works have never been forgotten.

We are obliged, of course, to face the fact that for long Machiavelli has been taken to be the representative of a man without conscience and without shame, and this is the connotation of his name popularly received. Historians have long pointed out the injustice of the popular idea, and after looking at the record of his life and work it is self-evident. Machiavelli himself lived up to the ordinary moral code of his times, and was, in addition, a trustworthy and highly respected public official. Yet in his works we do find a disregard of the code accepted as between man and man. The reason is that as a political writer he did not consider himself concerned with morals. He was not a moral philosopher. He was not dealing with the ultimate problem of what men ought to do; he was dealing with a limited practical problem of what an Italian of the fifteenth century ought to do in the sphere of politics. This is made the more easy to attack because of the particular form which his style imposed upon his work. He was a master of epigram, of short, startling phrases, and he utilized this to the utmost in *The Prince*. Thus that book is full of unqualified statements which catch the attention at once, as they were probably meant to do, but which were not intended to act as philosophical maxims for all time.

The fact that the book has survived indicates that the situation which Machiavelli faced in Italy recurs in the history of other nations, and men of action, wishing to restore the fortunes of their country, like to reassure themselves by appealing to the arguments which Machiavelli stated so clearly. Modern Europe has seen nations who felt themselves weak and disintegrated, and who eagerly hailed a leader who should reunite and revivify them. Such leaders, faced with an analogous situation, have acted on the lines of Machiavelli's theories. They have believed unity and strength must be achieved at whatever cost to the individual. We need perhaps to realize, in justice to Machiavelli himself, that the arguments to justify the establishment of a strong ruler—or, as we should say, a dictator—are developed in his other writings to show that, once the ruler had restored order and made his country strong, personal rule should give place to popular government, for the State, in reality, must always represent the community.

He has been accused of formulating 'the code of tyranny' that a deed takes its character from its success. Yet what he aimed at was to induce men to take life seriously. The development of culture and art had gone side by side with political decay. Machiavelli wanted to remedy this, and he advocated the founding of a State by force, but he wished conquest to be made secure by good government. He thought that to suffer, and to bear suffering, was weak and enervating; he wanted men to fight and struggle. He took the modern view, for he stood on the threshold of the modern world. The Empire and the Papacy were collapsing, and he, first amongst political thinkers, saw that something new must take their place. That 'something' was the national State, and thus he has come to be the prophet of nationalism.

As to him the State replaced the older order, so his individual hero is a new type. He praises not the saint, but the patriot. He does not appeal to philosophy or ethics. His stand is on reality. To him reason and logic are important; man must be intelligent. He must realize what aim he sets before him, and must grasp the truth that 'if you accept the end, you accept the means.' Thus the laws laid down in *The Prince* are not moral laws, but they are logical laws. He lays out his plan of life quite clearly. Man has a duty; he must be intelligent, and he must be strong. History proves that men are ruled by forces we can comprehend. Men must work, they must not be idle, and their lives must centre round their country and the community. The moral force doing away with individual selfishness will be the nation.

All the faults of his exposition lie in their exaggerations, which in turn are due to the times in which he lived. The exaggerations are no longer applicable, but the core of his teaching is. The means men adopt may change, and do change, but the end can remain the same. Certain means which in Machiavelli's times were a commonplace, are now no longer tolerated by public opinion.

"True Machiavellism," says de Sanctis, "is the considering of man as an autonomous being, containing within his own personality the laws of his development."

These political theories, immortalized in the 'little book,' *The Prince*, have left a very deep impression on mankind and roused much antagonism. The Roman Church attacked his doctrines from the outset, seeing in his glorification of the State the denial of the claims of the Church. Cardinal Pole, cousin of Mary Tudor, was one of the first to attack him. The Jesuits continued the campaign. On the other hand, the Emperor Charles V studied *The Prince*, and the Valois rulers of France were accused of making it their text-book, so much so that Henri III was said "to have been doomed to die, by reason that he took the advice of Machiavellians." Richelieu was familiar with it, and put many of its precepts into practice. One of its most interesting students was Christina of Sweden, whose copy, with her own annotations, still exists. She approved of most of his theories, especially any which dealt with a display of courage and ruthlessness, and, like many another, she begins by refusing her agreement and ends by giving it. She sums up her attitude when she writes: "Force is the secret of success."

Following on Christina came Frederick the Great of Prussia and his *Anti-Macchiavell*. He is the strongest exponent of Machiavelli's theories of fraud and treachery at their worst. He acted on Machiavelli's theories, but he stressed their ultimate justification: "The ruler must be the instrument of his people's welfare." He denied that ambition was an adequate motive for ruthless action, but his own deeds showed that he considered any action justified which led to the advancement of his State.

This is the secret both of Machiavelli's attraction and of the instinctive resistance we offer to his theories. He does encourage strong men to do the things they want to do, and he leads them to justify their immediate acts by looking to the future. He has suffered because the part of his teaching which encouraged a belief in ruthless action was emphasized at the expense of his corollary. He held that force and fraud could be employed in the service of the State, because he believed the State was necessary to the development of mankind. He wanted to see the lot of man made easier and better, and to him, living when he did, the force likely to ameliorate the lot of humanity was the strong State. He never justified private advantage; he aimed at the common good, and the facts of his career prove the truth of this.

This fundamental conception was lost sight of and distorted, and with it his other belief, that the State represented mankind at its best. He believed in the State as rising above individual selfishness; he saw in the community something better than the one. Yet he never would have agreed that the State should retain its position by force and that its component parts should be coerced. He knew, and said, that the people must be behind the State, their willing co-operation must be its motive power. This is as true now as then. When we see a State which uses force against its members we are tempted to believe that it is founded on force, and we do not see this is mistaken; the majority are behind it, and are in agreement with the coercion of a minority.

Machiavelli was one of the most intelligent men who ever lived, and such things were not hidden from him. He looked to the true end, and declared that the State must "be strengthened with good laws, and good arms, with faithful friends and good deeds."

END

APPENDICES

I

THE MACHIAVELLI FAMILY

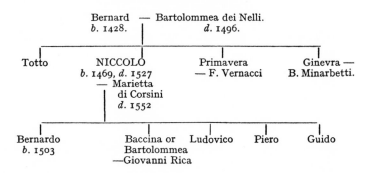

Bernard — Bartolommea dei Nelli.
b. 1428.   d. 1496.

| Totto | NICCOLO
b. 1469, d. 1527
— Marietta
di Corsini
d. 1552 | Primavera
— F. Vernacci | Ginevra —
B. Minarbetti. |

| Bernardo
b. 1503 | Baccina or
Bartolommea
—Giovanni Rica | Ludovico | Piero | Guido |

II

THE MEDICI (ELDER BRANCH)

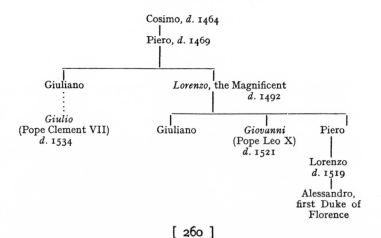

Cosimo, d. 1464
Piero, d. 1469

Giuliano
⋮
Giulio
(Pope Clement VII)
d. 1534

Lorenzo, the Magnificent
d. 1492

Giuliano   Giovanni
(Pope Leo X)
d. 1521

Piero

Lorenzo
d. 1519

Alessandro,
first Duke of
Florence

[260]

APPENDICES

III

SPANISH CLAIM TO NAPLES

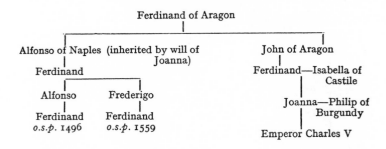

Ferdinand of Aragon

Alfonso of Naples (inherited by will of Joanna)

Ferdinand

Alfonso — Ferdinand *o.s.p.* 1496

Frederigo — Ferdinand *o.s.p.* 1559

John of Aragon

Ferdinand—Isabella of Castile

Joanna—Philip of Burgundy

Emperor Charles V

IV

FRENCH CLAIM TO NAPLES

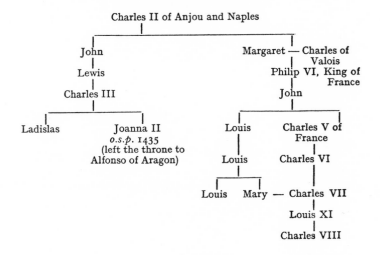

Charles II of Anjou and Naples

John

Lewis

Charles III

Ladislas — Joanna II *o.s.p.* 1435 (left the throne to Alfonso of Aragon)

Margaret — Charles of Valois

Philip VI, King of France

John

Louis — Charles V of France

Louis — Charles VI

Louis — Mary — Charles VII

Louis XI

Charles VIII

V

FRENCH CLAIM TO MILAN

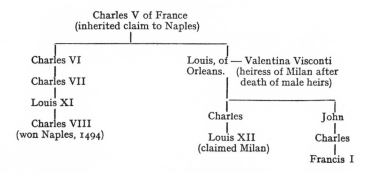

Charles V of France
(inherited claim to Naples)

Charles VI
Charles VII
Louis XI
Charles VIII
(won Naples, 1494)

Louis, of — Valentina Visconti
Orleans. (heiress of Milan after
death of male heirs)

Charles
Louis XII
(claimed Milan)

John
Charles
Francis I